Improvisation in Music and Philosophical Hermeneutics

ALSO AVAILABLE FROM BLOOMSBURY

The Dialectics of Music: Adorno, Benjamin, and Deleuze, Joseph Weiss
The Aesthetics of Imperfection in Music and the Arts: Spontaneity, Flaws and the Unfinished, ed. Andy Hamilton and Lara Pearson
Relational Hermeneutics: Essays in Comparative Philosophy, ed. Paul Fairfield and Saulius Geniusas
Rethinking Dwelling: Heidegger, Place, Architecture, Jeff Malpas

Improvisation in Music and Philosophical Hermeneutics

Sam McAuliffe

BLOOMSBURY ACADEMIC
LONDON • NEW YORK • OXFORD • NEW DELHI • SYDNEY

BLOOMSBURY ACADEMIC
Bloomsbury Publishing Plc
50 Bedford Square, London, WC1B 3DP, UK
1385 Broadway, New York, NY 10018, USA
29 Earlsfort Terrace, Dublin 2, Ireland

BLOOMSBURY, BLOOMSBURY ACADEMIC and the Diana logo are trademarks of
Bloomsbury Publishing Plc

First published in Great Britain 2023
This paperback published in 2024

Copyright © Sam McAuliffe, 2023

Sam McAuliffe has asserted his right under the Copyright, Designs and Patents Act, 1988,
to be identified as Author of this work.

For legal purposes the Acknowledgements on p. viii constitute an extension of this
copyright page.

Series design by Charlotte Daniels
Cover image: Geometric patterns (© a-r-t-i-s-t / Getty Images)

All rights reserved. No part of this publication may be reproduced or transmitted in any
form or by any means, electronic or mechanical, including photocopying, recording, or
any information storage or retrieval system, without prior permission in writing from the
publishers.

Bloomsbury Publishing Plc does not have any control over, or responsibility for, any third-
party websites referred to or in this book. All internet addresses given in this book were
correct at the time of going to press. The author and publisher regret any inconvenience
caused if addresses have changed or sites have ceased to exist, but can accept no
responsibility for any such changes.

A catalogue record for this book is available from the British Library.

A catalog record for this book is available from the Library of Congress.

ISBN: HB: 978-1-3503-3801-2
PB: 978-1-3503-3805-0
ePDF: 978-1-3503-3802-9
eBook: 978-1-3503-3803-6

Typeset by Deanta Global Publishing Services, Chennai, India

To find out more about our authors and books visit www.bloomsbury.com and sign up for
our newsletters.

For Kelsey

Contents

Acknowledgements viii

Introduction 1

Part I The structure of improvisation, derived from music 11

1 The conversation of improvised musical performance 13
2 Place and the origin of improvisation 29
3 Where are we when we improvise music? 64

Part II Improvisation in the philosophical hermeneutics of Hans-Georg Gadamer 93

4 Improvising with Gadamer? 95
5 Hermeneutics and the call to improvise 102
6 Improvisation, ethics and factical Life 139

Coda 159
Notes 181
Bibliography 211
Index 222

Acknowledgements

I would like to sincerely thank Jeff Malpas and Cat Hope for the support and encouragement they extended to me while I worked on this project, and for the invaluable insights they both offered after reading an earlier draft of this book. Nicholas Davey and Bruce Ellis Benson offered valuable suggestions that undoubtedly helped to strengthen the text, and Cynthia R. Nielsen's encouragement to publish provided a timely confidence boost. I would also like to acknowledge those musicians with whom I've been fortunate to engage with over the years – in particular, Ren Walters, David Brown, Stephen Magnusson, Tony Hicks, Mark Shepherd and the late David Tolley – those discussions and musical experiences were the catalysts for this book. Thanks also to my parents, Tim and Barb, and sister, Emily, for their continual encouragement. Last, but by no means least, I would like to express immense gratitude to my wife, Kelsey, whose unwavering support guided me through this project, without which this book would not have been possible.

Chapter 1 of this volume incorporates some ideas and materials that have been previously published. I would like to thank Taylor & Francis Ltd. for allowing me to make use of material from 'Defending the "Improvisation as Conversation" Model of Improvised Musical Performance.' *Jazz Perspectives* 13, no. 1 (2021): 1–13.

Introduction

The practice of improvisation is universal. Everyone is an experienced improviser, even though not everyone is aware of this fact. To improvise, put simply, is to *attend and respond to the situation in which one finds oneself*. And so, improvisation is essential to how we engage with the world. Improvisation is commonly associated with artistic practices, such as quick-witted improv comedy where comical scenes are created 'on the fly', and jazz music, where performers improvise on the melody and harmony of a tune. But equally, if improvisation is attending and responding to the *situation* more broadly, audience members improvise when they experience these performances, attending and responding to the arc of the comic's jokes or the musician's rendition of the tune. Further, we improvise when we converse with one another. Interlocutors can never know with certainty what the other person will say, and neither can they know exactly how their words will be interpreted by the other person. Conversation is inherently indeterminate – interlocutors rely on their ability to spontaneously interpret and respond, that is, improvise, to understand one another. While the way in which improvisation is manifest in different practices varies, such that, for instance, there is a certain novelty in comedy, jazz and dance commonly absent in verbal conversation, this does not negate improvisation's ubiquitous nature. It simply points to the myriad ways in which improvisation is manifest in human activity. The fact that improvisation is routinely relied upon in a wide range of activities is worthy of our attention.

Improvisation is discussed in a variety of disciplines, most notably the arts but also in areas including but not limited to cognition, education, creativity, social process and philosophy of language.[1] Despite a recent upsurge in interest, however, it is still not clear why or how improvisation is essential to such a wide range of human endeavours. Improvisation is rarely interrogated at a conceptual level so that the basic structure that must underpin all manifestations of improvisation can be recognized. It is precisely this basic or fundamental structure that is outlined in the pages to follow. This book comprises two main parts and presents two related claims for which it also argues:

1. *The structure of improvisation is essentially hermeneutic-topological.* Adopting a Gadamerian hermeneutical approach to philosophical inquiry, Part I of this book is concerned with the ontological structure of improvisation.[2] Given the dominant presence of music in discussions of improvisation,[3] improvised musical performance (particularly jazz[4] and free improvisation[5]) is taken as a case study to uncover this structure.

2. *Improvisation is at the heart of Hans-Georg Gadamer's philosophical hermeneutics.* In Part I it becomes clear that improvisation and hermeneutics share an almost identical structure. Exploring this relationship between improvisation and hermeneutics, Part II situates improvisation at the centre of Gadamer's philosophical hermeneutics, reading back into Gadamer the account of improvisation originally derived from his thinking. Part II examines the way in which Gadamer's account of truth and understanding, language and ethics each possess an essentially improvisational character.

Topology and ontology

The inquiry to follow seeks to uncover the fundamental structure of improvisation. The manner by which this structure is interrogated takes as its starting point Jeff Malpas's assertion that 'the objects of philosophical inquiry [are] properly understood only through the inter-relation and inter-connection of distinct, irreducible, but inter-related components'.[6] Uncovering the structure of improvisation involves identifying those components and noting their essential relatedness. This mode of inquiry – philosophical topography – prioritizes 'place' as the basic ontological structure of human experience and engagement. Philosophical topography, as Malpas conceives it,[7] draws from and advances aspects of Martin Heidegger's thought (particularly his later thinking), Donald Davidson's philosophy of language (especially his notion of 'triangulation'[8]) and Gadamer's philosophical hermeneutics. Put simply, philosophical topography may be understood as an interpretive (hermeneutic) philosophy that gives priority to the *topology* of interpretation and experience.[9] It seeks to uncover the way in which elements in the world are always *already* situated in a certain relationship with one another. A central concern of this book is to identify and understand the elements that comprise the structure of improvisation in their proper *place*.

The idea that improvisation might be characterized as an attending and responding to place echoes the thought of Heidegger. The question of being that Heidegger pursues throughout his thinking is, almost from the very beginning, tied up with the question of place.[10] That is, philosophy itself has its origins in our experience of finding ourselves already *there* in the world. Heidegger notes the historical nature of human being-in-the-world – we are always already *there* in the world with other humans and things. There are multiple attempts in Heidegger's thinking to articulate the relationship between being and place through central ideas such as 'being-in-the-world', 'equipmentality', 'dwelling', the 'fourfold' and the 'Event', for example (each of these themes is taken up in the main body of this book).[11] A key point in Heidegger's thinking is that thought arises from one's encounter with the world[12] – that is, the world as it is given in a particular place. Thinking, for Heidegger, arises from one's attending and responding to the world or place in which one is always already situated.

As noted, the basic understanding of improvisation advanced in this book is that it is *an attending and responding to the situation in which one finds oneself*. Improvisation is presented as an essentially *situated* activity; what one attends and responds to is always *encountered* in a certain situation, in a certain place. The activity of performing a musical work, for instance, is never independent of the situation or place – and the circumstances that arise within that place – of the work's occurrence. The situation, however, is not merely a neutral backdrop against which improvisation plays out. Rather, it is a bounded region that bears within it the players (and the subjectivities of those players) as well as the broader histories and traditions of the play in which those individuals are involved, and the other elements of that region *there* with the players, such as the work the players perform, their instruments, the furniture and the audience. The improvisational situation is not merely a space in the sense of extendedness or quantifiable volume, although it is that, but also a place of action and experience connected to the broader world within which it is nested. It is within this situation that both situates and is created by improvisation that improvisation plays out. It is that which emerges from within this situation that players encounter and engage with, and it is the peculiarities of the situation that players attend and respond to.

A focus of this book, as is particularly evident in Part I, is a three-part conception of place that emerges in Heidegger's thinking:[13] (1) as the 'focus' of thinking where place is that with which thinking is concerned and so is that which thinking attempts to articulate; (2) as the 'origin' of thinking, where place is that from out of which thinking emerges and from which it gains content and context; and (3) as the 'horizon' of thinking such that place 'bounds' thinking and allows it to appear as thinking. It is this idea of place that is of concern in this book – the place or situation that comprises the focus, origin and horizon of improvisation.

Part I of this book focusses on elucidating that with which improvisation is concerned, from where improvisation gains its content and context, and what 'bounds' improvisation and so allows it to happen. It is argued that the *improvisational situation* is that which provides this focus, origin and horizon. While focus, origin and horizon are not distinct from one another or amenable to being separated – each are elements of a single unifying structure, that is, the improvisational situation – the structure of Part I, which comprises three chapters, may be seen to work through ideas of focus, origin and horizon with respect to improvised musical performance. Each chapter has a broad or general focus on the foregoing concepts, without attempting to hold those concepts apart. It is the broader, overarching structure of Part I that is important, where Part I as a whole takes up and addresses the way in which the improvisational situation constitutes the focus, origin and horizon of improvised musical performance, as will be made clear in the chapter overview.

Improvisation and hermeneutics

In this book, philosophical hermeneutics finds relevance within a distinctly musical context in Part I,[14] and a critical commentary of Gadamer's hermeneutics is undertaken in Part II. In Part I, a hermeneutical approach is central to uncovering the hermeneutic-topological structure of improvisation in music. This task of elucidating the structure of improvisation is hermeneutical insofar as Gadamer's hermeneutics is not readymade to be applied to improvisation or music. The task requires engaging in hermeneutical conversation and assuming a certain reflective comportment. What will become evident over the course of this inquiry, especially in Part II, is that hermeneutic engagement relies upon the same improvisational structures present in music.[15] And so, reciprocally, musical improvisation can be understood as an essentially hermeneutical activity. That the structure of improvisation uncovered in Part I turns out to be an essentially hermeneutical structure consistent with key themes from Gadamer's thinking has certain implications that relate to the fundamental structure of hermeneutics itself. Part II of this book is concerned with addressing those implications.

At the heart of Gadamer's hermeneutics is a certain reflexivity or circularity where hermeneutical understanding is not merely an understanding of a particular subject matter, it equally constitutes a mode of *self*-understanding – understanding that reflects back on the inquirer. Thus, given that the structure of improvisation is uncovered hermeneutically, and the structure of improvisation turns out to be consistent with the structure of hermeneutics, the reflexivity at issue in hermeneutics calls into question the way in which this understanding might be reflected in hermeneutics, suggesting that hermeneutics is itself improvisational.

Given that the basic structure of hermeneutic reflexivity refers to the outcomes of one's questioning reflecting back upon the nature of that questioning, the overall structure of this book may be viewed as circular. The first half of the circle is completed by assuming a hermeneutical stance with respect to inquiring into the structure of improvisation in Part I. In line with the reflexive methodology of hermeneutics, if one can derive an understanding of improvisation from hermeneutics, one might ask in what way this outcome reflects upon the nature of hermeneutics itself. Thus, Part II takes up a critical commentary of Gadamer's thought, reading back into Gadamer the account of hermeneutics that surfaced in Part I.

If we view the overall structure of this book as an 'out and back' adventure, Part II is the return trip, a circling back along the road already traversed in Part I. However, it is a return with new insight and a transformed perspective. On the return trip there will be a degree of familiarity, which ought to be expected given that a key point of the argument is that musical improvisation and philosophical hermeneutics share a variety of similar features or structures. Notwithstanding a difference in subject matter, the road itself, given the shifts in perspective as a result of Part I, will appear quite differently.

It will become apparent in Part II that key themes from Gadamer's magnum opus *Truth and Method* – truth and understanding, language and ethics – possess an essentially improvisational character.[16] It should be noted, however, that the nature of the improvisational situation is not simply 'worked out' in Part I and then 'applied' in Part II. Rather, the improvisational situation is worked out, clarified and illuminated throughout this book as a whole; insight is gained by attending to it in different ways and from different perspectives. It is important to emphasize that it is the *same* topology that is attended to throughout this book – the topology of music and hermeneutics is one and the same.

Chapter overview

Chapter 1, 'The conversation of improvised musical performance', introduces the basic structure at issue in improvised musical performance: the conversational relationship between player and the work the player performs. A recurring theme throughout this book is the notion that improvisation is attending and responding to the situation in which one finds oneself. The 'focus' of improvised musical performance, then, is that which the player attends and responds to, that is, that with which they converse. In the context of musical performance, the player attends and responds to – converses with – the work. It is argued that improvisation is not primarily a subjective process of intentionally contributing musical themes, nor is it principally an intersubjective process where players respond to one another directly. Instead, improvising music involves turning towards and engaging with the work itself. Drawing on the work of Gadamer and Davidson, improvisation is presented as an essentially conversational activity.

Chapter 2, 'Place and the origin of improvisation', focusses on the character of the 'situation' at issue, where the idea of 'situation' calls into question notions of 'place' and 'circumstance'. It is argued that what players encounter and conversationally attend and respond to is given by, and wholly contained within, the 'improvisational situation'. It is the *situation* itself that constitutes the 'origin' of improvised musical performance. The broader situation in which players find themselves necessarily includes characteristics that are familiar to them, as well as those that are strange or alien. By orienting themselves in the situation, players attempt to hold in balance both the familiar and the strange. Consistent with the conversational structure discussed in Chapter 1, it is argued that the actions of the players should not be understood as exclusively subjective or intentional. Instead, the actions of the players should be understood as being structured by and responsive to the interdependent and interrelated elements *there* in the improvisational situation.

Chapter 3, 'Where are we when we improvise music?', focusses on the 'horizon' of improvised musical performance and considers the way in which the improvisational situation comes forth with a distinct boundary that demarcates the region where improvisation occurs and limits that with which players are concerned. By outlining how the work that is listened to by the players situates those players, the way in which the happening of the situation itself constitutes the horizon or boundary of improvised musical performance is outlined. Moreover, given that the 'placed' character of improvisation is in fact an engagement with the world in which we are always already situated, such that improvisation is not merely an engagement with one's own subjectivity but an engagement with that which is beyond oneself, improvisation enacts a return to the world as such. This engagement occurs within a certain 'horizonal field' – a particular field within which improvisation happens, the boundary of which is silence.

Chapter 4, 'Improvising with Gadamer?', the first chapter of Part II, initiates the 'turning back', where the structure of improvisation that was hermeneutically uncovered in Part I is read back into Gadamer's philosophical hermeneutics. This chapter is largely introductory in nature. It situates Gadamer's thinking within a broad historical context and highlights the significance of his thought. This sets the stage for the chapters to follow and will be of particular interest to those approaching this book with limited prior knowledge of Gadamer's philosophy. This chapter also addresses the dialogical mode of interpretation in evidence in Chapters 5 and 6, where the structure of improvisation that was hermeneutically uncovered in Part I is read back into Gadamer's philosophical hermeneutics.

Chapter 5, 'Hermeneutics and the call to improvise', is an investigation into the improvisational character of Gadamer's account of truth and understanding, and language. The chapter begins by sketching key hermeneutic themes, such as the circularity of understanding, the historicity of understanding and the task of hermeneutics, to give a preliminary indication of the way in which hermeneutics calls for a certain improvisational comportment. Then, a detailed interrogation of the improvisational character of hermeneutic engagement is undertaken. This discussion deals with the idea of the 'encounter' as well as the conversational engagement of hermeneutic interpretation, before moving on to consider the improvisational character of Gadamer's conversational understanding of language. The chapter concludes by arguing that the happening of truth, in philosophical hermeneutics, is necessarily tied to improvisation.

The final chapter of Part II, Chapter 6, entitled 'Improvisation, ethics and factical life', is concerned with a practical application of hermeneutics: ethics. While ethics may seem of peripheral importance in Gadamer's thinking, given he did not write a treatise on ethics, there is good reason to suggest that an account of the ethical is central to Gadamer's hermeneutics, as will be explained in this chapter. Further, given the practical nature of ethics, noting the improvisational character of ethics provides insight into the practical nature of improvisation itself. In this chapter, certain prescriptive consequences that arise from the ontology of improvisation presented in this book are addressed. Namely, that the way in which one improvises is directly tied to what they are becoming.

One of the aims of this book, as is particularly evident in Part II, is to demonstrate the universality of improvisation. The idea that improvisation is universal may, however, be met with a degree of resistance.[17] One of the issues thought to arise as a consequence of any claim for the universality of improvisation stems from a misguided conviction that universal concepts erase cultural difference. What is at issue here is a perceived aporia concerning universality and particularity, where the universal is thought to efface the particular. Such a view, Malpas observes, 'derives from a misunderstanding of the nature of "universalism" that such discourse invokes, as well as from a tendency to treat such universalism as *univocal* in character, rather than as actually allowing for the possibility of a discourse that is genuinely *multivocal*'.[18] Any talk of music, art or understanding necessarily requires a commitment to *both* the universal and the particular. That is, if one's characterization of improvisation is to be anything more than mere abstraction, it must bear relevance and be given meaning with respect to particular instances of improvisation. But at the same time, as musician-academic Dan DiPiero recognizes, the way in which improvisation manifests itself in the particular differs not only across cultures and media 'but also between each instance within the same paradigm or context as it is enmeshed in diverse social relations'.[19] If one's thinking on improvisation is not grounded by a unifying concept it must necessarily be defined anew each and every time it is invoked. The structure of improvisation presented in this book, intended precisely as such a unifying structure that goes beyond the particular, is a structure that offers a certain limit or boundary of improvisation, without obscuring improvisation's essential singularity.

Further, while there can of course be great value in directing one's attention to the idiosyncrasies of a particular cultural practice, one should not overlook the ways in which one's account of a specific practice, if it is to have any meaning to those outside that practice, necessarily relies upon unifying concepts. The example of translation is a case in point. It is because of, not in spite of, universal concepts that one is able to effectively communicate with others; it is because of basic universal concepts that we can translate words and ideas from one language to another. Attending to unifying concepts is of critical importance to ensure those concepts provide an appropriate foundation for those discussions concerned primarily with the particular.

Unifying concepts have the potential to illuminate significant truths about our being-in-the-world without erasing difference. It is perhaps only by attending to the ontological character of improvisation that it becomes clear that the practice of music has something to offer philosophical inquiry. Indeed, it is precisely this relationship that is explored in the Coda, the final chapter of this book, entitled 'Soon we shall be song'. In line with both improvisation and hermeneutics, where there can be no distinct end or final, complete understanding, this chapter does not attempt to offer a conclusion in the sense of a final judgement or decision. Rather, the Coda brings together Parts I and II. The key idea expressed in this chapter is that a consideration of music offers a certain insight into the 'poetic turn' or *poiesis* at issue in Heidegger's and Gadamer's thinking. While both Heidegger and Gadamer demonstrate a special sensitivity to the poetic word as a means to explicate the *poiesis* of thought, it will be argued that a consideration of music illuminates certain characteristics of *poiesis* that while present in poetry are largely obscured or overlooked in the poetic account. Noting the 'musicality' of thought highlights the musicality of hermeneutics itself, and so, while music may be understood as hermeneutical, so too may hermeneutics be understood as musical.

Developing these arguments results in a renewed understanding of improvisation, the performance of music and hermeneutics. A certain equivocity emerges where the hermeneutical may be seen to be essentially musical, the musical essentially hermeneutical and both the musical and the hermeneutical as necessarily improvisational. This is an equivocity, however, that does not weaken or obscure, but instead draws out and illuminates salient characteristics, drawing attention back to the significance of each concept. As a result, improvisation emerges as an ontological mode of being-in-the-world that extends across all human engagement.

Part I

The structure of improvisation, derived from music

1
The conversation of improvised musical performance

Improvisation is typically conceived as something people *do*. Most theorization about improvised musical performance tends to focus on the personal histories, narratives and mental processes of the player, that is, the subject who improvises.[1] And so, in much music scholarship, the player and the work that the player performs are often separated and theorized independently from one another, or, when taken together, the work is presented as reducible to the player.[2] It is the individual player and the way in which they improvise that is typically of interest. With respect to artistic practice more broadly, this focus on the subject is not new. Philosopher and theologian Bruce Ellis Benson writes, 'I think it's safe to say that making art – somewhere between the Renaissance and romanticism – became such that it was less about the *object* depicted than the *subject* depicting it.'[3] Such a view leads to the assumption that what is ontologically significant for works of art is that they were *made*.

A consequence of this now mainstream assumption is its obfuscation of an essential characteristic of art highlighted by Heidegger when he asserts that 'the artist is the origin of the work. The work is the origin of the artist. Neither is without the other.'[4] This statement calls into question any view that maintains works are merely *created by* people. Moreover, separating the player from the work and giving priority to the score, for instance, as opposed to the player, obscures the idea that, as Gadamer writes, 'every performance is an event, but not one in any way separate from the work – the work itself is what "takes place" . . . in the event . . . of performance',[5] which, as far as improvised musical performance is concerned, highlights the folly of attempting to theorize the work independently to its instantiation in the event. The work, insofar as it is experienced *as a work* and not merely as a representation of a work, lives only in the event of its happening. In the context of improvised musical performance, both Heidegger and Gadamer draw attention to the essential interconnectedness or inseparability of subject and object – artist and artwork.

The event of the work's happening involves an irreducible relationship between player, work, and the broader situation, which calls into question any subjectivist approach to theorizing about improvised musical performance.[6] The work is not independent to its instantiation in the event, and yet, despite the work necessarily needing to be performed, the work is not simply reducible to the subjectivity, intent or purposiveness of the player. Moreover, that the performance of the work is intelligible to others – the work is *always for others* – alludes to a tripartite structure comprising player, work and other.

As we will discuss in more detail later, this tripartite structure also underpins conversation – subject, subject matter and other – and so we may say that improvisation, in the broadest sense, is conversational. The idea of conversation at issue here, however, is not synonymous with the way in which jazz improvisation was metaphorically characterized as conversational in the 1990s (discussed later). Rather, the conversational structure presented here is more akin to Gadamer's 'hermeneutic conversation' and Davidson's notion of 'triangulation', where a player is concerned with something that is beyond them – a work – and they engage with that work in a conversational manner such that in their attending to the work there is a back and forth that follows the basic structure of question and answer. We may say that it is the work that the player conversationally attends to in the improvisational situation that is the 'focus' of improvised musical performance – although the idea of the 'work' at issue here requires further clarification and will be discussed further. The player's actions are always in response to a particular set of circumstances that arise *in* the improvisational situation. That is, that with which players are engaged is not merely their subjective 'take' on the situation but rather a set of circumstances *there* with them in the performance event.

The player's responses to the circumstances they encounter during performance contribute to the complex situation in which they find themselves, such that there is a giving and a receiving, a conversational to-and-fro between player and work. That this back and forth is intelligible necessarily requires an 'other'. If improvised musical performance is to be meaningful or intelligible, the player necessarily presupposes an other who is (also) capable of recognizing that which the player attends and responds to. The conversational structure at issue here is not metaphorical. The structure of both verbal and 'hermeneutic' conversation (where one converses with a text rather than an interlocutor, for instance) is taken to be identical to that which is at issue in improvised musical performance. Moreover, players are not presented as holding a dominant position in this structure, where the work might be thought to come about by virtue of the player or the player's contributions alone. Instead, just as the agreement reached between verbal interlocutors cannot be reduced to just one member of the dialogue but instead emerges from both and rests upon a shared understanding of the subject matter towards which those interlocutors are oriented, players comprise one part of an irreducible tripartite structure consisting of player, work and other.

Player, work, other

As noted, this tripartite structure is evident in the work of both Davidson and Gadamer. Davidson discusses three varieties of knowledge related to self, other and world, and outlines three basic problems of the mind: 'how a mind can know the world of nature, how it is possible for one mind to know another, and how it is possible to know the contents of our own minds without resort to observation or evidence'.[7] For ease of discussion, these might be simplified to objectivity, intersubjectivity and subjectivity. Davidson argues that 'it is a mistake . . . to suppose that these questions can be collapsed into two, or taken in isolation'.[8] It is Davidson's conviction that the very basis of knowledge demands their essential irreducibility and interconnectedness.

Although presented in different terms, the interconnectedness of objectivity, intersubjectivity and subjectivity is central to Gadamer's philosophical hermeneutics. As one learns from Gadamer, understanding is always already structured by one's historical situatedness and thus understanding always involves at least some awareness of other views. Intersubjectivity – one's (at least partial) awareness of the thoughts of others – is not, however, the foundation upon which understanding occurs. Rather, intersubjectivity emerges on the basis that self and other both exist in a shared world and experience the same things and subject matters in that world. One can only converse with another about a particular object or thing insofar as both interlocutors can identify that object as such, and that each person knows the other person is referring to the same object that they are. Davidson refers to this tripartite structure in terms of 'triangulation' and it appears in Gadamer's work with respect to his model of 'conversation', where a person (subjective) directs their attention towards a subject matter (objective) and converses with another on the basis that they both understand their interlocutor is also directing their attention towards the same subject matter (intersubjectivity).

As noted, this same structure is present in improvised musical performance. There is always something beyond the individual player towards which they orient themselves. Their acting is always towards and in virtue of a common matter of concern, typically thought of as the 'work' or 'artwork'. The idea of the 'work', here, perhaps goes beyond what one might typically think of as a 'work' in terms of something supposedly complete or clearly defined. The 'work', as I refer to it here and in subsequent chapters, is better understood in terms of 'a common matter of concern'. There is no singular thing towards which players may be said to orient themselves – they attend to the work in a broad sense, but they may also attend to individual sounds, the movements and gestures of the other players and so forth. The 'work', then, refers to those elements *beyond* the player that contribute to the way in which the work is 'worked out', if you will. The 'work', insofar as it is wholly contained in the happening of the improvisational situation, is that which is the 'focus' of improvised musical performance; it is *there* with the players as that towards which players orient themselves. The 'work' is always the 'happening of the work', or, better, 'the happening of the *situation*' and is thus dynamic and indeterminate; it demands attentiveness and responsiveness on behalf of the players.

When one performs with others in collaboration there is at least an implicit understanding that the other ensemble member(s) is/are equally engaged with a similar set of circumstances: that which is a common matter of concern. The actions of the other are only meaningful or intelligible insofar as each party understands that the other is attending to the same work that they are. The intersubjective relationship between players that is commonly explored in the literature on improvisation in music only emerges on the basis of this tripartite structure, despite the broader structure itself rarely being acknowledged. That is, an intersubjective relationship only makes sense on the basis that there is equally a subject-object or player-work relationship, where the work that players attend and respond to possesses and retains its own authority, and yet, like the players, is not independent of the happening of the situation.

This tripartite structure also exists in solo performance. The very intelligibility of the performance, such that it can be apprehended and appreciated as music, depends upon it. Ludwig Wittgenstein hints at the reason why this is the case in his rejection of the idea of a 'private language'.[9] It is only on the basis that someone else knows the language one speaks that one's propositions bear any real meaning. Equally, it is only on the basis that someone else understands the musical practice of the solo performer that their performance is intelligible. The solo performer presupposes that someone else (the other) will be able to identify their performance as musical and intelligible on the basis of being musical. As Gadamer asserts, 'artistic presentation, by its nature, exists for someone, even if there is no one there who merely listens or watches'.[10] Thus, solo performance includes not only a subject-object (player-work) relationship but also intersubjectivity. As such, the same basic structure is at issue in all improvised musical performance regardless of how many players comprise the ensemble.

Any attempt to understand what is at issue in improvised musical performance by appealing to only one or two elements of this threefold structure, or by attempting to hold those elements apart, unquestionably obscures part of what is at issue. Indeed, Davidson writes that these three elements form a tripod: 'if any leg were lost, no part would stand'.[11] While the subjective and the intersubjective relationship have been explored in great detail in the literature, albeit largely in isolation, what I am particularly interested in drawing out is the role of the 'work' or the object in this structure, and, as this book progresses, the broader structure of the situation in which this conversation between player and work takes place. What is at issue here is the way in which what *comes forth* from the improvisational event is not reducible to the intentionality or purposiveness of the players, nor only to what the player contributes. The performance is not meaningful solely based upon the supposed meaning given to it by the players. Players do not stand apart from the work, creating it absolutely as if they are the sole arbiters of truth. Rather, they are 'called' by the work to respond, a result of being an interconnected element of the tripartite structure at issue. In their conversational attending and responding to the work, the work draws out certain responses from the players. Work and player are inseparable and mutually irreducible.

Conversation and *Spiel*/play

It was in the 1990s that the metaphor commonly employed to theorize about improvisation in jazz, 'improvisation as conversation' came into prominence, notably through the work of Paul F. Berliner, Ingrid Monson and Keith Sawyer.[12] This model of musical improvisation, which argues that jazz musicians are able to improvise with one another by virtue of having learned a shared musical 'vocabulary' of musical components and a 'grammar' of how those components should be put together, remains popular. While the 'improvisation as conversation' model may be seen to bear fruit within the specific context that Berliner, Monson and Sawyer employ, it has since been taken out of its original context and widely deployed as a means to understand improvisation in music more broadly. This is problematic. Psychologists Graeme B. Wilson and Raymond MacDonald note that despite its widespread application, the 'improvisation as conversation' model is inappropriate to understand musical improvisation, broadly construed, due to its reliance upon a 'rule-based' understanding of language and conversation.[13]

The problem with a rule-based model, according to Wilson and MacDonald, is that musicians, both amateur and professional, demonstrably improvise with other musicians from vastly different musical backgrounds and with musicians of varying degrees of musical proficiency. This calls into question the assertion that the basis of musical improvisation is a shared understanding of a musical language. If this were the case, just as one fails to meaningfully converse with someone speaking a foreign language, so too would musicians be unable to improvise with other musicians who do not understand the rules of the common language. This leads Wilson and MacDonald to argue that 'a rule-based language learning model of musical improvisation may be inadequate to explain [musical improvisation]'.[14] In agreeance with this viewpoint, the inquiry that follows rethinks the 'rule-based' model of 'improvisation as conversation' and presents a model of improvisation that draws from a conversational, rather than a 'rule-based', understanding of language.

The conversational model of improvised musical performance presented here, then, is not analogous to the well-known metaphor, 'improvisation as conversation'. The model presented here is consistent with Gadamer's understanding of a hermeneutic conversation, where conversation involves the tripartite structure discussed earlier and does not necessarily rely upon an interlocutor, for one can converse with the subject matter of a text just as the solo performer converses with the work. But more clarification is needed if this conversational model is to bear fruit in the context of improvised musical performance. As noted, the problem with the metaphor, 'improvisation as conversation', is its association with an understanding of language as 'rule-based'. Like Wilson and MacDonald, I do not believe a 'rule-based' understanding of improvisation (or language), broadly construed, is adequate. Rules and conventions of language are always secondary, they arise by virtue of conversation. We learn the 'rules' of our mother tongue only after we learn to converse; language is a prerequisite of rules and convention, not the other way around. The conversational model of improvised musical performance advanced here is consistent with the understanding of language and conversation evident in the work of Davidson and Gadamer, both of whom argue against understanding language as being based on syntactic, semantic or grammatical rules, and instead present language as being social or conversational.[15]

Conceptualizing improvised musical performance in terms of conversation is beneficial on two counts. First, the idea of conversation provides an effective and insightful 'way in' to understand improvisatory practice because we are each familiar with the basic idea of conversation. Second, and more importantly, as noted earlier, the tripartite structure that underpins conversation is identical to the structure that underpins improvised musical performance. The idea that improvisation is conversational, then, is not merely metaphorical; the basic structure underpinning conversation is literally, not just metaphorically, present in improvisation.[16]

Players find themselves in a particular situation attending and responding to the work. This basic mode of attending and responding is indicative of the basic structure of conversation in Gadamer's thinking, which, at its core, asks us to take seriously the idea that the other has something to say as a condition of conversational engagement. Conversation is predicated on a certain openness to the other, which also means, of course, a certain openness to the event of conversation, which is also the event of understanding.[17] Conversation, even in its ordinary sense, is itself improvisational, but here conversation, as Gadamer understands it, offers insight into the nature of improvisation. It is the genuine openness to what comes, not only from the other as interlocutor but also from the 'otherness' (that which is beyond oneself) that is encountered in the improvisational situation, that allows for the genuine productivity evident in improvised musical performance and, indeed, in improvisation more generally.

The indeterminacy of improvisational engagement

Both Davidson and Gadamer assert, each in their own way, that understanding is always tied to the situation or encounter; understanding is always tied to the happening of that understanding. One arrives at understanding, to use Davidson's terminology, by virtue of 'passing theories', as opposed to 'prior theories'. For Davidson, 'prior theories' refer to a shared system of understanding 'governed by learned conventions or regularities',[18] which is indicative of the account of conversation given by Monson, mentioned earlier, with respect to jazz improvisation. 'Passing theories', on the other hand, are those *geared to the occasion*, where interpreters derive information *from the situation* as it emerges, and they spontaneously adjust their theories of understanding in light of the evidence presented – a distinctly improvisational process.

Davidson argues that we employ certain 'theories' of interpretation to understand regardless of whether or not we are aware of those theories. He writes,

> An interpreter has, at any moment of a speech transaction, what I persist in calling a theory.... I assume that the interpreter's theory has been adjusted to the evidence so far available to him: knowledge of the character, dress, role, sex, of the speaker, and whatever else has been gained by observing the speaker's behaviour, linguistic or otherwise. As the speaker speaks his piece the interpreter alters his theory, entering hypotheses about new names, altering the interpretation of familiar predicates, and revising past interpretations of particular utterances in the light of new evidence.[19]

Davidson suggests that one does not know what theory of understanding one must use to interpret particular phrases until those phrases are encountered. This is an example of 'triangulation' at work: one's understanding is tied to both the speaker and the subject matter that is of common concern. By attending to the subject matter towards which both parties are oriented the interpreter can 'triangulate' an interpretation. This is a necessarily spontaneous, dynamic and active process riddled with indeterminacy comparable to improvising music. Player 1 in a duet, for instance, understands the contributions of Player 2 (and vice versa) by triangulating between each player and the work to which they are both contributing.

To highlight a flaw in rule-based understandings of language, Davidson uses the example of malapropisms, which he claims 'introduce expression not covered by prior learning'.[20] What is of note is how we are often able to interpret and understand expressions that include malapropisms. Further, Davidson examines how one can interpret 'words [one has] never heard before, to correct slips of the tongue, or cope with new idiolects'.[21] He offers the following example:

Mrs Malaprop's theory, prior and passing, is that 'A nice derangement of epitaphs' means a nice arrangement of epithets. An interpreter who, as we say, knows English, but does not know the verbal habits of Mrs Malaprop, has a prior theory according to which 'A nice derangement of epitaphs' means a nice derangement of epitaphs; but his passing theory agrees with that of Mrs Malaprop if he understands her words.[22]

It is the passing theory that allows the interpreter to understand Mrs Malaprop. If one adheres only to a prior theory, one understands the *words* Mrs Malaprop speaks but misses what she is *trying to say*. Davidson provides a variety of examples of simple and everyday malapropisms that people 'get away with' in everyday communication, where neither speaker nor interpreter notices the malaprop, yet understanding has not been impeded. Davidson elucidates how even if we are not aware of it, we routinely rely on passing theories in everyday communication.

Of course, Davidson acknowledges that one's prior understanding of language is important, but only insofar as it allows the interpreter to arrive at a passing theory. A similar position is held by Gadamer, where language is understood as conversation, that is, language is not predetermined but emerges in its application. For both Davidson and Gadamer, language and understanding can never be reduced to pre-established rules, that is, what Davidson refers to as 'prior theories'. Similarly, in improvised musical performance, prior understanding of music is certainly important, but only insofar as it affords a foundation to offer meaningful responses to that which is encountered in the dynamic performance event. When players encounter the work in performance they do not attempt to rethink or remember the appropriate action that is known to correlate with the work. That is, they do not cohere to pre-given rules or meanings. Instead, the actions of the improvising musician are determined by the work as the player encounters it in the improvisational situation and converses with it *there* in the happening of the event. Thus, the conversational model of improvised musical performance proposed here is dependent on the musical equivalent of 'passing theories', rather than being derived from a rule-based model of language and conversation.

When speaking of the work, it is important to be clear about what players attend and respond to. Players rarely experience 'bare' intervals and rhythms, for example. Of course, jazz musicians, for instance, may perceive shifts in tonality – they may hear the cycle of fourths, notice a harmonic shift up or down a semitone – or perhaps horn players are momentarily startled by an unexpected rimshot from the drummer. But this is more often than not captured in the broader structure of the *work*, which, as noted, is best characterized as a common matter of concern – a constellation of phenomena 'playing out' in the happening of the situation. Players rarely hear just intervals and rhythms. Rather they perceive these things in a particular context; the difference between playing the same melody staccato or legato, clean or with distortion, is significant, just as the same words take on a different meaning when yelled aggressively or gently whispered, spoken matter-of-fact or sarcastically. It is the situation itself that gives meaning to what is encountered. Distortion guitar has a different emphasis in jazz than it does in heavy metal, for instance, just as two people yelling at the top of their voices while sailing in strong winds is not the same as two people yelling in the quiet carriage of a train. As the American phenomenologist Don Ihde writes of listening to speech, 'when I listen to an other I hear him speaking. It is not a series of phonemes or morphemes which I hear, because to "hear" these I must break up his speech, I must listen "away" from what he is saying'.[23] What one attends to during a conversation is, for the most part, what the other person is trying to say. This is consistent with the way musicians converse with the work; they attend to the work as a structure situated within a particular context.

A player's actions cannot be wholly attributed to any prior theory of action or interpretation any more than verbal conversation can be wholly attributed to prior theories of language. Players need not share common prior theories of interpretation or action. Music is *not* a universal language as is sometimes claimed, at least not if language refers to sharing a system of syntactic and semantic rules. Indeed, Davidson goes so far as to say that 'there is no such thing as language',[24] if by 'language' one refers to a rule-based understanding of language. Just as language is inherently indeterminate and understanding arises only on the basis of conversation (Gadamer) or triangulation (Davidson), so too is improvised musical performance inherently indeterminate and conversational. Players converse with the work by attending and responding to the possibilities offered by the work in the happening of the event of the work's coming forth.

The play of improvisation

To conceptualize the way in which the conversation of improvised musical performance always goes beyond the subjectivity of the player, we might consider Gadamer's concept of '*Spiel*'. The idea of *Spiel*, as Gadamer employs it, is used to describe aesthetic experience,[25] specifically, as American philosopher Cynthia R. Nielsen notes, the way in which aesthetic experience is a 'dynamic, communicative, and communal event'.[26] While Gadamer does not predominately employ the concept with respect to creating art, focussing more on experiencing art, his thinking on this topic is insightful. It is important to note that the German word *Spiel* can be translated as either 'play' or 'game' (or even 'dance'), and in many ways they should be thought of together. What is important for Gadamer is the way in which, for those who play, as in playing a game, play contains 'its own, even sacred, seriousness'.[27] Even a game that from the outside may seem inconsequential, such as children playing with a ball, bears within it this seriousness. Indeed, while players may know that what they are engaged in is 'only a game', it is precisely the inherent seriousness of play that draws them into play; Gadamer notes, 'someone who doesn't take the game seriously is a spoilsport'.[28]

But Gadamer's concern is less the players and more the concept of 'play' itself. Considering the actions of the player leads to the subjectivity of the player. The concept of play itself on the other hand implicates the player while also indicating the way in which play goes beyond the purposiveness and subjectivity of the individual. What is important with respect to improvised musical performance is Gadamer's assertion that 'the mode of being of play does not allow the player to behave toward play as if toward an object'.[29] A great deal of scholarship on improvised musical performance, particularly that which separates players from the work, presents improvisation as an activity where performers engage with objects. Performers are presented as autonomously and selectively engaging with 'x' idea here and 'y' idea there, as if the performance itself were a collection of divisible objects towards which players subjectively direct their purposiveness.[30] Gadamer suggests we have become so accustomed to understanding activities such as the playing of games from the perspective of subjectivity that we 'remain closed' to the idea that 'the actual subject of play is obviously not the subjectivity of an individual who, among other activities, also plays but is instead the play itself'.[31] It is from this perspective that we should approach the conversation of improvised musical performance; not from the subjectivities of the players, but from the play of improvisation itself.[32]

Much in the same way that Gadamer suggests interlocutors attend not to one another directly but to the subject matter that exists between them, players do not primarily attend to one another; they attend to the work – that which is a common matter of concern. The work does not exist solely in the minds of the players but materially exists as that towards which players orient themselves and attend to (discussed further in Chapter 3). It is the work that offers possibilities for engagement to players and calls for action. Take the song 'Stagger' from Australian jazz musicians, Julien Wilson (saxophone and bass recorder) and Stephen Magnusson's (guitar) album *Kaleidoscopic*,[33] as a musical example.[34] 'Stagger' follows the basic structure of a typical jazz performance where a pre-composed theme bookends the performance. Between these statements of the theme, the group engages in free improvisation reminiscent of Ornette Coleman's pioneering ensembles from the 1960s. The playing styles of each musician on 'Stagger', however, demonstrate a contemporary approach to jazz performance, particularly with respect to the disjointed rhythmic interplay between Jim Black (drums) and Mark Helias (bass), which gives the performance a unique, modern sound.

Immediately, when the track begins, one is greeted with a particular sense of rhythmic fluidity; ensemble members push and pull against one another, creating what one reviewer equates with 'a drunk's night out'.[35] This rhythmic 'looseness' establishes a context for that which is pre-composed and for the broader ensuing performance. In many ways, it is this rhythmic 'drunkenness' that broadly characterizes the track. In a sense, it is both the rhythm and the pre-composed material that might be considered an underlying matter of concern that underpins the broader improvisational conversation. As the work develops it offers certain possibilities for action that increasingly structure the ensuing performance.

As the performance increasingly becomes more established, the possibilities for action become both narrower and increasingly demanding. That is, as the work increasingly becomes more defined it begins to establish a trajectory for itself that players are tasked with attending to. Or, as can be seen particularly clearly with respect to free improvisation, players are drawn to work towards bringing what were at first merely traces of a structure into fuller being until it is fully formed. The work itself cannot come forth without the players, but neither can the players 'play' – improvise – without attending and responding to the work in the happening of the improvisational situation.

One notices the way in which the work exists between players when, on the track 'Stagger', just mentioned, having stated the pre-composed melody, players begin 'filling in' the subsequent blanks. Magnusson is at the forefront of the performance, at least in its early stages. As one hears from the continuous nature of his contributions, it seems he has little interest in 'taking turns' with other players in the sense of an intersubjective call and response. Yet one gets the sense that there is a call and response between player and work. For example, at approximately 2'09 pianist Barney McAll interjects with a low frequency contribution that contrasts the high frequency contributions of Magnusson. The fleeting contribution from McAll – it lasts only two or three seconds – offers a welcome contrast in the broader context of the work towards which the players are oriented. One may say that McAll is not so much responding to Magnusson, nor Magnusson to McAll, but that they are both responding to the demands of the work that exists between them, and they both know the other is engaged with the same work that they are. McAll's contribution is what the *work* called for – he attends to the work as it emerges and calls to the players, and he is drawn to respond – he is 'played by' the work, which is precisely what is at issue in Gadamer's idea of *Spiel*.

As mentioned, the nature of *Spiel* in Gadamer's work predominately relates to one's experience of artworks. Contra Immanuel Kant and Friedrich Schiller, for Gadamer, aesthetic experience is not merely subjective. Instead, just like the player who is drawn into the game and 'played by' the game just as much as they 'play' the game – that is, they are caught up in the to-and-fro of the movement of the game such that their subjectivities are suspended – so too is the person experiencing an artwork swept up by, or 'played by', the artwork; one becomes so captivated or enraptured that they temporarily forget themselves. Aesthetic experience, which is relevant to both players and audience members alike, is not merely a subject regarding an object but a transformative event. The role of the player is to draw out, or illuminate, what is *already there* in the improvisational situation by allowing oneself to be caught up in the situation, to be 'played by' the improvisation itself (this idea is developed further in the following chapter).[36] On such an account, the productive outcome of improvised musical performance is not the subjective determinations of the players in response to certain stimuli but the presentation of a musical event.

The participatory nature of improvisation

The broad appeal to subjectivist understandings of improvised musical performance might be said to derive from a sceptic epistemological worldview where it is thought that all we can know is the contents of our own minds. Such a Cartesian[37] worldview holds that we have no direct knowledge of the world, or of others. As should be clear from the earlier discussion, Davidson and Gadamer assert that this view is untenable, a position that I endorse. The very basis of truth and understanding relies upon the fact that we each have a certain access to the world and the minds of others. A simple command such as 'look at that tree' is only meaningful on the basis of a shared understanding of what a tree is. Shared understandings such as these rely upon the fact that we each have at least some access to a shared world. Moreover, we develop the language to express such commands by virtue of the world; we have the word 'tree' because there are trees in the world. Davidson writes, 'though *possession* of a thought is necessarily individual, what gives it content is not. The thoughts we form and entertain are located conceptually in the world we inhabit, and know we inhabit, with others.'[38] There can be, then, no priority given to the subjective. There is no subjectivity that is not already tied to objectivity and intersubjectivity.

The epistemological worldview expressed by Davidson (a worldview that errs strongly towards ontology) is largely absent in the literature on improvised musical performance. The idea of world, which is taken up further in the following chapters, is of utmost importance and yet largely overlooked. The work is not solely created by the players. Rather, the work predicates the responses of the players in the situation, and so, insofar as the work is given in the improvisational situation and is that towards which players orient themselves, that which players converse with constitutes the 'focus' of improvised musical performance. Moreover, as will be discussed in detail in the following chapter, the broader improvisational situation that situates this conversation and so may be said to be the 'origin' of improvisation is not merely a structure that bounds and limits, it equally gives content and context to, and therefore *structures*, improvisation. On the basis of such an argument, rather than suggest improvisation is something players *do*, it would be more accurate to say that improvisation is something players *participate in.*

Outlining the participatory nature of improvisation and the significance of world takes an important step towards conceptualizing improvised musical performance in a way that does justice to Heidegger's and Gadamer's convictions, mentioned at the beginning of this chapter, that artists and artworks irreducibly *belong* together.[39] Improvisation necessarily involves an irreducible relationship between player, work and other. Thus, improvisation *is* conversational in the sense that there is an active to-and-fro between player and work that is meaningful on the basis that the 'play' of improvisation is intelligible to others. Improvised musical performance is not merely a subjective act of self-expression or intentionality, for one's actions are always mediated by the broader conversational structure at issue.

2

Place and the origin of improvisation

It has been argued that the conversation of improvised musical performance occurs on the basis of a shared world or situation in which players find themselves. Given that players attend and respond to the situation as that which is the 'focus' of improvised musical performance, several questions arise: What exactly does the term 'situation' refer to in this context? How does the situation structure the actions of the player? If improvised musical performance is as indeterminate and spontaneous as it appears to be, what facilitates the player's capacity to act in and navigate the situation? These questions are addressed in this chapter, the concern of which, broadly construed, is the 'origin' of improvised musical performance. If the situation really is a 'place', literally, not metaphorically, then what is at issue here is the way in which players *are* in the situation, how they orient themselves in and engage with that place.

The term 'situation' is commonplace in the music literature. In most authors' deployment of the term, however, the word itself carries no real conceptual weight. Ideas of 'place', 'circumstance' and 'orientation' – ideas central to the concept of 'situation' – are invariably implied but are typically passed over and are rarely thematized. Thus, despite the prevalence of the term 'situation' in the music literature, rarely is it acknowledged that to be situated, and to contribute to one's situation in some meaningful way, requires the ability to orient oneself and attend to the peculiar circumstances of the improvisational situation in a manner not entirely dissimilar to the way in which one might attend to and navigate any other place.

When navigating a foreign town, for instance, a person may seek certain landmarks to orient themselves so that they might explore the less familiar territory and acquire a more holistic experience or understanding of the town. This process of orientation and engagement is always specific to the features of the place. The way in which the person perceives select features of the place as meaningful or useful in helping them maintain a basic orientation is specific to the relationship between the person and the other things in that place. For example, in simple terms, one person may use street names as a means to orient their exploration of a foreign town, another may attempt to keep a certain tall building in view. Each person's ability to navigate, however, is reliant upon there *already* being street names or a tall building.

Despite the radical change in features, this process of orienting oneself by attending to familiar characteristics of a place to explore its less familiar features is no less apparent in improvised musical performance. Rather than attend to the visual characteristics of a jazz club, for instance, during performance, musicians primarily attend to the sonic and acoustic characteristics of the place. These characteristics might include a certain tempo, harmony, melody, rhythm, timbre and compositional structure. Just as vision is typically accentuated in an art gallery because of that which is salient in the gallery-place, sites for musical performances bear within them distinct phenomena for those in that place to attend to. Precisely what salient features the player attends to, however, is dependent on the place itself. Each improvisational situation – which, as will become clear, is related to but distinct from the 'site' or 'venue' in which the performance occurs – will give rise to a distinct set of features that players may use to orient themselves while performing. For example, the jazz bassist may attempt to orient themselves within the structure of the tune, which involves attending to the tempo and harmony, among other things, to ensure they play the appropriate chord progression during each section of the tune. In contrast, an electronic noise musician is likely more concerned with a certain intensity and/or textural density and orienting themselves with respect to particular durational parameters.

Simply because different situations comprise unique features, sometimes requiring a different emphasis with respect to the dominant mode of perception, does not mean that one situation or place is any more real or concrete than another. Just because one can reach out and touch the walls that demarcate the boundaries of the kitchen-place or see the field lines that demarcate a particular region of a football field, but cannot touch or see the boundaries of the audible region specific to improvised musical performance, does not mean that musical practice is any less situated than any other activity (the boundary of the audible region is taken up in the following chapter). What is important to acknowledge is that a distinct set of features and circumstances arise in a particular situation that is specific to *that* situation that players attend and respond to. Improvising is a conversational attending and responding to that which is encountered in the situation in which one finds oneself. And it is the peculiarities and the salient features of the situation – a situation that comprises the players no less than the work – that structure the happening of the situation itself.

American jazz and classical music pianist and composer Keith Jarrett's 1975 performance at the Cologne Opera House, the live recording of which is entitled *The Köln Concert*,[1] offers a preliminary exemplar of the way in which the situation might be said to structure the actions of the player. Upon arriving at the Opera House Jarrett discovered problems with the Bösendorfer piano. 'There were some keys that did not release properly when used, the pedal was deficient, and the overall tonal balance of the instrument was unsatisfactory',[2] notes musicologist Peter Elsdon. The wrong piano had been put on stage and there was no way to swap in the intended piano with the time available. By considering Jarrett's subsequent performance on the Bösendorfer piano, the influence of the situation on one's acting is made apparent.

Dissatisfied with the way the piano played and sounded, Jarrett was forced to explore the possibilities *given by* the deficient piano – the piano itself became a matter of concern. Jarrett found himself in a situation where he had to attend and respond to the possibilities afforded by the piano, the way in which Jarrett presumably expected to play disappeared. As record producer Manfred Eicher says of Jarrett's approach to playing the defective piano, 'he played it the way he did because it was not a good piano. Because he could not fall in love with it he found another way to get the most out of it.'[3] While Jarrett possessed a certain knowledge and skill set that allowed him to act the way he did during the performance, one must acknowledge that the context and content of his acting were given by and emerged from the situation in which he found himself. By virtue of the conversational structure of improvisation, the situation 'drew out', as it were, particular responses from Jarrett that are not reducible to Jarrett alone.

This basic mode of attending and responding to the situation, exemplified by Jarrett's *The Köln Concert* – where it is clear that the happening and outcomes of the performance are not reducible to the player alone nor to something only the player contributes – is at issue in all improvisation. Extending the conversational model of improvisation presented in the preceding chapter, the present discussion explores the way in which the situation in which the improvisational conversation occurs is the 'origin' of improvised musical performance – the situation itself gives content and context to the performance and is that which structures improvised musical performance. To reference the discussion of *Spiel* from the preceding chapter, what is worked out here is the way in which players are 'played by' the situation in which they find themselves.

The position advanced here begins from the idea that when one acts in the world, as a skilful musician does, one is not, for the most part, intellectually apprehending an alien world, building an internal picture of that world, planning movements and then executing those movements. While common, as American philosopher of mind Alva Noë recognizes, such a view supposes that 'the closest analogy of our relation to the world is that of the computer or robot; the latter are designed, precisely, to embody the kind of detached, intellectual attitude . . . that the intellectualist wrongly thinks is the defining feature of our mental lives'.[4] One's deliberations, one's abstract thoughts and so forth are never separate from the world. Rather, they are always involved with and embedded in the world. Moreover, one's intellectual capacities, those celebrated by traditional neuro and cognitive scientists, only account for a small part of our everyday being-in-the-world. For the most part, the way in which one understands and acts in the world is given by virtue of the world already being as it is – one is *in* the world, not alienated or detached from it.

The improvisational situation in which players find themselves is not separate or accidental to improvised musical performance but is in fact essential to it, indeed, is its 'origin'. Rather than merely give an account of the *player* who improvises, in this chapter, it will be made clear that the player is one element of a larger topological structure, referred to as the 'improvisational situation'. For example, the way in which the player's instrument structures their actions, as well as the way in which a player's habits are structured by the world already being as it is, will be discussed. Improvised musical performance involves the interconnection and interrelation of distinct, irreducible elements that include but necessarily go beyond the player, all of which are wholly contained within and situated by the *improvisational situation*.

Exploring the idea of situation

The idea that place, in the sense of society and culture,[5] is influential with respect to the cultivation of the self is not an uncommon theme in music studies. The 'influence of place' with respect to 'self' or 'identity' is a topic common to ethnomusicologists, and more recently popular music and jazz musicologists concerned with the topic, 'music and identity'. Given this strong ethnomusicological association, most discussions focussed on music and place are closely tied to cultural studies.[6] Discussions typically focus on the ways in which musicians question their self-definition or self-understanding, particularly in relation to the way in which they feel they belong to or identify with (or at least desire to belong to or identify with) particular social groups.

The way in which music and improvising musicians are connected to place in the standard musicological and ethnomusicological literature is exemplified by musician-academic, George E. Lewis in *A Power Stronger Than Itself*.[7] Lewis considers the 'foundations and prehistory' of the Association for the Advancement of Creative Musicians (AACM) primarily with respect to place and experience. He writes that 'the roots of AACM discourses of mobility and atmosphere can be traced to the decades-long movement known as the Great Migration'.[8] The narrative of the Great Migration (the movement of approximately six million African Americans from the South to Northern,

Midwestern, and Western states to escape poor economic conditions and the racial oppression of Jim Crow), Lewis contends, 'turns upon the question of loss – in particular, the loss of land'.[9] The story Lewis offers with respect to the prehistory of the AACM is one that revolves around the importance and influence of place. The narrative emphasizes where people came from, where they were going, and how and where the founding members of the AACM came together. One also gains insight into the places in which the musicians gained their early musical experiences, such as churches and high schools. Broadly speaking, one gains a sense of the way in which one's experiences in, and relationships to, a place are closely tied to musicality. Indeed, Lewis acknowledges the role and influence of place and, more importantly, displacement – not in the sense that one can ever not be in place, but rather in the sense that one experiences a sense of nostalgia for, or loss of, the familiarity of a place in which someone once was[10] – with respect to one's development as a musician and improviser.

Berliner, too, notes the influence of place and situation with respect to musical development. He writes, 'it is within the soundscape of the home and its environs that children develop their early musical sensibilities'.[11] Berliner refers to the home as a particular environment, a place, where children are afforded the opportunity to develop an appreciation for and understanding of music. He provides a variety of examples where jazz musicians cite gaining a musical education in their homes via 'osmosis'.[12] For example, he writes, 'Vea Williams's mother sang jazz "all the time" at home; she possessed a beautiful, powerful voice that passed easily through the apartment's screens and resonated throughout the courtyard', and 'Tommy Turrentine fondly recollects his father's "saxophone section" that practised regularly in their living room. Music literally "surrounded" Turrentine as a child.'[13] Examples such as these broadly point to the influence of place; one's approach to music is connected to one's experience of culture and society.

Despite an increasing preoccupation with 'place' in music and improvisation studies, rarely is the idea of 'place' or 'situation' taken up directly. While Lewis and Berliner, for instance, offer fascinating insight into the lives and experiences of the musicians they write about, their consideration of 'place', consistent with the vast majority of musicological and ethnomusicological writing concerned with 'place', tends to err on the general or metaphorical at the expense of the conceptual; an ailment that extends beyond music scholarship.[14] Making a comparable argument, the geographer Doreen Massey asserts that while a range of authors rely heavily on terms such as 'space' and 'spatial', assuming a clear and uncontested meaning, the way in which these terms are deployed varies greatly. She writes, 'buried in these unacknowledged disagreements is a debate which never surfaces; and it never surfaces because everyone assumes we already know what these terms mean'.[15] Indeed, tracing the philosophical history of the concepts of place and space, American phenomenologist Edward S. Casey acknowledges the different ways in which philosophers have regarded the concept of place,[16] highlighting that the concept is by no means as self-evident as many authors tend to assume.

To gain insight into what is at stake in the term 'situation', which, as noted, is understood here in terms of 'place', we might consider the different ways the term 'situation' emerges in everyday activities: One may claim to 'have found oneself in an awkward situation'; one may simply say, 'we've got a situation here'; or one may speak of a cottage that 'enjoys a pleasant situation surrounded by trees'. These examples hint towards key themes with respect to the term 'situation'. That is, 'circumstance' – the awkward situation, for instance – and 'place' – the cottage's location in the trees. However, as noted, the idea of 'situation' itself is rarely thematized, and thus the term rarely carries any real conceptual weight. A broad survey of the literature on music for different ways in which the term 'situation' is employed yields at least: 'concert situations',[17] 'working situations',[18] 'professional situations',[19] 'performance situations',[20] 'gender situations',[21] 'personal situations',[22] 'cultural situations',[23] 'desperate situations',[24] 'unexpected situations',[25] 'peculiar situations',[26] 'social situations',[27] 'conversational situations',[28] 'aesthetic situations',[29] 'difficult situations',[30] 'weird situations',[31] 'noise situations',[32] 'concrete situations',[33] 'everyday situations'[34] and, of course, 'the situation'.[35]

The fact that the term 'situation' is so readily employed without explanation suggests that for the most part, authors do not mean much by it. It is a simple term that apparently conveys something so obvious that one need not waste time explaining its meaning. This is not altogether problematic; in communication one necessarily employs terminology of which the meaning is assumed. The problem at issue here is that when one pushes the term 'situation' it becomes apparent that the concept goes far beyond the way in which it is commonly employed. Thus, the task is to draw out the weight and depth of the term 'situation' so that it is clear that the idea of 'situation' at issue in this book should not be seen to be synonymous with the weightless, insignificant ways it typically figures in the literature.

As mentioned, the common yet implicit threads that connect the disparate ways in which the term 'situation' arises in the literature refer to 'place' and 'circumstance' or perhaps 'relations'. Malpas writes,

> To talk of 'situation' almost invariably introduces topological, that is, place-related, considerations. To be in a situation is to be 'placed' in a certain way, and, typically such 'placing' involves an orientation such that one's surroundings are configured in a particular way and in a particular relation to oneself – just as one is also related in a particular way to those surroundings.[36]

The term 'situation', as it occurs in the music literature, invariably implies these topological considerations but rarely makes them explicit.

All situations rely upon certain materialized conditions such that the topological ordering identified by Malpas can occur; situations always rely upon more than merely the subjective feelings of the individual. Even a hypothetical situation where one plays out certain scenarios in one's mind involves taking seriously, and attempting to place oneself within, the concrete. The hypothetical must bear within it and be based upon the concrete if it is to offer any real insight. Further, there must always be an objective (thing) that gives rise to the subjective feelings about a thing that leads one to entertain the hypothetical. The hypothetical is always based upon 'playing out', as it were, concrete relationships and circumstances. All situations – concrete or hypothetical – occur within the context of the material place in which one finds oneself. In this sense, even imaginary situations do not stand completely divorced from material conditions. It is only on the basis that one is already there and already in possession of prior experience of certain material conditions that the imaginary arises. The imaginary does not supplement the material but arises from out of, and is given in terms of, what is materially given. As soon as one takes seriously this idea, one encounters those topological considerations mentioned earlier by Malpas. The affective character of the situation is always affective with respect to certain materialized conditions.

Even one's historical situatedness relies upon concrete, materialized conditions. One's historical situation does not merely float through the air in the abstract but is something one encounters in their everyday being-in-the-world. Musicians, for instance, inherit certain practices handed down through tradition – musical forms, techniques, scales, rhythms, technologies and so forth – and they understand the significance of those practices because of a broader understanding of musical practice more generally. They literally encounter those practices in the world in which they *are*. Indeed, as Gadamer writes, 'the individual is never simply an individual because he is always in understanding with others'.[37] One's historical situatedness is enacted by one's being-in-the-world with others; it is something one encounters in concrete experience. People are affected by their historical situatedness – it intimately affects their thinking and doing – precisely because of the topological structures at issue in their situatedness. The conditions of their historical situatedness are material – one is always already *in* the world and therefore in relation to other things and people. The materialized conditions of history are an aspect of one's own concrete situatedness.

It cannot be stressed enough, then, that it is not a metaphorical assertion to claim that the improvisational situation is a place. The idea of 'situation', here, is consistent with the original meaning of the term. According to the *Oxford English Dictionary*,[38] the term 'situation' has multiple origins, partly borrowing from Middle French and partly borrowing from Latin. With respect to the Middle French, in the late fourteenth century, situation refers to 'position of a person or thing in relation to another', and later, in the early fifteenth century, a 'set of circumstances affecting a person or thing'. The fourteenth-century Latin refers to both 'place, site' and 'act of setting in place'. Consistent with these origins, the 'situation' at issue here is *the setting in place of player and work in relation to one another such that a set of circumstances arise affecting both player and work.*

Being 'set in place'

To be 'set in place' in an improvisational situation suggests that during performance players do not merely find themselves in the same place that they were prior to performance. The place in which the player is when setting up their equipment is not identical to the place in which they find themselves when performing, for place is tied to action and circumstance. This is not to suggest that if one is performing in the Primrose Potter Salon (henceforth, the Salon) at the Melbourne Recital Centre, one is suddenly no longer there in the Salon during their performance. Rather, just as there are places within places – the Salon is in the Melbourne Recital Centre, which is in the suburb of Southbank, which is in the city of Melbourne, which is in the country of Australia and so forth – to *be* in the improvisational situation is to be 'set in place' within a broader place. The Salon 'houses', we may say, the improvisational situation, or to employ Malpas's terminology, the improvisational situation is 'nested' within the Salon.[39]

Unless one was concerned with, for instance, the architecture of the Salon, it is unlikely that the Salon itself is attended to in any focussed way. Rather, while one attends to a situation that is unquestionably tied to its being nested in the Salon, particularly with respect to acoustics, for instance, what concerns most performers and patrons in the Salon is not the Salon itself. Of course, one goes to the Salon as opposed to another establishment because the Salon routinely houses certain situations and not others, and offers an appropriate atmosphere, where 'atmosphere', Finnish architect and theorist Juhani Pallasmaa says, refers to 'the fused, over-all, and enfolding inside experience of a place or space'.[40] The atmosphere of a place is that multisensory feeling one gets when, for instance, upon entering an ancient site one is immediately met with a certain 'feeling' that seemingly arrives prior to any intellectual understanding. The atmosphere of the Salon, the presence of which can be deeply affecting, nests and gives rise to the improvisational situation such that the improvisation becomes the focal place of the broader Salon-place that houses the performance.

It is the *activity* 'set in place', housed by the Salon, that is largely the concern of both patrons and performers. Simply because the spatiality of the 'nested' situations that occur in the Salon may not be immediately clear, such that one might visually differentiate one place from the broader place in which it is nested, as one can differentiate the stage from the audience's seating in most venues, should not be recourse to dismiss the idea that the improvisational situation within which musical performance occurs is not itself a distinct place nested within a broader place. Which is also not to suggest that the two places are altogether separate, either. The nature of situation and place at issue here is distinctly phenomenological – it does not refer to a purely physicalist understanding of space, which concerns itself primarily with simple location,[41] but refers to a practical and historical field within which action occurs.

Pallasmaa argues,

> We tend to think of space and place as something outside of ourselves, as external contexts for human existence and events of life. Yet, space and self, forum and collective, place and I, are fused and inseparable, as the notions of space and place only arise through experience.[42]

Place is not simply a context or backdrop for one's actions or something one enters and departs at will. The idea of place at issue here is not independent of the player. The player does not enter the place as something external to them. It is more accurate to say that the place gives rise to the player – the individual comes forth because they find themselves placed in a meaningful relation to other things in that place. One does not 'enter', 'view' or 'hear' place as something separate from them; place is as much interior as it is exterior – place is lived.

To be 'set in place', then, is to find oneself in a specific space of disclosure where one's relationship to and engagement with that place is limited by a certain 'horizon' or boundary (discussed in the following chapter). Which is to say that the improvisational situation is a distinct bounded region, albeit a region housed within a broader place and atmosphere. Particular features of that region are disclosed to the player, features that constitute the common matter of concern that is the basis of improvisational conversation. The situation in which one finds oneself possesses infinite richness with respect to possibilities of conversational engagement. However, the prior experience and prejudice of the player limit the selection of possibilities available for conversational engagement; not in the sense that the player deliberately or methodically 'selects' certain attributes of the place to attend to, but in the sense that only a limited number of those attributes will be apparent to or disclosed to the player by virtue of their prejudice.[43] The nature of 'prejudice' at issue here should be understood positively in line with Gadamer's understanding of the term, an understanding that predates French and English Enlightenment.[44] Conceived in such a way, one's prejudices do not distort or blind them from the truth so much as they 'constitute the initial directedness of our whole ability to experience'.[45] It is because of, not in spite of, one's prejudice that one becomes curious about and pursues some topics and not others (which is not to suggest that one should not question one's prejudices[46]). Thus, it is by virtue of the prejudice of the player that a *certain* conversational engagement arises with respect to the possibilities given by the situation.

The 'horizon' at issue here refers to the limit of disclosure, demarcating the region within which what is disclosed comes into presence. Precisely *what* is disclosed is itself dependent on the situation within which that disclosure occurs. It is within the horizon of one's knowledge and experience – one's prejudices that form the background or context for the way in which we encounter and understand the world – and within the horizon of the concerns of the situation more broadly (i.e. that which has significance as being relevant to the situation and that which is given by the situation) that the player's actions take on a certain meaningfulness. Meaningful, in the sense that the player's actions arise in response to possibilities given by the situation in which they find themselves. One's actions are not arbitrary (which is not to suggest one's actions are always successful or appropriate). Rather, just as in verbal conversation, as discussed in the previous chapter with respect to 'passing theories', one acts in response to that which one encounters in the situation.

To be 'set in place' is to be confronted by a set of possibilities for action that emerge from within the horizon of one's playing. By virtue of being *in* the situation the conversation between player and work brings forth a work that is *there* – it emerges from and is determined by a set of circumstances that arise in the open region of the improvisational situation. Indeed, the happening of this being 'set in place' is itself the happening of place, because, as noted, place is never something static or predetermined that one simply 'walks into'. It is not that an arbitrary boundary encircles the players and improvisation occurs within that boundary, as shoes are placed in and subsequently contained in a box. Rather the play (*Spiel*) of improvisation is the *play of place* – the player is not separate from the place, but along with the other elements that comprise the place, *is in and of place*. We may go so far as to say that place subjectifies the player; the player becomes a subject – the player *is* – precisely because they *are* in place. The improvisational situation extends no farther than the concerns of the improvisational play itself and is as dynamic as the improvisational activity occurring within it (precisely how the boundary of the situation is configured is the focus of the following chapter).

Encountering possibilities for improvisational engagement

As noted, the term 'situation' refers to ideas of 'place' and 'circumstance'. To find oneself in a situation with respect to improvised musical performance is to find oneself in a certain place in relation to other things, the circumstances of which affect both player and work, and therefore place itself. It is by finding oneself 'set in place' that the conversational engagement between player and work emerges. It is by being situated in a common place that the player encounters the work, and an essential relatedness arises between the two. It should be noted, however, as Malpas acknowledges, 'although the place of the encounter is itself partly configured by the encounter, it is nevertheless within that common place that the encounter occurs and on the basis of which it "takes place"'.[47] Which is to reiterate that the 'place' at issue here should not be thought to be determined by the player. Such a view, Malpas notes, takes as its focus that the encounter is 'something brought about', when in fact it is 'something that happens'.[48]

To be 'set in place' is to be already engaged with those possibilities that disclose themselves by virtue of them being *there* with the player, and by virtue of the player's predisposition to notice and attend to those possibilities and not others. To be 'set in place' is the enactment of the improvisational conversation. In this sense, the improvisational situation refers to a practical situation. To be in the situation is to navigate the dynamic circumstances that arise in that situation.

Insofar as the idea of conversation discussed earlier echoes Gadamer's concept of *Spiel* – where it is the back and forth between player and work that constitutes play – the possibilities for engagement that emerge from this conversational structure largely constitute the circumstances that affect both player and work. That players *encounter* certain possibilities disclosed in the situation suggests a topological orientation and directionality. Again, while players may for the most part remain stationary during performances (a pianist, for instance), the idea that players are oriented in and navigate place is not a metaphorical assertion. Rather, the topology at issue here is an ontological structure that bears a similarity to Heidegger's Event (*Ereignis*),[49] which we might think of as an improvisational happening in which players are 'taken up by', in the sense that musicians typically refer to as being 'in the moment' (discussed in the following chapter), the circumstances present in the situation in which they find themselves.[50] As Gadamer says, not only do players 'play' the game but 'all playing is a being-played'.[51]

At issue in Heidegger's idea of the Event, as it is relevant to the present discussion, is the basic idea that the situation goes beyond a purely individual or even human frame. Indeed, the happening of the Event is also the happening of what Heidegger refers to as the 'fourfold', where the world is said to comprise 'earth, sky, divinities, and mortals'.[52] According to Heidegger, the world cannot be reduced to any one, or any partial combination, of those four elements. The Event draws out the appropriative nature of the fourfold. The Event is the co-responsive happening – the 'mirror-play',[53] as Heidegger says – of the fourfold. Players appropriate the broader structure of the situation while simultaneously being appropriated by the situation. To use Heidegger's language, it is an 'event of appropriation'.[54] No single element directs or conducts the Event. Rather, in much the same way that players refer to being 'in the moment', which is analogous to the idea of being 'appropriated', each element of the fourfold draws upon and appropriates the other in a single happening or 'round dance',[55] as Heidegger says. That is to say, simply, the happening of the work involves more than what the players alone contribute – improvising musicians allow themselves to be directed and influenced by those elements of the performance that are *beyond* them, and thus the happening of the improvisational situation is not merely reducible to the player.

Importantly, the idea of the fourfold accounts for the way in which players *receive* possibilities for action in the improvisational situation. At issue in the fourfold is an irreducible tension or interplay between concealing and unconcealing. In any situation, musical or otherwise, there is infinite richness. The individual however, by virtue of their prejudice, experiences the world in a *particular way* and thus encounters only a finite amount of that richness. One never has absolute access to the world and thus one is always situated between the concealed and the unconcealed. This tension or interplay, however, is essential. When something is unconcealed, Heidegger says that it 'stands out'.[56] What that 'something' stands out from, is concealment. That is, if everything were to be unconcealed the world would become homogenized, and everything would be of equal significance. As a consequence, nothing would grab our attention, nothing would appear any different to anything else – nothing would *stand out*. Thus, unconcealment needs concealment from which to *stand out*.

To the extent that players are 'played' (Gadamer) or 'appropriated' (Heidegger) by the situation and the happening of the work is not solely reducible to that which the player contributes, players cannot predetermine precisely what they will encounter during their playing. To understand the way in which players *receive* possibilities for action we might return to Heidegger's fourfold, specifically, the 'divinities'.[57] The unexpected elements that one encounters when one improvises may be said to be given by the divinities, where the divinities can be understood as hitherto concealed possibilities of engagement with the world that extend beyond a human lifetime.[58] When something is said to *emerge* from concealment and be revealed to us it is on the 'earth' and under the 'sky', present to the 'mortal' by virtue of it being offered by the 'divinities'. Such that possibilities are offered by the divinities in the fourfold, and so in the Event, the possibilities emerge from the richness of the improvisational situation itself.

We might simply understand the relationship at issue between players and the divinities as a tension between the familiar/expected (that which comes from the player or is in alignment with the player's expectations) and the strange/unexpected (that which comes from the divinities or the situation). In improvised musical performance players orient themselves between the familiar and the strange, between the expected and the unexpected, turning or oscillating between the two, always bringing one near at the expense of the other. The play of improvisation is reminiscent of Heidegger's 'event of the turning',[59] where players orient themselves towards that which is disclosed in the situation, where what is disclosed comes from both the 'mortals' (humans) and the 'divinities'. Indeed, this turning towards the divinities or the strange/unexpected is precisely what is at issue in the Latin *improviso*, from which our current word 'improvisation' is derived, which means 'unexpected' or 'unforeseen'. To improvise is to turn towards and open oneself up to the unexpected and unforeseen that emerges from the happening of the Event or fourfold, or what has been otherwise referred to as the *situation*. Thus, we may say, in simple terms, the possibilities for engagement encountered by the player emerge from the happening of the *situation*.

Orienting oneself towards the strange or unexpected, however, is not a conscious act that one achieves via a certain technique or method. Due to the indeterminacy of the improvisational situation players can never know in advance precisely what they will encounter and thus they can never be wholly prepared for what may be offered by the situation. But insofar as they are improvising, participating in the situation, players allow themselves to be *led* by possibilities disclosed in the situation. In this context the 'experienced improviser' might be likened to Gadamer's 'experienced person':

> The experienced person proves to be . . . someone who is radically undogmatic; who, because of the many experiences he has had and the knowledge he has drawn from them, is particularly well equipped to have new experiences and to learn from them.[60]

It is the experience of the player that allows them to spontaneously and habitually turn towards and engage with the strange or alien. This experience comes forth in a certain 'tactfulness' or tacit knowledge of how to allow oneself to be appropriated by the event and allow the event to 'happen' in an improvisational manner (habit and tact are discussed further, later).

It is in the happening of the situation that one encounters those circumstances that affect both player and work. It is this situation in which the 'play' of improvisation occurs that is the event of appropriation. The conversational structure – the back and forth between player and those common matters of concern disclosed within the horizon of the situation – is indicative of the player's 'turning' in the situation. The 'turning' is not something the player 'performs'. Rather, having given themselves over to the event (in the sense of *Spiel*) they find themselves already there, already engaged in the 'event of the turning' by virtue of their experience – it is something that *happens* to them as they participate in the improvisational situation.

Moreover, for one to be genuinely improvising, that is, attending and responding to the unexpected and unforeseen disclosed in the situation, and not merely 'going through the motions', there must be an engagement with that which is strange or unfamiliar. That is, in their 'turning' or oscillating, players balance the familiar and the strange. If one concerns oneself only with the familiar one is merely concerned with oneself and one's prior expectations at the expense of attending to the unexpected and unforeseen – that which is beyond oneself. On the other hand, if one attempts to completely give oneself over to the strange or unfamiliar, one risks losing one's basic orientation in the performance and becoming overwhelmed, disoriented or, as jazz musicians say, 'lost', and therefore unable to meaningfully contribute to the situation.

To take an example from jazz, if a player becomes 'lost' in the structure or form of a tune they might listen out for certain familiar 'landmarks'. Take Miles Davis's well-known tune 'So What?'[61] as an example. 'So What' is a modal tune based around the Dorian mode and has an AABA form, where each section comprises eight bars. The A sections are based around the D-Dorian mode (Dmin) and the B sections are based around the E^b-Dorian mode (E^b min). If an amateur horn player, for instance, becomes 'lost' in the AABA form – perhaps in their pursuit of the unfamiliar they lose track of how many bars of Dmin have passed since the last B section – they may listen for the distinctive semitone movement that distinguishes the A sections from the B section. They attempt to re-orient themselves by seeking out something familiar in the strange that has disoriented them. The harmonic movement in 'So What?' acts as a familiar landmark that can re-orient the player within the form of the tune. Thus, simply because players receive unforeseen possibilities for engagement from the divinities does not necessarily mean their improvising will result in a particularly significant work. The divinities make only offerings; they do not explain themselves. They illuminate a 'pathway' as a possibility for action – this does not mean the player necessarily possesses the experience or is in the position to follow that pathway and illuminate it in a particularly meaningful or insightful manner.

The happening of the situation

Earlier it was suggested that the prejudice of the player informs the way in which they spontaneously and appropriately respond to the indeterminate situation. This directs us to consider the relationship between one's memories and what one encounters in the situation. Furthermore, it leads to a consideration of the ways in which players 'read' or attend to the situation such that they can orient themselves in the indeterminacy of the situation and respond with the spontaneity expected of improvised musical performance.

The idea that one's prejudice structures one's performing is not uncommon in the literature.[62] Less common are discussions that acknowledge the role of place or world with respect to that prejudice. The idea that one's experiences in place, broadly construed in terms of embodied memories, structure one's approach to performing music is sketched by music theorists Mandy-Suzanne Wong and Nina Sun Eidsheim when they posit that 'personal and cultural memories . . . "shape and train" [the body]'.[63] They assert that performers draw upon the resources of the body, which have been shaped by their experiences and memories, in order to improvise. Wong and Eidsheim write, 'the repository of experience harboured in each musicking body is revealed in the sonic results of improvisatory music-making practices'.[64] Improvising, then, is not only encountering something *beyond* oneself but, by virtue of one's engagement with that which is beyond oneself and the way the situation *draws out* certain actions as one improvises, it is equally a mode of encountering *oneself*. Through performance, aspects of one's prejudices come to the fore and are revealed by the situation.

Drawing from Gayl Jones's novel *Corregidora*,[65] particularly the character Ursa, Wong and Eidsheim provide an example of how violent trauma can 'shape and train' one's body and consequently affect musical performance.

They write, 'memories of rape penetrate and scar Ursa's body, so that every aspect of her singing – from her original lyrics to the timbre of her voice – is audibly influenced by these memories. In other words, her blues singing manifests her embodied memories.'[66] Commenting on Jones's novel, Wong and Eidsheim describe how after Ursa's traumatic experience, Ursa feels her voice has changed of its own accord – her body has been reconfigured:

> Despite her efforts to sing as she normally would, 'it's still changed', she says. Because of its inadvertent quality, the change can be likened to a scar, as something left unwanted in and on her body, like the physical consequences of violent rape. Try as she might to move beyond the trauma by going back to work, Ursa's body retains and betrays, in her singing, working voice, the memories of the trauma.[67]

Ursa's voice is altered because of the experience. She cannot easily rid herself of the embodied memories – they have been inscribed on her body. Through her performances these memories come into presence; audience members note the 'scarred timbre' of her voice, with one person likening it to 'callused hands'.[68]

Despite Ursa's attempts to sing as she might have prior to the traumatic experience, she finds she cannot; she literally cannot escape the place of her trauma. To understand this relationship between self and place the following statement by Casey is insightful:

> In every case, we are still, even many years later, *in the places to which we are subject* because (and to the exact extent that) *they are in us*. They are in us – indeed, *are us* – thanks to their incorporation into us by a process of somatisation whose logic is yet to be discovered. They constitute us as subjects.[69]

The place of Ursa's experience has become a part of her. While it would seem Ursa did not intend, prior to performance, to portray a 'scarred timbre' in her voice, the traumatic experience 'makes sense' of her singing, for the place is still *with* her, *in* her, *is her*. She comes to understand the nature of her experience, its effects, and indeed the place itself through the act of performing. Which is to say, there is no reality that stands *behind* the performance, only the reality *within* it, in the place of its occurrence. The way in which identity and place come forth during improvised musical performance is not something *represented* in action but is characterized by the very happening of performance. Performing music is to participate in the music of place.

Beyond examples of extreme trauma, however, one might ask why it is that some memories are drawn out during improvised musical performance and not others. Of memory and remembering Casey suggests that 'memory involves something more than the purely temporal in its . . . makeup'.[70] He elucidates,

> But if memory is not simply or exclusively 'of the past,' what does it involve in addition? The very embodiment of remembering hints at an answer. To be embodied is *ipso facto* to assume a particular perspective and position; it is to have not just a point of view but a *place* in which we are situated. It is to occupy a portion of space from out of which we both undergo given experiences and remember them. . . . As embodied existence opens onto place, indeed *takes place in place* and nowhere else, so our memory of what we experience in place is likewise place-specific: it is bound to place as to its own basis.[71]

The player's ability to perform is tied to the way in which the situation appropriates memory and experience. The very idea of action at issue in improvisation is tied to the situation in which one undergoes experience. One cannot separate place and memory. Not only does place give rise to memory, but one's memory also orients them in place, and to a certain degree those memories *are* the place in which one finds oneself.

Moreover, Malpas argues that one's mental states, which are tied to the memories and prejudice of the player, are structured holistically. He writes,

> The unity of subjectivity . . . cannot be like the unity of a planetary system with the 'subject' or self in the role of the sun, and holding all other bodies in systematic relation through the force it exerts upon them. Instead, the unity of subjectivity is a dynamic unity that operates through the constant articulation and re-articulation of the interconnection between mental states – interconnections that belong or are 'internal' to those states.[72]

Further, Malpas argues that one's attitudes, beliefs and desires, and therefore action more generally, are tied to those mental states.[73] Thus, we may say that mental states make sense of one's acting, but the structure of those states derives from one's experiences in place. We come to recognize the nature of one's reason primarily through practical experience, that is, engagement with the world.

Not only are the player's mental states bound to place in the sense that Casey, earlier, discusses the way in which memory is place-bound, but Malpas argues that one's mental states themselves are organized topologically.[74] He writes,

> If we view mental states as forming a 'web' in which each state is connected with many other states, then it is a web that is always being pulled in some particular direction. Like a spider's web in which a fly has been caught, and in which all the threads are under stress from a single point, mental states are similarly organised in relation to, or 'pulled towards', the current activity of the agent – and, just as some parts of such a web will be stretched more than others, some states will be 'pulled' more than others.[75]

It is the possibilities for action encountered in the improvisational situation that 'pull' on certain mental states of the player. The player does not so much 'perform' or 'direct' their mental states towards certain phenomena so much as, by allowing themselves to be appropriated by the situation, certain mental states are 'pulled' by the situation.

That one's knowledge and skill set underpinning one's improvising is structured as a web suggests how different aspects of one's prejudice can surface. Indeed, thinking back to the discussion about Jarrett, one may argue that it was largely the defective piano that 'pulled' on particular aspects of Jarrett's web. That the situation pulls on certain areas of the player's web to varying degrees suggests how particular responses to the improvisational situation arise. It also indicates how potentially unexpected responses may emerge during improvised musical performance. For example, pioneering English avant-garde guitarist, Derek Bailey acknowledges that the base of his 'improvising language' came from his interest in 'Schoenberg's pre-serial, "free" atonal period, the later music of Webern and also certain early electronic music composers'.[76] But he acknowledges that this 'language' was 'superimposed upon another musical language; one learned . . . over many years as a working musician'.[77] The web that Bailey stands within while improvising, then, comprises not only the 'language' inspired by Schoenberg, Webern and select electronic musicians but also, perhaps less prominently, his knowledge of performing music in clubs, dance halls, recording studios and so forth. While the latter may no longer form a prominent part of his web, it may still be there, and, under the right circumstances, if it is pulled in the right way by the situation in which he finds himself, can perhaps come forth. Bailey notes, 'the unexpected, not to say unnerving, can . . . occasionally appear. Recently, it seems to me, some reflection of the earliest guitar music I ever heard occasionally surfaces in my solo playing; music I have had no connection with, either as a listener or player, since childhood.'[78] It is the peculiarities of the improvisational situation – the encounter – that the player appropriates and is appropriated by that draw out the prior understanding of the player.

The play of place

While the preceding discussion highlights the ways in which place might be said to draw out certain responses from players, it does so in broad terms, riffing on examples derived from the literature on improvised music. We might now delve deeper into the way in which place may be said to structure the thinking and doing of the improviser. The view that intentionality, one's mind or even the individual is not solely responsible for the way in which one *is* in the world is largely consistent with the literature on embodied cognition, extended mind and enactive cognition.[79] Indeed, Noë states that 'it is now clear, as it has not been before, that consciousness, like a work of improvisational music, is achieved in action, by us, thanks to our situation in and access to a world we know around us. We are in the world and of it. We are home sweet home.'[80] Noë suggests that consciousness is not relegated to the brain alone but extends to our bodies and even into the situation in which we find ourselves.

Let us begin by considering the way in which individual things in the world, such as musical instruments, structure the way in which we engage with the world. Noë argues that 'tool use can modify our body schema.'[81] He provides an example of someone who is blind using a cane to perceive the ground as they walk; the person, via the cane, is able to feel the ground's texture. The point here is not that the cane somehow has nerve endings that extend from the hand.

Noë argues, 'the brain and nervous system, insofar as they enable perceptual awareness of the environment, are not in the business of generating feeling; rather, they are in the business of enabling us to interact dynamically with the environment'.[82] What we are and how we interact with the environment depends upon more than the brain alone. When one gains a certain degree of experience with a particular tool such as a walking cane, the tool can extend one's ability to interact with their environment in a manner that goes beyond what the brain alone could achieve. Noë offers, 'drivers can come to feel where the back of the car is as they back into a parking spot . . . . In this same way, the baseball glove or lacrosse stick extends the athlete's reach.'[83] Tools are not merely things one comes to master via use of one's brain. Rather, tools modify the way in which one interacts with the world.

This is, despite Noë's criticism of Heidegger's ideas of 'equipment', 'presence' and 'absence',[84] not entirely dissimilar to the argument put forward by Heidegger with respect to his idea of 'equipmentality'. For Heidegger, equipment is 'something in-order-to . . . '.[85] A guitar plectrum, for instance, is a piece of equipment used 'in-order-to' strike the strings of the guitar. That the proficient player simply uses the plectrum without apprehending it theoretically, Heidegger would say, is because the relationship between player and plectrum 'has in each case been outlined in advance in terms of the totality of such involvements'.[86] The way the player acts when using the plectrum is already structured by the use the plectrum is known to serve the player. One plays the guitar with a plectrum because it serves a particular use, but in using the plectrum, as is now being recognized in contemporary cognitive science and philosophy of mind,[87] the way in which one acts in the world is altered.

For example, when an experienced player sits with an acoustic guitar, they are not conscious of all their actions towards the guitar. Largely, the guitar structures the bodily position and movements of the player. The instrument brings a mode of being with it. By virtue of the way in which the instrument structures the actions of the player, the player's right hand (assuming they play right-handed) moves vertically between the highest and lowest strings, and horizontally, achieving brighter tones as they strike the strings closer to the bridge of the guitar, and warmer tones as they move up the body of the guitar towards the neck. The fingers on their left hand press strings to the fretboard to alter the pitch, and the hand stretches to execute certain large intervallic leaps. The right arm wraps around the guitar, gently holding it in position against the player's body as the left arm holds the player's hand in position such that their thumb rests on the back of the guitar neck, stabilizing the fretting fingers to enable them to apply the appropriate pressure to the strings.

For the experienced guitarist, assuming they play in this traditional manner, the instrument demands this basic configuration. The instrument configures the body and brain of the player. Noë observes,

> The expert's performance . . . deteriorates if he focuses on the mechanics of the task. . . . It has been shown, for example, that highly trained experts – musicians, athletes, etc. – show a decrease in overall level of brain activation when they are engaged in the performance of their skills compared to beginners.[88]

The player is not consciously acting towards the guitar. Rather, in their knowing how to play the guitar, where the guitarist possesses a certain tacit knowledge that allows them to take a 'step back', as it were, they allow the guitar itself to structure their acting.

Just as the player is not separate from the situation but *a part of the situation*, so too does the instrument comprise an interrelated part of the situation. Indeed, the situation may comprise a great many things such as the player, their instrument, the other players in the ensemble, the stage, the audience, the atmosphere of the broader place that nests the improvisational situation and the work. While the prejudice of the player is obviously integral to their actions in the situation, so too is the presence of their instrument. Equally, the chair upon which the player sits structures the player's relationship with the situation. Various elements that comprise the improvisational situation demonstrate this influence to varying degrees on the happening of the situation. Thus, while it is largely that which is 'of concern' (the work) that is the 'focus' of one's improvising, the improvisational situation itself, such that it is the 'origin' of improvisation, goes beyond that which is of concern to the players and extends to those elements *there* in the situation that afford improvisation but are not perhaps 'of concern' to the player.

To know how to play a guitar, then, is to know the *topos*[89] the instrument brings with it – the player comports themselves, thinks and acts in a manner consistent with that which is required of the instrument in the given situation. Playing one's instrument is the enactment of certain topological structures such that inasmuch as the player plays the instrument, the instrument plays the player. To spontaneously engage with one's instrument while one improvises music, then, is, in part, to allow oneself to be *played by* the instrument. There is a certain relationship between player and instrument that comes about only when player and instrument relate to one another in this way. If the relationship breaks down, as it were, perhaps the guitar breaks or malfunctions in some unexpected way during performance, the topological structures that afford the decrease in brain activation mentioned earlier are interrupted, and new relationships emerge – perhaps the guitarist perseveres with a broken string and for the most part, the original relationships are reconfigured, or perhaps the interruption is so severe the performance is forced to an early close.

The 'play' of improvisation is determined by the topological structure of the situation. The way in which we each *are* in the world is structured by the world itself – the topology in which we always already are. Musicians develop certain skill sets because there already exists in the world a reason to have such a skill set; musicians assume the *topos* of their instrument because that is what the instrument demands. Players are 'played by' the situation insofar as they are *there* with an array of things that are equally *there* with them, and players become *a part of* the situation. In a very literal sense, the improvisational situation is a place with a distinct topological ordering of things that relate to one another and affect one another. One's being-in-the-world is itself structured by the world in which one is. In a certain respect the way in which we are simply happens as we engage with the world.

The spontaneity of improvisation

Based on the account offered in the previous section, the idea that improvised musical performance is reducible to the subjectivity or mental processing of the player is surely misguided. Such a view not only undermines the complex topological structures outlined earlier but also oversells the player's ability to consciously reflect upon their actions and undertake conceptual thought during performance. While I do not wish to argue that players undertake no intellectual thought during improvised musical performance, I do want to argue that, for the most part, players act in the situation via what American philosopher Mark Johnson refers to as 'qualitative determinations'. He writes, 'we are in and of the world via qualitative determinations, "before we know it," by which I mean, before we relate to it as knowers'.[90] Johnson argues that our most immediate access to the world is via our perception of qualities, rather than concepts, where qualities are often perceived 'at a level beneath conscious awareness'.[91] For instance, prior to conceptual thought, the increasing density and intensity of the work spur the players into a crescendo; the silence of the audience suggests their attentiveness; the brightness of the reverb signals the proximity, density and reflectivity of the floor, ceiling or walls of the performance venue; a slight nod from the jazz trumpet player to the saxophonist indicates a transition in 'soloing' responsibilities. Much of what might be thought to be indicative of conscious decision-making on behalf of the player is in fact indicative of qualitative determinations.

Players demonstrate what Johnson refers to as 'aesthetic attitude', which, in contradistinction to its usual definition of 'disinterestedness', Johnson (re) defines as, 'sensitivity to the forms, images, patterns, qualities, emotions, and feelings that constitute the stuff of meaningful experience'.[92] It is not the ability to undertake complex conceptual reflection that describes improvisation or one's being-in-the-world more generally, but the ability to spontaneously derive qualitative meaning from the dynamic and indeterminate situation in which one finds oneself, and respond habitually and spontaneously. Such that players are engaged in the situation in this way suggests that their acting in the situation is equally not primarily evaluative, intellectual or abstract, but is largely reliant on body schema, habit and tact; each of these is discussed further.

Body schema

Previously, it was suggested that experienced musicians possess a tacit knowledge of how to be with their instruments. To play an instrument, it was said, was to embody a certain topological structure with respect to the way one relates to their surroundings, the posture they assume, and one's subsequent actions, for instance. The way in which the musician is in the world with their instrument, among other things, is, then, for the most part, automatic or habituated, and structured by the topological ordering of the *situation* in which the player *is*. One's playing, more often than not, operates below the level of consciousness.

Many of a musician's actions relate to the idea of 'body schema', which, Shaun Gallagher writes, is a subconscious system that regulates the way in which 'the body acquires a specific organisation or style in its relations with a particular physical and social environment'.[93] Such organization, Gallagher argues, is 'neither reducible to neurological functioning nor equivalent to ... an intentional object of consciousness'.[94] Body schema explains the way in which one is able to seamlessly act in the world and be responsive to the situation in which one finds oneself, without being conscious of or intending each and every action. Indeed, one relies upon body schema in a great many activities. For example, body schema is that which affords guitarists the ability to, when prompted under normal circumstances, strum their guitar without having to consider the spatial location of their hand or the guitar or the trajectory in which the hand must move to appropriately strike the strings of the guitar. With respect to musical performance or playing sports, for instance, Noë argues that 'paying too much attention to what [one] is doing, to the mechanics of the task ... will interrupt the flow and likely cause the expert to choke'.[95] When one performs standard movements while playing their instrument, for the most part, their movements are guided by their body schema.

It is uncommon for someone to consciously consider their body in their everyday being-in-the-world. For example, someone might walk into a high-school music room full of instruments with no thought of their own body; they make it through the doorway without wondering how to appropriately orient their body in relation to the opening, they navigate the desks without intending to take one path or another despite the numerous ways in which the room might be traversed, and they walk by a violin hanging on the wall without worrying that they might accidentally bump the violin from its wall mount. Upon picking up the violin, however, if they do not know how to play a violin, the person may suddenly be very aware of their body. They wonder how to stand, what to do with each arm, how to grip the bow, how to place their fingers on the strings and so forth. In this instance, the individual's body schema does not extend to the topological relationality of how to *be* with a violin.

Body schema can, however, extend beyond the body, as alluded to earlier with respect to the *topos* of the guitar. Take, for example, an individual who has recently had their leg amputated. That one's everyday being-in-the-world is largely subconscious is made apparent when we consider the idea of phantom limbs. A phantom limb can remain a part of the body schema.[96] It is not uncommon for the amputee, particularly in the early stages after their amputation, to simply try to walk. It is only when one fails to walk that one finds the leg is in fact not there. Over time, however, Gallagher writes, 'a prosthetic device may be incorporated into a schema, just as a carpenter might incorporate a hammer'.[97] Extending this assertion, one may say that the equipment one uses during improvised musical performance can be incorporated into one's body schema as one develops an understanding of that equipment. Just as one can walk through a doorway without consciously intending each and every action, so too can experienced musicians subconsciously play their instruments, at least in a basic sense, and assume the *topos* associated with their equipment, as mentioned earlier. The instrument becomes what the prosthetic becomes for the amputee, or what the hammer becomes to the carpenter, by virtue of body schema.

The way in which one acts with respect to body schema, however, is not mere repetition, it is not the exact same movement every time. Rather, the body schema is, Gallagher writes, 'selectively attuned to its environment'.[98] This is particularly important with respect to improvisation. There are countless movements that one's body is physiologically capable of. But the particular movements of the player, despite them largely operating at a subconscious level, are, for the most part, appropriate to the indeterminate situation in which they find themselves. The happening of the situation draws out actions from the player with very little intentionality or selectivity. The improvisational situation motivates the action. One's spontaneous responding to the situation in which one finds oneself, then, is not arbitrary – it is responsive to the particularities and peculiarities of the situation – but it is equally, for the most part, not intentional, either. As mentioned, it simply happens.

Habit and place

'Traditional approaches to the mind in cognitive science have failed to appreciate the importance of habit, for they start from the assumption that the really interesting thing about us human beings is that we are very smart', writes Noë.[99] As mentioned, the dominant view of human beings is that we are thinkers; it is our rationality that separates us from other animals. It is our capacity to rationalize, deliberate, make propositions and think abstractly that has garnered the most attention from those who seek to understand us. Consequently, we tend to think of ourselves as thinkers first and foremost – we tend to operate under an intellectualist conception of human beings. Of course, human beings *are* thinkers. But what an intellectualist conception of human beings tends to overlook, Noë argues,[100] are all those habitual skill sets that underlie our capacity to make intellectual judgements. The musician engaged in collective free improvisation, for instance, who patiently waits while the rest of the ensemble performs, judging the situation, perhaps seeking the opportune entry point to begin playing, can only do so on the basis that they have already taken for granted what music is, and that they understand how to play their instrument.

Moreover, in their engagement with the improvisational situation, not only do players rely on body schema, but for the most part, they also do not intend to be deliberate. Whereas an intellectualist conception of expertise tends to present the expert's mind as being capable of undertaking immense computational tasks very quickly, Noë argues that 'the expert isn't someone who simply uses rules quickly or unconsciously; the expert is someone for whom, a good deal of the time, the question of rules does not even arise'.[101] Indeed, as was discussed in the preceding chapter, any appeal to rules, such as with respect to a rule-based understanding of language, cannot account for the indeterminacy of our being-in-the-world. Understanding, thinking and acting, is not something that can be entirely understood by appealing to the subject's prior understanding of rules.

In the play of improvisation there are certain habitual responses readily available to be 'pulled' by the situation. Which is to suggest that non-habitual actions are those that require a greater deal of thought or concentration to execute, a process that requires more concentration on oneself, which can detract from one's ability to attune oneself to that which is beyond oneself – the broader situation. 'In the progress of habit, inclination, as it takes over from the will, comes closer and closer to the actuality that it aims to realise; it increasingly adopts its form', writes nineteenth-century French philosopher, Félix Ravaisson.[102] As one develops a habit, through practising their instrument for instance, the interval between potentiality and the goal diminishes, which is to say, the subject and the object of thought come closer together. Once a habit has been established, Ravaisson asserts, this 'middle ground' between subject and object disappears and 'the end whose idea gave rise to the inclination comes closer to it, touches it and becomes fused with it'.[103] Habit brings together and unites one's tendency that determines a particular action and the being of the movement that realizes it. Habits are actions readily available to be 'pulled' by the situation.

Moreover, consistent with the argument that players are but one part of the broader situation, one's habitual actions are not independent of the world. That is, not only are they *drawn out* by the circumstances of the situation, but the world itself structures one's acquisitions of habits. Such that to improvise music is *the setting in place of player and work in relation to one another such that a set of circumstances arise affecting both player and work*, one may say that those circumstances that routinely tend to arise in certain improvisational situations give rise to the habitual. For instance, a recurrent jazz chord progression is the ii-V-I progression, which in the key of C major is: Dmin^7-G^7-Cmaj^7. In any given improvisational situation that jazz musicians find themselves in, they will likely negotiate countless ii-V-I progressions. Experienced jazz musicians know how to 'find their way around' ii-V-I progressions. There may well be a certain degree of intentionality or deliberateness with respect to how the player attends to the progression, but that intellectual achievement is dependent, as noted, on an array of habituated concepts. What is important is that it is the situation itself that enables the player to orient themselves within it. That is, it is because they routinely encounter ii-V-I progressions in the improvisational situation that players are familiar with them and have reason to practice negotiating those chord progressions outside of performances. Place gives rise to the habit; habits are made possible by the world being as it is.[104]

Atmosphere, qualities and tact

Earlier, it was noted that the place in which the improvisational situation is nested imbues the situation with a certain 'atmosphere'. I want to return to this idea with respect to the atmosphere of the situation and the way in which players 'read' or 'feel' the atmosphere of the situation. What the idea of atmosphere conveys is that one's experience of a place is not reducible to any one of the senses. Rather, as Pallasmaa notes, 'an atmospheric perception involves judgements beyond the five Aristotelian senses, such as sensations of orientation, motion, duration, continuity, scale, density, intimacy, temperature, humidity, air movement, and the dynamics of illumination'.[105] While auditory perception is typically the primary mode of perception at issue in improvised musical performance (discussed further in Chapter 3), one should not disregard the affective quality the overall atmosphere has on the player.

Not only does the place in which the improvisational situation is nested imbue its atmosphere into the situation, but the players and emergent work also alter and affect the atmosphere. The conglomeration of affective qualities comes forth as a complex constellation of 'diffuse, unfocused, peripheral, emotive, an emergent phenomena',[106] according to Pallasmaa. This is the immediate situation in which players find themselves. Given the complexity of such a situation and the spontaneity with which players respond to the improvisational situation, it is difficult to disagree with Johnson when he argues that 'human organisms inhabit their world most immediately through their perception of qualities, often at a level beneath conscious awareness'.[107] What is at issue in improvised musical performance with respect to the player's ability to attend to and navigate the situation is largely their ability to habituate themselves to the atmospheric qualities of the situation.

The player's acting in the improvisational situation, one may say, is a demonstration of their 'tactfulness'.[108] Gadamer describes 'tact' as 'a special sensitivity and sensitiveness to situations and how to behave in them, for which knowledge from general principles does not suffice'.[109] He writes further, 'the tact which functions in the human sciences is not simply a feeling and unconscious, but is at the same time a mode of knowing and a mode of being'.[110] Tact can refer to the way in which one broaches a particular subject matter with someone; depending on how one goes about such a discussion could result in it being either tactful or tactless. The tactful individual possesses the sensitivity that Gadamer describes so as to broach the topic by making certain things explicit and passing over those things that do not need to be said. Gadamer writes, 'tact helps one to preserve distance. It avoids the offensive, the intrusive, the violation of the intimate sphere of the person'.[111] This mode of knowing and being is characteristic not only of verbal conversation but also, it is suggested, of music and improvisation.

Gadamer tells us that tact is not merely synonymous with manners and customs but is a tacit mode of knowing. He provides the following example:

> Someone who has an aesthetic sense knows how to distinguish between the beautiful and the ugly, high and low quality, and whoever has a historical sense knows what is possible for an age and what is not, and has a sense of the otherness of the past in relation to the present.[112]

Equally, it might be argued that someone who has a musical-improvisational sense knows how to appropriately orient oneself in the improvisational situation, such that one gives oneself over and to some extent surrenders oneself to the situation. Whereas body schema and habit allow the player to respond spontaneously, it is tact that allows the player to read the situation, as it were, and habituate themselves to the atmosphere of the situation to become a part of it – *belong* to it. Tact is that which affords the player the ability to orient themselves between the familiar and the strange and receive what is given as they appropriate and are appropriated by the improvisational situation.

On the idea of tact as it appears in Gadamer's thinking, British philosopher Nicholas Davey writes,

> Tact is a speculative skill insofar as it can grasp the meaning of what is immediately said or disclosed in terms of what lies beyond the self-evident.

> ... Tact, then, involves an ability to sense the flow and direction of a given dialogue, to 'read' it in the full hermeneutical sense of the term. Such 'tact' – to know what is appropriate – is, of course, a matter of practice rather than method.[113]

What is important is Davey's description of tact as a skill where a subject can immediately grasp the meaning, sense the flow, of a situation and orient themselves appropriately without recourse to method. Indeed, anyone familiar with performing music will acknowledge an affinity with this idea of 'sensing the flow and direction' of performance and being drawn to act accordingly. The flow and direction sensed by the player are the qualities given by the situation. It is not an abstract, conceptual or intellectual sensing, but an 'aesthetic attitude' consistent with Johnson's definition, mentioned earlier.

Such tact is in evidence in improvised musical performance. Consider the track 'Larf' from Icelandic jazz and experimental guitarist Hilmar Jensson's album *Ditty Blei*,[114] especially Jensson's guitar solo that occurs from approximately 3'34" until the end. For the most part, this section comprises Jensson on guitar, Trevor Dunn on double bass and Jim Black on drums, with Herb Robertson on trumpet and Andrew D'Angelo on saxophone re-entering towards the end. There is a sense in which the trio, during the guitar solo, are intimately attuned to the situation. While there is an established trajectory to the performance consistent with the role of the bassist and drummer prior to Jensson's solo that largely permeates through the solo, it is clear that no member of the trio is merely 'going through the motions', or that they are not attentive to the situation. One can discern subtle responses from each player as the work unfolds and develops, offering the players possibilities for engagement.

With the definition of tact in mind from the discussion earlier, one can clearly notice that each player exemplifies a certain tactfulness. As one listens to the accompaniment of bass and drums, one hears each musician being 'pulled' towards certain actions by virtue of the happening of the situation; a slight pause from Black (drums) here, a short ostinato from Dunn (bass) there. Jensson, too, appears habituated to the situation unfolding around him. All three performers immediately grasp the significant qualities of the situation, they sense the atmosphere of the dynamic situation, and orient themselves accordingly in the situation; they are a part of the broader situation that goes beyond their individual subjectivities. The immediacy by which this responsiveness occurs is demonstrative of body schema and habit at work, and the appropriateness of their responses is demonstrative of their tactfulness.

Jensson, Dunn and Black each demonstrate a confidence and a willingness to enter into a dialogue with the work and exemplify what Davey describes when he writes that 'tact demands a sensitive ear'.[115] Each musician is attuned to the situation and responds with an immediacy that highlights they do not need all the implicit terms of the situation made explicit in order to orient themselves while being *led* by the situation. That is, they do not undertake conceptual reflection or abstract thought, rather they attend to the complex qualities of the situation, relying, for the most part, on their body schema, habits and tactfulness to respond spontaneously and appropriately.

The improvisational situation

To improvise, it has been argued, is to find oneself set in place, attending and responding to the circumstances that arise by virtue of the conversational structure at issue in improvised musical performance. In this chapter the idea of 'situation' at issue in this book has been interrogated and laid out. It was argued that the situation, and subsequently the idea of place, is not merely a metaphorical assertion, but an ontological concept underpinning improvised musical performance. Such a claim builds upon the idea of conversation from the preceding chapter, where to converse, whether with another person, a musical work, or a text/score, is to *encounter* something beyond oneself – a subject matter, a work of art and so forth – and allow oneself to be *led* by the happening of the situation.

When one finds oneself in conversation, such that one is improvising in the manner described in this chapter, one always experiences a certain distance from that which they are attending to. The distance at issue here is twofold. First, it is proximal in the sense that the work is *there* with the player as a distinct 'thing' and is therefore not merely confined to or reducible to the mental capacities of the player. Second, it is indicative of the 'circumstances' facing the player, insofar as the player, by virtue of this distance, is always separate to the work and yet not so removed that they stand beyond the situation, looking in, objectively. Thus, the player always encounters a certain indeterminacy – they are always responding to a particular, predominately qualitative, character of the situation as it happens.

By virtue of their conversing, players find themselves charged with responding to a certain set of circumstances that emerge in the place of the conversation's occurrence. Players converse with that which is disclosed to them. And insofar as they are genuinely conversing, that is, attending and responding to the indeterminacy of the situation, players must come to recognize, to quote Gadamer, 'the value of the alien'.[116] Which is to say that in the improvisational situation players necessarily encounter that which is alien, strange or unfamiliar, in the sense of *improviso* – improvisation is a spontaneous attending and responding to a situation that is without antecedent, and so is unprepared for and unanticipated. The 'event of the turning' is this recognizing the value of the alien and habitually turning towards it to receive the possibilities for action offered by the divinities in the happening of the situation. Thus, as will be discussed in subsequent chapters, improvisation might be thought of as a 'traverse' or sorts, where players are led by the possibilities encountered in the situation such that their improvisational engagement illuminates a certain character of the place in which they *are*.

The way in which players undertake this situated conversation relies upon the player's ability to spontaneously orient themselves and respond habitually and tactfully to the complex indeterminate situation. This situation, however, includes not only that which is of concern – that which is the 'focus' of improvisation – but also all those things that enable improvisation to happen, irrespective of whether they are recognized by the player or not. Thus, it is the *improvisational situation* from which improvisational activity may be said to emerge that is the 'origin' of improvised musical performance. The spontaneous conversation is not something that one 'performs' or 'directs', but as noted, is something that *happens* – it emerges from and is given by the situation.

3
Where are we when we improvise music?

The previous two chapters have broadly concerned themselves with the 'focus' of improvisation – the way in which players orient themselves towards and conversationally attend and respond to the work – and the 'origin' of improvisation – the way in which one's thinking and acting is structured by and is responsive to the situation in which one finds oneself. What remains to be articulated is the 'horizon' of improvisation – the way in which the player's improvisational engagement is both enabled and limited by their situatedness in the improvisational situation. The concern of this chapter – the final chapter of Part I – is the 'horizon' of improvised musical performance. While this topic was alluded in the previous chapter, it will now be discussed directly and pursued by considering the question, 'where are we when we improvise music?' Which is to ask, what is the horizon or boundary from which improvised musical performance may be said to emerge? Given that the question 'where are we when we improvise?' appears to be intimately tied to that which is the 'focus' and 'origin' of improvised musical performance, this question may also be understood as an inquiry into where one is when one listens to and converses with the music that one is playing. That is, the question of 'where' implicates the nature of 'listening' at issue in improvised musical performance.

While on the face of it, the answer to the question 'where are we when we improvise music?' would appear to be obvious: in the practice room, the auditorium, the studio, the concert hall – in whatever place the players engaged in the practice of improvisation are located – perhaps this answer emerges too quickly, especially in its assumption that the question is simply one of bodily location. It is common to find talk of music as taking us to a different place – and even of the player as being 'caught up in' or 'taken up by' the music that they are playing so that they are no longer fully aware of their physical location; they are typically said to be 'in the moment'. How seriously should we take these ideas? Given that the 'focus' and 'origin' of improvised musical performance turned out to be the *improvisational situation* itself, and given the way in which the happening of the situation is intimately tied to the happening of the work that the player listens to and converses with, we should take seriously the idea that there may be an ambiguity in the question – and the possible answers – as to where one is when one improvises music. An ambiguity that is suggestive of a deeper and more nuanced inquiry into the question of 'where' and the nature of listening with respect to improvised musical performance.[1]

The question 'where are we when ...?' has been posed by others.[2] Notably, in 1993 the German philosopher and cultural theorist Peter Sloterdijk wrote an essay entitled 'Where Are We When We Hear Music?',[3] which, despite the focus on the audience rather than the player, also acknowledges the relationship between 'where' and 'listening' or 'hearing'. Curiously, Sloterdijk does not believe we are (wholly) in the world when we hear music. He writes, 'people can never be completely in the world when they are listening to music'.[4] He also suggests that music 'transport[s] us from dull hours to a better world'.[5] On precisely how we are to think of this 'better world', such that we are not 'completely' in the world when we hear music, Sloterdijk's account is ambiguous and offers no real topological insight that might assist the present inquiry.[6]

What is interesting, however, is the basic idea that Sloterdijk alludes to of finding oneself withdrawn from the ordinary world when experiencing music, something relevant to performers and audience members alike. As noted, it seems players do tend to find themselves 'somewhere else' while playing music. This 'somewhere else', however, is surely in the world. Indeed, Sloterdijk's assertion that people cannot be completely in the world when listening to music appears to be rather problematic. As ancient wisdom tells us (Archytas of Tarentum), 'to be (at all) is to be in (some) place'[7] and to be in place is *always* to be in the world. Thus, while there is something worth pursuing in the idea that players may tend to find themselves 'somewhere else' during their performances, we must be able to understand this 'somewhere else' in concrete and phenomenologically accurate terms; this is the goal of this chapter.

As mentioned, the idea of being 'caught up in' or 'taken up by' music suggests that the idea of 'where' is tied not only to one's situatedness but also to listening; to be taken up by the music that one is playing, one must be able to hear it. Thus, to address the question of 'where' depends upon addressing both the region within which improvised musical performance occurs and the nature of listening that is at issue in such performance. As will become clear, it is primarily, although not exclusively, that which players listen to – that which is of concern – that demarcates the boundary of improvised musical performance (as noted in the previous chapter, the structure of improvisation is given not only by that which is of concern but also by an array of elements that are necessarily *there* but are not considered by the player – it is the former that is the primary concern of this chapter). Since the boundary of the improvisational situation is constituted primarily by the happening of the work that the player auditorily attends to, we will first consider the character of listening and being 'taken up by' music before moving on to consider the boundary of improvised musical performance.

Listening at the threshold

While he does not develop his question primarily with respect to music, focussing on aesthetic experience more broadly, Finnish aesthetician Harri Mäcklin addresses the question, 'where do we go in and through a work of art?'[8] Mäcklin presents the idea of the 'poetic world' of works of art, which he claims is distinct from but related to the 'lifeworld' of the beholder. Mäcklin asserts:

> It is clear that when I am immersed in the happening of the work, I am not taken to another world, which I could inhabit as my own; instead, I am brought to a *threshold*, to a peculiar in-between of the piece's poetic world

and my lifeworld, where I am capable of seeing a glimpse of the other world without thereby being able to dwell in it.⁹

Following Mäcklin, to be 'caught up' in music as a player is not so much to find oneself *beyond* the world but to find oneself at the threshold of the poetic world of the musical. The poetic world, according to Mäcklin, refers to 'the combination of elements that constitute [the work of art] as that particular piece',¹⁰ such as the history and tradition in which the work is situated, as well as the rules, melodies, timbres, atmospheres and so on. The poetic world constitutes itself 'from possibilities inherent in the lifeworld' such that it is 'both a part of the lifeworld but separate from it'.¹¹ Indeed, as the French phenomenologist Mikel Dufrenne writes, 'there is nothing but *the* world, and yet the aesthetic object is pregnant with *a* world of its own'.¹² We are *entirely* in the world when we hear music but in aesthetic experience, we are brought to the threshold of the poetic world of the work. In improvised musical performance, which involves an intimate engagement with the work, players find themselves at a certain threshold – the threshold of the work that they conversationally attend to.

Multiple uses of the term 'world', however, in the excerpts from Mäcklin and Dufrenne, perhaps invite a degree of confusion. The 'poetic world' and 'lifeworld' constitute different experiences of *the* world. Both are embedded in and refer to the broader (singular) world that goes beyond any particular poetic experience of the world and beyond any single lifetime. What Mäcklin directs us to is the difference between *ordinary* and *poetic* engagement with *the* world. In ordinary experience the world mostly passes us by; as Heidegger would say, we tend to navigate the world 'circumspectly'.¹³ That is, we mostly engage with things in the world as a means to orient ourselves and get by in the world. For the most part, things do not stand out in everyday experience. Sound is typically experienced in this way; we typically pay no mind to everyday sound. It is there in the world, but we mostly do not concern ourselves with it in any direct or thematic way.

Poetic experience, in contrast, is *engaged*, *thematic* and invites *wonder*, and so, as far as sound is concerned, is distinct from both sound that we pay no attention to and irritating noises that grab our attention but which we attempt to ignore. The everyday sounds of Times Square, for instance, are made salient – are poeticized – by Max Neuhaus's 'Times Square' sound installation,[14] where Neuhaus installed a generator and loudspeaker under a subway grate by the intersection of Broadway and Seventh Avenue that emanated resonant drone-like sounds that both contrast and blend into the cacophony of Times Square. Works of art, regardless of their medium, borrow from and appropriate the 'ordinary' world and thematize elements of that which is appropriated, and in so doing make those elements salient, which draws us into poetic engagement. Everyday sounds of Times Square, for instance, are thematized by Neuhaus's installation in ways they are not in ordinary experience. Indeed, the sounds of Neuhaus's installation may easily be overlooked. But as one discovers or is directed to the installation, not only does one hear the installation as such but one's relationship to and consideration of other sounds in the world may also be altered. Thus, certain possibilities of those sounds – intriguing or thought-provoking characteristics of the sounds that were not previously considered – are revealed in poetic engagement.

Engagement with the 'poetic world' and engagement with the 'lifeworld', then, to employ Mäcklin's terminology are not engagements with different worlds; there is only one world. But engagement with the poetic world of the work reveals a certain character of *the* world that otherwise exists but is not thematic in ordinary experience. Being at the 'threshold' of the poetic world does not entail standing at the threshold of a *different* world to the one the player already inhabits. Instead, it is a standing at the threshold of *the world itself*, where the player's engagement with the work permits them to experience a certain aspect of the world anew.

The threshold, or what may also be referred to as the 'liminal', at issue here is that which stands *between* the everyday or ordinary world of the player and the poetic world of the work. The liminal, however, is always a crossing; it refers to a certain *movement* towards or away from, it is never a point of rest or stasis.[15] The threshold is best understood not as a 'here', that is, as somewhere static, but instead in terms of a certain relationality, as a 'there',[16] where one is oriented and moving towards the poetic world. The happening of improvisation is a *continual* crossing of the threshold towards the poetic; one never reaches a stable point within the poetic world where one might rest.

Those who find themselves at this threshold cannot wholly occupy the poetic such that the world at large may be thematized poetically. Instead, the player encounters a *particular* poeticization of *certain* elements that constitute the work as *that* particular work by virtue of conversational engagement.

The idea of the threshold, then, is essential. As noted in the preceding chapter with respect to Heidegger's fourfold, there must always be this balance, opposition even, between the poetic and the ordinary – unconcealment and concealment. What the work reveals in the sense of poeticization occurs only by virtue of concealment. That which is revealed always *stands out* against that which is concealed, and thus there is an essential and irreducible relationship between revealing and concealing, between the poetic world and ordinary world. Due to its reliance on *standing out* from concealment, the poeticization of the world is never absolute or complete; it necessarily requires concealment from that which to stand out from. Thus, as noted, to find oneself crossing into the poetic world during the performance of music, then, is not to move into a different world but to find oneself coming into *the* world, in a new way.

Precisely 'what' will be made salient to players during performance as they cross the threshold of the poetic world of the work, however, cannot be given in advance. Indeed, as noted by Mäcklin,[17] the poetic world that one finds oneself at the threshold of is always singular, it is always specific to the particular work. Moreover, it is always specific to *that* individual performance. What is thematized will be unique to the performance, not only by virtue of the work but also by virtue of the prior understanding of the player to whom the work reveals a character of the world. What it is that *stands out* is not solely determined by the work or the player. But not just *anything* will stand out. What stands out must be present in the improvisational situation. For the sake of example, what might stand out could be certain instrumental timbres, textures, rhythms, the reverberant qualities of the performance venue, the silence of the audience and so forth. It is by virtue of the player's engagement with the work – the player's listening at the threshold of the poetic world of the work – that the player encounters and engages with those salient characteristics of the world as they are given within the horizon of the singular event of musical performance.

Such that players open themselves up to receive possibilities given by the situation, we may say that they *listen towards* the poetic world – a straining towards a character of the world present in the poetic world of the work that one might improvisationally engage with. There is evidence of such listening, in, Australian guitarist and visual artist, Ren Walters's description of his improvisatory approach to solo performance:

> Listening for the unintended; being prepared to 'loosen the grip' of one's control over how sounds are being made and following the consequences of that, which requires using awareness rather than judgment, and patience to allow something initially unfamiliar/uncomfortable, its own space. Consider that whatever this sonic event/process becomes, will be a unique story, it then becomes a matter of commitment to elucidate. . . . Imagine observing a large and beautiful tree[,] its sculptural qualities are easily admired and enjoyed. After a while we begin to notice more details, like its bark and leaves. We may be drawn to get closer. Oozes of sap, insect lives, spider webs, soon it becomes apparent there is a thriving microecology that was not visible before. There is a world of sonic possibility.[18]

Walters describes an approach to listening where he does not merely settle for that which is familiar but *listens towards* that which may not be immediately apparent – he orients himself towards the unforeseen and unexpected (*improviso*), seeking to encounter possibilities given by the situation. Walters describes a mode of comportment where he opens himself up to receive the strange; by giving himself over to the situation he listens for possibilities that may arise from the improvisational conversation.

We notice this approach in action on the track 'Raphsody' from Walters and Magnusson's album, *de flection*,[19] which features the guitarists playing duets of free improvisation. One immediately notices both players exhibiting the patience described by Walters. Particularly as the track begins, Walters and Magnusson take their time, allowing the work to breathe, as it were, giving each musical theme its own space. Given the sparseness of the track in its early stages, one can quite clearly hear distinct themes emerge. Moreover, one can perceive the way in which Walters and Magnusson are drawn to develop certain themes and transition from one to the next. One can hear themes become catalysts for the 'unique story' Walters mentions, where the duo is tasked with elucidating that story and following the possibilities given by the happening of the situation. For instance, the track begins with an exploration of harmonics. Until approximately 1'10", one hears the way in which both players attempt to explore and be led by the possibilities of harmonics on the guitar. Rather than merely settling for that which is familiar, the players orient themselves towards the strange (*improviso*) by virtue of their listening. They listen towards and seek something that piques their interest – something that *leads* them to the threshold. Improvised musical performance, such that it relies upon an engagement with the strange or unfamiliar, relies upon listening.

The event of listening

So far, two assertions have been made:

1. Listening draws the player into conversational engagement with the poetic character of the improvisational situation.
2. The player's engagement is never with the world as a whole but the world as it is given in a certain place – the improvisational situation.

To address the question of 'where' one is when one improvises music, it is necessary to further detail the way in which players attend to the music that they are playing, before moving on to consider the horizon or boundary itself.

Given the nature of listening described before, listening can be characterized as an event that opens up or clears space for a certain character of the world to *stand out*. Thus, I agree with French philosopher Jean-Luc Nancy when, of 'sonorous time', he writes, 'it is a present in waves on a swell, not in a point on a line; it is a time that opens up, that is hollowed out, that is enlarged or ramified'.[20] He also speaks of the 'open and above all opening presence'[21] in which listening takes place. The event of listening appears to show something of the essential character of time or temporality: one does not find oneself *in* time in the sense of succession but as emerging from *out of* time. Rather than think of time in terms of duration or succession, Nancy alludes to a conception of time that echoes Heidegger's Event, which refers to an *opening* from which timespace (*Zeit-raum*) emerges.²² That is, as will be discussed later, the happening of improvised musical performance is not fundamentally temporal but should rather be understood topologically, such that the happening of the event is that from which both time *and* space come forth as timespace.

Understanding the improvisational situation in this way – as not merely temporal but topological – is in tension with the temporocentrism²³ that dominates much of the conversation around sound and music. Indeed, in contemporary music scholarship one commonly encounters statements such as, 'music is a temporal art which, unlike the visual arts, exists by necessity in time',²⁴ and 'music unfolds in time; in other words, one thing happens after another'.²⁵ Music is often referred to as the temporal art par excellence.²⁶ While such claims have a degree of validity about them, the priority given to time at the expense of space and place in the music literature is pronounced.

American philosopher Christoph Cox, for instance, upholds a preference for understanding sound and music from a predominately temporal perspective. For example, when Neuhaus writes, 'traditionally composers have located the elements of a composition in time. One idea which I am interested in is locating them, instead, in space, and letting the listener place them in his own time',²⁷ Cox undermines his consideration of space. In response to Neuhaus, Cox writes, 'the time/space distinction is a red herring. The real distinction is between two kinds of time: *pulsed time* (the time of music and meaning) and *non-pulsed time* or *duration* (the time of sound matter itself)'.²⁸ That space is thought to be such an issue relates to the supposed implications of conceiving the spatial in terms of stasis; spatial thinking is sometimes seen as a mode of conceptualizing the world as a collection of discrete objects at the expense of acknowledging the perpetual flux or process of the world.

For French philosopher Henri Bergson, whose distinction between 'time' and 'duration' largely informs Cox's argument, time refers to a 'medium in which our conscious states form a discrete series so as to admit of being counted'.²⁹ He writes further, 'time . . . is nothing but space'.³⁰ Thus, time, as we see with respect to the way in which we typically divide time into seconds, minutes, hours, days, etc. is divisible and therefore spatialized and measurable. Duration, on the other hand, according to Bergson, 'is the form which the succession of our conscious states assumes when our ego lets itself *live*, when it refrains from separating its present state from its former states'.[31] Bergson argues that the succession or flow at issue in duration, in contrast to the divisible succession of spatialized time, is 'pure succession' – a primordial conception of temporality where past, present and future form a genuine continuum; a flow that produces beings and events.

For Bergson, the goal is to demonstrate how we must suspend spatial thought and give priority to duration. Such a view, however, demonstrates a fundamental misunderstanding of the character of time and space, for it assumes they are mutually exclusive and therefore amenable to being separated and theorized independently of one another, or that one is derivative of the other. Indeed, Heidegger points out that Bergson's account of duration ultimately fails to understand authentic time.[32] Regardless of whether one thinks in terms of divisible moments (time) or the permeation of past, present and future (duration), both, for Bergson, are understood in terms of *succession*. A quantitative 'space' of time, an hour, for instance, is not eliminated in the qualitative account of duration, for the spatiality is still present, it is simply that no distinct beginning or end is given in the qualitative account.

On the prioritization of temporality, Malpas writes,

> One of the problematic features of the prioritisation of temporality alone is . . . it prevents any adequate thinking of world – of that prior mode of engagement in which we are already implicated – and in this sense it prevents us from any adequate thinking of *transcendence*, understood as an opening up of that which goes beyond the immediately present or presented (and which is surely at the heart of any creative engagement with the world, whether through thinking, making, or acting).[33]

Malpas argues that the unity of time and space – timespace – emerges from the 'active opening' of place,[34] consistent with the account of situation given in the preceding chapter. Time constitutes the dynamicity of place, and space the extendedness of place – they emerge together in the unified happening of place. One can only think of time and/or space separately if one does so abstractly. It is only through the unity of time and space that one properly understands sound and music, and, particularly, improvised musical performance.

The temporality at issue in improvised musical performance is evident in the Latin *extempore*, from which, along with *improviso*, mentioned earlier, the term 'improvisation' is derived. *Extempore* is literally 'out of time' – *ex* (out of) *tempore*, ablative of *tempus* (time) – but in the sense of being that which is *of* time or '*of* the moment', and so *stands out* from time, which is not dissimilar to Nancy's idea of 'sonorous time', mentioned earlier. Time, here, is not to be conceived in terms of duration or succession but as the temporalization of the event – an opening from which the happening of the event or situation itself comes forth. Thus, time comes forth with space from the happening of the situation. The temporality at issue in the improvisational situation emerges from the situation itself, such that the happening of the performance is responsive to the *extempore* of the event.

Being 'in the moment'

To attend to the music that one is playing is to perform from *out of* time. It is to participate in the happening of the timespace of the event. 'Timespace', Heidegger writes, 'as the unity of the originary temporalisation and spatialisation, is itself originarily the site of the moment.'[35] The 'moment' at issue here is an opening from which the event of performance emerges. To listen to the music that one is playing at the threshold of the poetic world is to open up the world 'in the moment', or, better, *in the situation*, such that one's participation in the situation thematizes a certain character of the place in which one is situated, poetically. The idea of being 'in the moment', then, is perhaps best understood as being 'in the situation'. Although, as will become clear, the idea of being 'in the moment', such that it tends to evoke ideas of 'engagement' and 'singularity', draws attention to both the dynamicity and participatory nature of the *situation* in which players find themselves.

Given the prevalence of the idea of playing 'in the moment' in both the academic literature and everyday conversation, it is worth discussing more thoroughly. Typically, the phrase seems to be employed to describe the mode of attunement demonstrated by performers. For example, George E. Lewis offers, 'you can justify it after the fact or you can try to rationalise it before the fact, but in the moment you are just there and you commit',[36] and Ellen

Waterman writes of improvising musicians that 'all their decisions are made in the moment'.[37] There is no shortage of quotations that link improvisation in music to being 'in the moment'. Less common, however, are explicit explanations regarding what being 'in the moment' actually means. Even less common is any detailed interrogation of whether or not the commonplace idea of being 'in the moment' does justice to the issues at stake.

From the perspective of cognitive psychology, Andrys Onsman and Robert Burke offer the following explanation of being 'in the moment':

> The sublimation of the cognitive processing to ignore input that does not have direct impact on the decision-making equates to a state of heightened awareness of and exclusive focus on the task at hand. It is this that musicians refer to as 'being in the moment'.[38]

Here Onsman and Burke make explicit what is often only implicit when the phrase 'in the moment' is invoked. Their definition is one that suggests a mode of focus where musicians attune themselves to the 'task at hand' while blocking out thoughts unrelated to performing that particular task. This definition is an adequate summation of how the phrase 'in the moment' is readily employed. This understanding, however, highlights an implicit preoccupation with subjectivity – the focus is on the cognitive processing, decision-making and awareness of the player at the expense of any real account of unity,[39] which has been the focus of the preceding chapters. Further, what is left unsaid is what the 'moment', in the phrase 'in the moment', refers to.

One can infer from the music scholar Daniel Fischlin that the phrase 'in the moment' has a strong connection with temporality:

> Improvisation is . . . an invocation of the event horizon of what is thinkable, doable in the moment in which it occurs. . . . Being 'in time' necessitates a response to time, expresses a relationship to time that is at once intensely ludic in the moment but also memorialisation of all past times, and a salute to times that could be. Histories flow from these improvisatory acts in time. Improvisation responds to time, is responsible to the potential always found in time.[40]

While the conclusion that the term 'moment' bears a connection to 'time' perhaps seems obvious, it is interesting to see how the concept of time is invoked, because Fischlin employs it in two different ways. He refers to improvising in the moment as 'intensely ludic' – suggesting an understanding of the 'moment' as spontaneous, or as occurring 'now'. But he also suggests that improvisation involves not only the 'now' or the present but also past and future.

Fischlin's conception of time or being 'in the moment' bears a similarity to Edmund Husserl's, principal founder of phenomenology, notion of 'internal time consciousness'[41] with respect to Husserl's tripartite view of the composition of the 'now'. Husserl suggests the 'now' is comprised of three components:[42]

1. Primal impressions: Live experiences, the 'now'.
2. Retentions: As primal impressions transition into the past, they remain in one's consciousness as 'retentions' before they gradually fade from consciousness and become memories.
3. Protentions: The expectation that the future, or something, will come.

Thought of in this way, being 'in the moment' is always more than a mere instant – there is a certain depth to the 'now', not entirely dissimilar to Bergson's account of duration. Drawing from Husserl's conception of internal time consciousness Gary Peters writes on the topic of being 'in the moment' that 'the moment is no longer identical to the instant but, through the temporal reach of intentionality, becomes an *event* that is sustained as long as attention, retention, and protention hold together and flow into each other'.[43] For Peters, the 'moment' is not a mere 'instant' but a temporal event that encompasses past, present and future.

Whereas Onsman and Burke,[44] for instance, assert that one moment springs into the next, which suggests understanding performance as a sequence of moments (perhaps implicitly reflecting the Bergsonian notion of time), Peters argues the event constitutes the performance as a whole. He suggests there is a continuum between attention, retention and protention that improvisers 'hold together' for the duration of the event. He writes,

> The beginning and the end of a written/composed work coexist within the simultaneity of the originary document, but in a completely improvised work they do not and, thus, the improviser has to both begin the improvisation and then retain this beginning as a (the) moment of the work's unfolding and its ultimate end. In other words, the beginning is not just the commencement of the work (the instant) but also an originary phase of the moment of the work as a whole; once this beginning phase expires, through insufficient attention, the work expires with it.[45]

What players attend to, in Peters's account, is the event or situation as a whole, a view that I endorse. There is no moment to moment as Onsman and Burke suggest but rather a unified event. But the unfolding of the event or the moment cannot merely be conceived in terms of succession or temporality, regardless of whether that succession is conceived quantitatively (time) or quantitatively (duration), to employ Bergsonian distinctions. The 'moment', as issue here, is an opening from which the event or situation emerges.

The phrase 'in the moment' should not, then, be understood in exclusively temporal terms, nor in terms of the subjective focus or the mental processing of the player. To be in the moment is not to find oneself situated with respect to a certain durational succession but to play from *out of* the moment itself, in the sense of *extempore*. Indeed, it would be accurate to say that inasmuch as players are 'in the moment', they are '*of* the moment', in much the same way that one is *of* the situation. To say that improvisation is *of* the moment is to say that improvisation is *of* the world; indeed, the work is a thematization of the world. It is the topological unity of place that is the opening of the moment. To be *of* the moment is to be engaged in the happening of the situation to the extent that one surrenders oneself, by virtue of listening to the music that one is playing, to the immanent happening of that situation. It is to find oneself at the threshold of the poetic world and, by engaging with the world, allow the poetic to stand out from the ordinary world in the happening of the improvisational situation.

The performance of listening can be understood in terms of an opening up or a making present, where to listen allows that which the work poeticizes to *emerge* or *come forth* from *out of* the 'moment' of performance. The poetic character of the world that the work illuminates to the player does not *arrive* so much as it comes to *stand out* in the situation in which one *is*. Thus, it was already there, albeit, prior to the event of listening, concealed. The participatory engagement of improvisation – where one attends and responds to the work, that is, listens – clears a space for that which was *already there* to emerge. To listen is to allow the sound that was already there to *re*-sound, poetically, as if for the first time. The music that one plays genuinely emerges from the happening of place – the improvisational situation. It is the 'moment' or 'situation', as opposed to simply the 'site' or 'venue', that establishes the boundary of improvised musical performance, as will be discussed further.

Listening as a creative engagement with that which is *there*

It is from within the happening of the improvisational situation that players encounter the world as thematized by the work. The improvisational situation emerges in the midst of things – nested in a certain history, tradition, culture and discourse – and is itself a bounded opening within which things emerge. As entwined with performance, the work emerges in the world from this bounded opening. But as something that emerges in the *world* and not merely in the *present*, the work brings forth the world; the work is the happening of the world, musically-poetically. In this sense, the nature of 'transcendence' mentioned by Malpas, earlier, can be understood. Of this transcendence he writes, 'it is not the transcendence that brings about world transformation, but rather the small flicker of light which suddenly shows us who and what we are, which illuminates what is around us and then dies out'.[46] This reflects the character of the work. The work emerges in the world not as a distinct thing unrelated to everything around it but in a complex relationship with that which it emerges in the midst of. As players find themselves at the threshold of the poetic world of the work their improvisational conversation illuminates a certain character of the world.

The improvisational situation, as noted, is the emergence of timespace in and from place. But it is not merely that which is present in the happening of the situation that is meaningful. What makes what is present significant is relative to absence, just as unconcealment depends upon concealment. Thus, music, it might be said, is a way of giving voice to silence. The presence of the work brings forth a small flicker of light that not only illuminates what is around us but also can make salient that which is absent. That which is illuminated by the happening of the situation always goes beyond that which is made sonorous and is essentially indeterminate; one can give no prior determinations as to what will be made salient by the work's coming-into-presence.

As something that happens in the world, improvised musical performance always goes beyond a strictly musical frame. To play music is not merely an engagement with the musical. Rather, in finding oneself at the threshold of the poetic world, to play music is to participate in the happening of the world. One participates in an activity that is truly productive – one's engagement with the world illuminates a particular character of the world itself, of which music is a part. Improvised musical performance allows the world to come forth in a way that is unforeseen and new – *improviso* is also *innovare* – it is original and originary, as Heidegger would say. It is important to note, however, that the 'original' character of the productivity of improvisation is not creation in the sense of *ex nihilo* (out of nothing) but, as Benson says, '*creatio ex improvisatione*', where 'artistic genesis', he writes, 'always begins *somewhere*';[47] the productivity of improvisation is a bringing forth or making salient that which is already *there*, in the situation.

To improvise music is to create from that which is *there*. As noted in the preceding chapter, players *receive* possibilities given by the situation. To encounter those unexpected elements that give rise to improvisational engagement the player must listen. It is by listening as one plays that allows the player to engage with those elements of the work that *stand out* in the situation, those that, when attended to in the 'right' way (whatever that may be in the context of the particular performance), renders a performance *inspired*, as we say. Those salient characteristics of the work capable of illuminating the world in a particular way never appear to the player who does not listen. Non-listeners remain firmly planted in the ordinary world, sealed off from the wonder and difference that exists beyond their own subjectivity. They remain closed to the possibilities of musical performance that may come forth 'in the moment'.

Listening offers players the means to *receive* and creatively engage with possibilities for action previously not considered. This idea of creativity is the creativity of *participation*, or, as mentioned, what Benson refers to as '*creatio ex improvisatione*', where to create is to 'fabricate out of what is conveniently on hand'.[48] Creation is thus not absolute, in the sense that the demiurge may be said to create from inchoate matter, but rather involves engaging with that which is *there* to produce something new so that an unforeseen character of the world may *stand out* and become present. The creativity at issue in improvisation is a mode of creativity that echoes the idea of the muses who were thought to inspire, guide and assist poets, authors and musicians. The 'inspiration' at issue here, however, may be said to come from the world, specifically, from the situation in which the player *is*. What is available to inspire, what is 'conveniently on hand', as would Benson say, is not only the player's prior understanding of the world but also those possibilities for action that are *received* through listening. The player's creative engagement with the work hinges on their attending and responding to the situation in which they find themselves. Thus, the creativity and participation at issue in improvised musical performance are intimately tied to listening.

Every aspect that enables improvisational engagement is *there* in the situation. Everything that constitutes a common matter of concern for the players is wholly contained in the moment or situation of the performance's occurrence. Thus, the 'where' of improvised musical performance refers to and is limited by that which is the 'focus' and 'origin' of improvisational engagement. The boundary of improvisational engagement is given by that which is a common matter of concern – the work. To understand that boundary, we will now turn to the way in which players may be said to be 'situated' or 'placed' by the work that they are playing.

The horizon of the improvisational situation

While players do not experience the 'outside' of the work, as it were, always attending and responding to a common matter of concern that is *there* with them *in* the improvisational situation, there is nonetheless a horizon or boundary that situates this engagement. Horizons are simple to conceptualize in visual terms; the horizon is the limit of one's vision. Beyond the horizon, nothing is visible. Indeed, the region that lies beyond one's field of vision is the realm of the *in*visible, but it also constitutes the boundary within which what one does experience comes forth. It is only *within* the horizon of the visible that one encounters visible phenomena towards which one orients oneself.

Given the centrality of the concept of the horizon in Husserl's phenomenology,[49] and given that phenomenology is sometimes charged with a certain ocularcentrism,[50] the concept of the horizon may at first seem to be of peripheral importance to a discussion focussed on music and listening. But horizonality is at issue in sound, no less than sight.[51] The idea of 'horizon', here, relates to the notion of 'boundary', in line with Heidegger's assertion that 'a boundary is not that at which something stops but, as the Greeks recognised, the boundary is that from which something *begins its presencing*. That is why the concept is that of *horismos*, that is, the horizon, the boundary.'[52] The horizon or boundary demarcates a particular place or region within which action occurs, which holds for hearing as much as it does for vision. Indeed, as Ihde notes, 'until the question of a horizon is raised, it would be quite possible to fail to discover silence'.[53] According to Ihde, silence is the 'other side' of sound.[54] Just as in visual perception where objects have an 'other side' that we cannot see that gives the object a certain 'depth', the depth of sound is given by silence. Sound is always situated, always given within, and limited by the horizon of silence.

The significance of the horizon for the current inquiry can be gleaned from the following statement by Ihde: 'The horizon situates the field which in turn situates the thing.'[55] To understand where one is when one improvises music is to understand the horizon that situates improvisational engagement. Acknowledging that the horizon 'situates the thing' brings to the fore the situatedness, or placed character, of improvised musical performance. Players are located within the horizon of the work's happening, the relative boundary of which is the 'other side' of the work – that which is beyond the 'common matter of concern', as discussed in Chapter 1. To conceptualize the way in which the happening of the work situates the players requires attending to the nature of sound.

Audible phenomena, like visual phenomena, conveys spatial information such as direction and distance. One can orient oneself with respect to sounds similarly to the way in which one can orient oneself with respect to the objects of vision. Objects of hearing, no less than objects of vision, exist externally to the subject. Philosopher of perception Casey O'Callaghan writes that 'sounds are in the world. Sounds are the entities that, in the first instance, we auditorily perceive.'[56] This view, which echoes and extends the thinking of *Groupe de Recherche de Musique Concrète* founder Pierre Schaeffer,[57] holds that sounds are not secondary qualities – they are not merely the auditory properties of objects we see or feel, nor are they dependent on one's perception of them. Just as the tree stands in the woods irrespective of whether or not someone is there to see it, so too does it make a sound when it falls, irrespective of whether or not someone is present to hear it. Sounds are ontological particulars that occur in time and space.

O'Callaghan, challenging the theory from acoustic science that sounds are waves, which implies that sounds 'exist or occur in different parts of the medium as time passes',[58] asserts that 'sounds . . . are located roughly where we hear them to be: at or near their sources'.[59] Thus, when a percussionist strikes a snare drum, the sound is located at or near the site of collision between the stick and the drum. Other ensemble members who may not be in immediate proximity to the drum hear the sound by virtue of the sound's displacement of a medium (in this example the medium is air). O'Callaghan's argument is that sounds themselves do not travel, but they are perceived at a distance from their sounding by virtue of a medium, for example, air, water, metal, helium. Just as a splash occurs at a particular locality but also creates a ripple effect in the medium (water) that travels outwards, sounds similarly displace a medium creating what are typically thought of as sound waves. Unlike a splash, however, which requires the medium to exist, O'Callaghan posits that sounds occur without the presence of a medium, such as in a vacuum.[60] Sounds exist regardless of whether or not there is a medium. However, since there is no medium to displace in a vacuum, and therefore no waves are generated for us to auditorily perceive, we do not perceive sound in a vacuum

– while sounds themselves do not rely upon a medium, our perception of sound does.

What this means for understanding the work that comes forth from the improvisational situation is that it materially exists as an entity in the world. The music that comes forth from the situation is a constellation of sounds that exist at or near where players perceive them to be. Those sounds are experienced by the players via the waves the sounds set in motion by disturbing a medium. Those waves are perceptible within distinct topological parameters. In order to attend and respond to the work – participate in improvisation – players must be situated and oriented in such a way as to listen to the work – within the right topological happening, that is, in the right place.

The topography of the situation is created by the happening of the work, and thus its qualities are necessarily dynamic. Take, for instance, Australian saxophonist and experimental musician, Jim Denley's album, *Through Fire, Crevice + the Hidden Valley*.[61] Of this album, Denley writes,

> From the 18th of May 2006, I spent 15 days armed with sax, camera, audio recorders, food and a solar recharger in the Budawang Mountains, a wilderness area in the Morton National Park, South West of Nowra on the east coast of Australia. These mountains are full of dramatic and rugged rock formations, caves, crevices and a hidden valley – it's a wonderland of natural acoustics. Presumably people have been making music in these spaces for thousands of years, but it's almost certain sax hasn't been heard there before.[62]

Despite otherwise being considered a 'solo' album, the work Denley converses with includes sounds generated by the immediate natural environment. Denley did not simply record himself playing solo in the remote Budawang Mountains of New South Wales. Rather the album documents Denley attending and responding to those sounds naturally occurring while playing his saxophone in that locale. In 'standard' performance settings it is not uncommon for such natural sounds to be relegated to the background while performers and audience members alike attend to the 'music'; naturally occurring sounds do not tend to constitute the common matter of concern that players attend to. Denley's performances, on the other hand, draw these natural or 'scenic' sounds to the fore and they become an active part of the work. Resultingly, Denley's performances draw attention to both the dynamic and situated character of improvised musical performance. By making salient the naturally occurring sounds of the environment one recognizes how that which is a common matter of concern can change over the course of the performance and yet, precisely what possibilities for engagement emerge are limited by virtue of both the broader region that nests the improvisational situation and the situation itself.

What is interesting with respect to understanding the dynamism of the work is that things that generate natural sounds, such as animals and wind, noticeably start, stop and move. Unlike a traditional jazz trio comprised of piano, double bass and drums, for example, where each musician is more or less stationary for the entire performance and sounds not generated by those three instruments are of little consequence, meaning that the sonic topography of the work is predominately altered only with respect to variability in dynamics, for Denley, the place of his performances is constantly mutating in a quite radical sense. Sounds, both loud and soft, suddenly emerge from variable directions at variable distances and then disappear, significantly altering and drawing attention to the topology of the work. The work is intimately connected to the environment of its happening, but the possibilities that constitute that which is a matter of concern are limited by what is *there* in the improvisational situation.

Denley's work offers insight into the situated character of improvised musical performance. It is from within the place of improvisation that Denley encounters that which is of concern. It is the improvisational situation that both limits the possibilities for engagement and constitutes the boundary within which those possibilities may stand out. It is the audible region in which those common matters of concern occur that constitutes the dynamic horizonal field of the situation. The 'other side' of the situation does not concern Denley for it is not present as something he can engage with. Denley is situated within the happening of the sounds that he attends to, sounds that materially exist, displacing the medium that allows Denley to perceive them as an audible topography. That which Denley listens to and concerns himself with is that which stands out within the distinct boundary of the happening of the improvisational situation.

The receding work

The bounded region or field in which players listen to and engage with the work, and the relative silence that exists beyond that horizonal limit of the situation might also be considered in terms of presence and absence – improvisation occurs in the situating *presence* of the work. The happening of the improvisational situation creates the opening from which the work itself emerges. The improvisational situation, then, possesses a distinct horizonal limit. The performance ends when the horizon that allows the work to begin its presencing disappears. To understand the way performances of improvised music end is to return to the idea of receiving possibilities for engagement, discussed earlier, where it was argued that the improvisational situation presents certain possibilities for engagement that *lead* the player. Simply put, it is argued that 'stopping' arises as a possible mode of action given by the situation. Which is to say, the improvisational situation bears within itself its own ending.

There are always durational restrictions on improvised musical performance. Often players are aware of these restrictions prior to performance. Perhaps they are to play multiple tunes over the course of forty-five minutes, or maybe they have agreed to participate in an extended duration performance and are required to play without break for several hours, or until they can play no more. Players generally have at least a rough idea of how long they will perform. It is not uncommon during performances of free improvisation for players to perform until an ending presents itself, stop, check to see how much time they have left, and then decide whether or not to 'play another one'. As significant as time restraints are for initiating the end of performances, these constraints are not the focus here. Regardless of time restrictions, in most instances an ending *presents itself* to the players from within the situation, as opposed to the performance being suddenly cut off by some external power. Even when musicians know they are short on time they generally do not stop haphazardly. Rather, they seek out possibilities and opportunities given by the situation to conclude their performance. Of course, the possibility to end a performance is relatively straightforward when performing within the constraints of a pre-composed structure. It is more complicated with respect to open form or free improvisation, which is our focus here.

There comes a point in every performance where players encounter the possibility to stop. One listens to the work that one is playing and perhaps hears the current musical theme reaching a natural ending and so acts upon the possibility or opportunity to conclude the performance. Or, perhaps, there is a sudden, unexpected gap in the performance where all players seemingly pause on cue, and this silence presents itself as an opportunity to cease playing and bring the work to a sudden and exciting close. By whatever means the work ends, the process by which it does is indeterminate and improvisational. In the example just given where the work unexpectedly ends because each player interprets and acts upon the unanimous pause as a possibility to end the work, there is always the possibility that one player may interpret the pause as simply that, a 'pause' rather than an invitation to 'stop' and will thus continue playing. In which case, the players await another possibility to stop to present itself.

Of course, when performances end more gradually, as opposed to stopping in response to an unexpected silence, players may act upon different possibilities for engagement. That is, they do not necessarily receive and act on the same possibility. Having received what one player interprets as an invitation to stop, that player may initiate a gradual winding down of their contributions. It might be that what the other players in the ensemble respond to is not the same possibility that the initial player responded to but rather they respond to the way in which the 'winding down' of the initial player is manifest in the work. But this does not negate the indeterminacy of such a process. Precisely how the 'wind down' will play out cannot be given in advance. Players are still tasked with improvising and therefore attending and responding to the situation. Thus, the way in which the work ends is a possibility that emerges from the happening of the situation that players attend and respond to.

One can notice players 'at the ready' as they act upon possibilities for ending a piece just in case their collaborator(s) interpret the work differently and they must spring back into action. Such a phenomenon is evident in video footage of Australian jazz musicians Scott Tinkler (trumpet) and Simon Barker (drums) performing together.[63] While one cannot know precisely when either player encounters the possibility of stopping and comes to act upon such a possibility, one can see Barker poised and at the ready lest Tinkler unexpectedly acts upon a possibility to continue the work. Barker ceases playing at approximately 42′46″, yet his posture suggests he is ready to resume if necessary – that is, if the situation calls for it. He maintains such a posture, as if ready to play, even after what we come to realize is Tinkler's final contribution. Barker relaxes his posture only at 43′14″ when the audience, having sensed the end of the performance, begins applauding. It is only then that both Barker and Tinkler show the first visual signs that they too believe that the performance has come to a close.

The indeterminacy of this process arises by virtue of the fact that players can never exhaust the possibilities given by the work. By virtue of their prejudice and experience (not to mention durational constraints on the performance and the physical capabilities of the player) the player will inevitably encounter and act upon a possibility to stop. This does not suggest that the improvisation could not have gone on. Indeed, John Coltrane is famous for his ability to improvise for extended periods. Upon asking Miles Davis how to stop playing such long solos, Davis is said to have quipped, 'take the horn out of your mouth'.[64] This suggests that 'stopping' has more to do with experience, etiquette and musicality than it does with exhausting the possibilities of the situation.

With regard to the horizon of improvised musical performance, it seems as if presence withdraws and is engulfed by absence when the call to stop, which emerges from the situation, is recognized and acted upon by each player. While the improvisation, we may say, begins from out of silence with an invitation to *sound*, the improvisation concludes and retreats back into silence after players accept the invitation to be *silent* and the horizon within which the work was situated is no longer exists. The work is no longer present, for the sonorous region in which it was situated has withdrawn. Without the boundary given by the horizon of the situation, the situation in which the players were said to participate no longer exists.

Engaging with the world

What this chapter has brought to the fore is the way in which improvisation always happens within a particular region; a horizontal field that simultaneously *opens up* a particular region within which possibilities for action can be encountered by players and *limits* the possibilities available to be encountered. The work that emerges from this region is not reducible to the players but emerges from the happening of the improvisational situation.

One might conceptualize the work that emerges from improvised musical performance through the analogy of topographical surveying. The improvisational situation can be likened to a particular region that the topographical surveyor traverses in order to build up a map of the area. For both the performer of music and the topographical surveyor there are distinct aspects of the region towards which they are oriented; neither subject has access to the region as a whole. Rather the improvisational situation is a region – demarcated by the horizonal field – that comprises distinct elements and qualities that players encounter and attend and respond to. In their participating in the situation there is a circling where players traverse, encounter and engage with the happening of the improvisational situation.

Using the analogy of topographical surveying with respect to philosophical topography, Malpas writes,

> The process of topographical surveying is one in which the complex structure of the region is arrived at through crossing and re-crossing the surface of the land and through sighting and re-sighting from one landmark to another. In that process, it may seem as if the region itself is lost sight of – as if it is forgotten in the emphasis on particular views and measurements. In fact, it is only at the end of the process that the view of the region as a whole can emerge in the form of the survey map. . . . It is only through such journeying, sighting, and re-sighting that place can be understood.[65]

What is of interest here is the idea that the surveyor eventually builds up a map of a region by attending to the region itself. One might think of the work that emerges from improvised musical performance in a manner similar to the way in which one considers the topographical surveyor's map. In each case, one through largely visual means and the other auditorily, someone encounters and traverses, or engages with, a particular region. The person's responses to that which they encounter in the situation, whether by sketching in a book or sounding on their instrument, articulate a certain character of the situation itself. That is, by continually moving towards the threshold of the poetic world a particular character of the world is illuminated – not merely a character projected on to the world by the person but a genuine character of the world as it is given in the situation.

The improvised musical performance, then, comprises an attending and responding to discreet elements that comprise a larger situation or structure. It is through the gradual articulation of different elements in relation to other elements encountered in the situation that give rise to a particular 'whole'. It is precisely through noticing the way in which the work comes into being – through the player's attending and responding to the situation – that one notices the inseparability of time and space. Players traverse or engage with a particular region, but the way in which they move from one discreet element to the next is enabled by the temporality of the situation. If the situation was purely temporal, the structure would not be expansive and therefore would be merely a linear succession. Equally, however, the situation cannot be purely spatial, for pure multiplicity, just like pure succession, does not result in the *unity* required for the complex structure to emerge. One needs both the expansiveness of space – the multiplicity of elements – and the dynamicity afforded by time, which allows those elements to relate to one another in complex ways. The overarching structure itself in which this timespace comes forth is what has been referred to as the 'improvisational situation'. It is only in the overarching structure of place – the situation in which players find themselves – that the timespace that refers to one's active improvisational engagement with the world comes forth.

The improvisational situation, then, emerges in a particular horizontal field. Players traverse the bounded region, encountering what is both strange and familiar by virtue of attending and responding to the work, which results in 'mapping out', as it were, the broader region, such that a 'whole' work emerges. Through their attending and responding to the situation, players articulate responses to the situation, that is, the world; the conversation of improvisation is an engagement with the world as it is given in the improvisational situation. And so, we may say, to return to the discussion from earlier in this chapter, it is through improvisation that players find themselves engaged with the world, such that they are *of* the moment, and therefore *in* and *of* the world.

Improvised musical performance occurs at the threshold of the poetic world of the work within a horizonal field, the limit of which is given by the presence of that which is of concern – the happening of the work.

Listening directs the player towards the world, as it is given in the happening of the improvisational situation, so that they may encounter the world, and indeed the work, as they have not encountered it before. For the performing musician, listening constitutes the way in which they receive possibilities 'in the moment' so that they may be creative in their performance, or, to invoke the idea of the muses, to give an *inspired* performance. The creativity at issue in improvised musical performance emerges from the possibilities one encounters in the situation by virtue of listening. That which is given and available as a possibility for creative engagement is that which is *there* with the player in the situation. To encounter possibilities for creative engagement – to be creative while one performs, that is, to improvise – one must listen. In improvisation, one encounters the world as the world presents itself in the situation, and thus the world, or a certain aspect of the world, is thematized and made salient. The 'where' of improvised musical performance, then, is the world, as it is given in the horizon of the improvisational situation.

* * *

Having now addressed the 'focus', 'origin' and 'horizon' of improvised musical performance in this and the preceding two chapters, the structure of improvisation has been elucidated. Improvisation can be understood, in simple terms, as a conversational engagement that occurs within the horizon of a common matter of concern where that engagement is given by the complex happening of the situation in which it takes place. The 'focus', 'origin' and 'horizon' of improvised musical performance is the *improvisational situation*. Anyone familiar with Gadamer's philosophical hermeneutics, which is the focus of the subsequent chapters, will notice that this improvisational mode of attending and responding is more or less identical to the happening of hermeneutic engagement.

While largely implicit throughout Part I, the nature of thinking and reflection to arrive at this understanding of improvisation has been guided by an approach that is distinctly hermeneutical; it has involved conversing with and reflecting upon – that is, attending and responding to – the subject matter that is improvisation. As noted, given that hermeneutics can guide an inquiry into improvisation, and the structure of improvisation turned out to be consistent with the structure of hermeneutics, it stands to reason that hermeneutic engagement itself possesses an improvisational character. Elucidating precisely how hermeneutics may be understood as improvisational is the focus of the following chapters in Part II.

Part II

Improvisation in the philosophical hermeneutics of Hans-Georg Gadamer

4

Improvising with Gadamer?

The word 'hermeneutics', Francisco Gonzalez tells us, has its origins in a family of ancient Greek terms: '*Hermêneuein* or *hermêneusai* and *hermêneia* to designate an activity, *hermênês* to designate the individual who carries out this activity and *hermêneutikê* to designate a particular discipline associated with this activity.'[1] As it further relates to ancient Greece, it is commonly said that *hermêneuein* was derived from the god Hermes, the bearer of messengers between heaven and earth. Regardless of whether or not there is any truth to the etymological connection between *hermêneuein* and Hermes, the nature of hermeneutics is certainly reflected in Hermes's role as messenger.[2] Despite these connections with ancient Greece, however, the history of hermeneutics as we know it today is generally considered to originate much later. While one could point to what might be described as the hermeneutical character or vocabulary of thinkers such as Plato, Aristotle and even some poets and philosophers up to the Classical period,[3] the word 'hermeneutics' emerged in the seventeenth century, referring to the art or science of interpretation.

The hermeneutics of this period, up until the end of the nineteenth century, was thoroughly methodological and taken up by those disciplines concerned with interpreting texts or signs, such as theological and judicial hermeneutics. Those who employed hermeneutics were concerned with avoiding misinterpretation or arbitrariness in interpretation.[4] While this style of hermeneutics was taken up by a range of thinkers in different ways – its prehistory is generally attributed to Saint Augustine and Martin Luther, and the tradition extends into post-Kantian thinkers such as Friedrich Ast and Friedrich Schlegel – the major developments of hermeneutics through this period relevant to 'philosophical' hermeneutics are commonly attributed to three key figures: Friedrich Schleiermacher, a theologian and philosopher; Johann Gustav Droysen, a historian; and Wilhelm Dilthey, a historian, psychologist, sociologist and philosopher.[5] Despite the significance of these thinkers for their contribution to the growing awareness of hermeneutic problems, however, philosopher and Gadamer biographer Jean Grondin notes that they did not primarily conduct their work under the rubric of hermeneutics.[6] Thus, the hermeneutics of this period, while significant in its own way, could hardly be described as fully formed or developed in the sense in which it later became 'philosophical hermeneutics'.

The step away from hermeneutics as a method towards what is now referred to as 'philosophical hermeneutics' was initiated by Heidegger. Heidegger's early work on hermeneutics rejected the idea that hermeneutics is an art or technique of understanding. That is, contra Schleiermacher, Droysen and Dilthey, for Heidegger hermeneutics does not and should not form the basis of a methodological foundation for the human sciences.[7] In Heidegger's hands the subject matter of hermeneutics shifts from a 'theory of' interpretation to 'interpretation' itself, or, more clumsily, the interpretation of interpretation. For Heidegger, hermeneutics comes to name a fundamental ontology – the self-interpretation of *Dasein*.[8] However, despite Heidegger's explicit engagement with hermeneutics at the beginning of his career, specifically in his 1923 lectures, published as 'Ontology: The Hermeneutics of Facticity',[9] and *Being and Time*, the term 'hermeneutics' largely disappears in his later work.

While one could make a convincing argument that Heidegger's later thinking remains hermeneutical, especially with respect to the way in which his thinking becomes based upon text interpretation in the traditional sense of hermeneutics, interpreting the work of earlier philosophers and poets such as Kant and Friedrich Nietzsche, Friedrich Hölderlin and Georg Trakl, the lack of any explicit engagement with hermeneutics in his later work meant that despite his substantial influence, it was not he who developed hermeneutics into a distinct and fully formed philosophical discipline. Thus, when one thinks of philosophical hermeneutics, while Heidegger's significant contribution must be acknowledged, it is generally not Heidegger who is considered the founder of the discipline. Indeed, in a letter to Otto Pöggeler, Heidegger himself states, '"Hermeneutic philosophy" – that's Gadamer's business.'[10]

Gadamer published his magnum opus, *Truth and Method*, in 1960, at sixty years of age. It is with this text that Gadamer established himself as the founder of philosophical hermeneutics.[11] Prior to the publication of *Truth and Method*, Gadamer had published only one other book, entitled *Plato's Dialectical Ethics*.[12] Thus, despite the maturity of *Truth and Method*, with respect to both the contents of the work and the age of its author, in the context of Gadamer's subsequent output, which was substantial and continued for another forty years, *Truth and Method*, Grondin writes, 'can almost be seen as a youthful publication'.[13] When one views the scope of Gadamer's thinking, however, *Truth and Method* unquestionably sits at the centre. And while Gadamer entered numerous debates regarding the hermeneutics explicated in *Truth and Method*, notably with Jürgen Habermas and Jacques Derrida, these debates did not lead to any substantial revisions.[14] Thus, with respect to Gadamer's thinking, as for philosophical hermeneutics more broadly, it is *Truth and Method* that is decisive and foundational.

The central concern of *Truth and Method* is to address the problem of the human sciences for philosophy. It is largely because the human sciences cannot be epistemologically justified under the methods of the natural sciences that the 'knowledge' of the human sciences has become a problem for philosophy. Against the backdrop of the human sciences being negatively characterized as the 'inexact sciences'[15] and thus inferior to the natural sciences, Gadamer tasks himself with elucidating and providing a foundation for the knowledge of the human sciences. He does not seek, however, any 'technical' foundation, because framing phenomena epistemologically – reducing phenomena to the methods of the natural sciences – does not elucidate their foundation.[16] Instead, Gadamer asks what understanding is, beyond any technical or methodological control of it. His concern, he writes, is 'not what we do or what we ought to do, but what happens to us over and above our wanting and doing'.[17] Gadamer is concerned with the 'event' of understanding – an event that *happens to us*; an event that has more to do with experience than method.

Gadamer turns away from the idea of modern scientific method to understand the human sciences and instead, as is evident at the beginning of *Truth and Method*, turns towards the humanistic tradition, taking up the related ideas of self-formation, education, cultivation and 'becoming cultured' (*Bildung*) as guiding concepts. In the ideas of culture and tradition, Gadamer, following Dilthey and Heidegger, acknowledges the historicity of being (discussed further in Chapter 5). By acknowledging the finitude of being, Gadamer overcomes the metaphysical presumption that one could uncover enduring or absolute truths about the world. Gadamer points out that human knowledge and practice emerge from and rely upon tradition and culture. For Gadamer, knowledge is not tied to scientific method where one may attempt to extract from the world and accumulate absolute and enduring truths, but is rather tied to *Bildung*, which he describes as 'the properly human way of developing one's natural talents and capacities'.[18]

The knowledge at issue for Gadamer, as reflected in *Bildung*, is not an elitist idea of possessing brilliant factual or cultural knowledge. Grondin writes,

> Those who have a fund of factual knowledge are often called pedants, and they are not proposed as a model to the human sciences. This is not culture. Cultivated people are those who can adopt a position of detachment, a distance in relationship to all of the items of knowledge that characterise the pedant.[19]

It is not simply about being 'acquainted with' knowledge that enables one to become cultured or knowledgeable. 'Becoming cultured' is not merely the intentional cultivation of one's talents or skillset, for this suggests working towards a specific goal or end. Rather, as Paul Fairfield puts it, *Bildung* is better understood as 'a life task that belongs to every human being'.[20] We are each educated or cultivated (*gebildet*) in ways related to and distinct from formal education or training. Thus, *Bildung* is a continuous journey for everyone.

By not taking any particular form of knowledge or understanding as its focus, Gadamer's hermeneutics becomes *philosophical* hermeneutics by breaking from the methodological concerns of romantic hermeneutics, where hermeneutics was applied as a tool to assist a specific disciplinary purpose. Gadamer concerns himself with understanding as such – the understanding at issue in one's life task of 'becoming cultured'. In the sense that Gadamer's hermeneutics asks about the nature of understanding itself, prior to any technical or epistemological conception of knowledge or understanding, hermeneutics becomes universal. One may argue it is precisely the universal character of hermeneutics and its rejection of method that not only established Gadamer as the founder of philosophical hermeneutics but is what gives his philosophy such broad appeal and application.[21]

Interpreting Gadamer

In his own work, Gadamer says little about improvisation and music. Yet, there is a sense in which the concept of improvisation uncovered in the preceding chapters may be said to run through key themes and concepts of *Truth and Method*, and indeed beyond into Gadamer's later thinking. For example, in light of the account of improvisation presented in Part I, it would be difficult to deny that the reflective, indeterminate nature of hermeneutics, characterized in Gadamer's ideas of 'play' and 'conversation' for instance, does not resonate with the structure of improvisation already outlined.

To view Gadamer's philosophical hermeneutics as essentially improvisational, however, requires a degree of interpretation; a mode of interpretation that stems from the very core of Gadamer's philosophy. While it is unlikely one would arrive at an improvisational account of hermeneutics through a standard reading of *Truth and Method*, by reading back into Gadamer the account of improvisation originally derived from his thinking, that is, through a certain interpretive angle, one can identify a particular characteristic of Gadamer's thought that may not be immediately clear in the original text but is present, nonetheless. The very act of illuminating the improvisational character of hermeneutics is an act of improvisation. This becomes apparent when one considers, for instance, the way in which jazz musicians take a theme given to them by someone else and then, through improvisation, 'make it their own', developing it in new and perhaps unexpected ways. The engagement with Gadamer in Part II of this book is analogous to such an improvisation upon a theme.

This improvisational engagement brings with it a certain interpretive tension, one particularly prevalent in music, where it becomes somewhat difficult to determine what extent the 'improvisation of hermeneutics' is actually Gadamer's position and to what extent it is my own. Benson asserts that such quandaries of authorship are always present, noting how he is only the author of his own texts 'to a certain degree'.[22] He writes, 'one starts with things gifted to us by other people and [we work] from there',[23] a process he describes as distinctly improvisational.[24] One might take Gadamer's account of 'truth' (discussed further in subsequent chapters) as a case in point – to what extent is Gadamer's account his own, and to what extent is it demonstrative of his improvising on a theme given to him by Heidegger? Although I assert my reading of Gadamer is well grounded with respect to both Gadamer's texts and the spirit of his thinking more broadly, my interests lie primarily in the questions that are addressed by improvising on the themes of philosophical hermeneutics. Thus, Part II may be seen first and foremost as an inquiry into the relationship between improvisation and philosophy – I offer an account of the improvisational character of truth and understanding, language and ethics – and secondarily as a contribution to the study of Gadamer.

The particular interpretation of Gadamer's work presented in Part II draws out the improvisational nature of truth and understanding, language and ethics. As mentioned, there is a reciprocity at issue here where on the one hand, in Part I, improvisation is read as emerging from out of the hermeneutical, establishing a connection between the hermeneutical and the improvisational. On the other hand, however, in Part II the praxis of hermeneutic engagement is seen to be intimately tied to improvisation. The universality of hermeneutics, it will be argued, implicates improvisation as essentially universal, too – this is a key theme that runs throughout Part II.

There is also a sense in which the central topics covered in Part II – understanding and truth, language and ethics – each lends themselves to being discussed in relation to improvisation. On the one hand, this could be seen as simply an all too convenient selection of themes pursued to 'push' a certain reading. On the other hand, if such central themes or topics of Gadamer's hermeneutics do seem to lend themselves to being understood in a particular way, then one is not so much 'pushing' a point at all but highlighting a particular characteristic of those themes that was already there to begin with.

While I do not directly thematize any methodological conclusions with respect to the work undertaken in this book, there is a sense in which Part II draws out what has been my own underlying theoretical stance throughout this book as a whole. That is, the extent to which my own thinking involves an interweaving of improvisation with philosophical hermeneutics. By elucidating the improvisational character of hermeneutics, however, I hope not to demonstrate a personal hermeneutic approach but to show how all philosophical hermeneutics is necessarily improvisational.

In accord with the conversational nature of Gadamer's hermeneutics, the thinking presented in the following chapters is considered genuinely dialogical. That is, the following discussions might be considered explorations into philosophical hermeneutics where the task is to illuminate a certain characteristic of Gadamer's thought. Just as all understanding is for Gadamer subject to revision and therefore not definitive, these chapters do not present the final word on the improvisational character of hermeneutics. The goal is to bring the conversation not to an end but to a new beginning.

5
Hermeneutics and the call to improvise

For Gadamer, as for Heidegger, aesthetic experience is an exemplary form of the way in which one encounters truth. Truth is an event; truth is the disclosure of what is *there* in the situation.[1] Commenting on Heidegger, from whom Gadamer inherits his account of truth, Gadamer writes that 'a work of art does not "mean" something or function as a sign that refers to a meaning; rather it presents itself in its own being, so that the beholder must tarry by it.'[2] The truth of the work comes forth in, and only in, one's active engagement with the work, and its truth is wholly contained in its presencing – wholly contained in the situation of its coming forth. The being of the work of art, Gadamer tells us, 'does not consist in its becoming an experience. Rather, by virtue of its own existence it is an event, a thrust that overthrows everything previously considered to be conventional, a thrust in which a world never there before opens itself up.'[3] The 'world' into which one is thrust in aesthetic experience may be seen to be analogous with the 'situation' of the preceding chapters, where the productivity of improvisational engagement opens up or clears a space for the self-presentation of the work.

Moreover, Gadamer asserts that the '*event of being that occurs in presentation* . . . belongs essentially to play as play.'[4] The 'event of truth' that both Gadamer and Heidegger speak of is an event of appropriation,[5] consistent with the way in which this was said to figure in improvised musical performance in Chapter 2. The idea of truth at issue here is not the methodologically derived truth of metaphysics or epistemology but a participatory *event*. Simply put, what is at issue in Gadamer's account of truth is the immanent happening of three basic elements:

1. An encounter: All interpretation begins with a certain encounter, for example, with a work of art or a text.
2. Participatory engagement: Not only does one encounter a work of art or a text but one is also *addressed by* that which one encounters. One is drawn to engage with the thing in a conversational manner such that one participates in the happening of the thing as an artwork or text.
3. The self-presentation of truth: Just as the agreement reached between two interlocutors is not reducible to either interlocutor alone but emerges, as if of its own accord, *between* them, so too does truth *emerge* from participatory engagement.

In this chapter we will explore these basic elements to elucidate the way in which improvisation sits at the core of Gadamer's account of truth.

Many of the themes presented further are adumbrated in the previous chapters on music. Thus, the following discussion may be seen as taking up the basic structure of the musical and placing it within the hermeneutical, highlighting the way in which the same improvisational structure – the same *topology* – is at issue in both music and hermeneutics. In addition to the methodological concerns outlined in the previous chapter, noting the way in which improvisation and hermeneutics share a similar set of features or structures further elucidates the ubiquitous nature of improvisation. That is, given the universality of hermeneutics, drawing attention to the improvisational character of hermeneutics substantiates a central tenet of this book: improvisation is universal.

Having already developed an account of improvisation in Part I, in this chapter, and, indeed, Part II as a whole, the idea of improvisation at issue is not rearticulated. Instead, the aim is to demonstrate how the idea of improvisation already elucidated is at work in philosophical hermeneutics, which will, in turn, illuminate the situated character of improvisation from a different perspective.

Therefore, the focus turns from giving an account of improvisation towards giving an account of philosophical hermeneutics and drawing out the way in which the conversational structure of understanding at issue in Gadamer's hermeneutics is necessarily improvisational.

Improvisation as a demand of finitude

Central to Gadamer's hermeneutics is the idea of finitude. All understanding is a historical understanding; one's prejudices are produced by and embedded in tradition. Knowledge, according to Gadamer, is never absolute and enduring. Rather, understanding is bound up in a perpetual dialogue where we seek to understand on the basis of history, such that we are always already there with that which we seek to understand. That is, we only understand insofar as we are *there* to understand.[6] Philosophical hermeneutics does not seek infinite, enduring knowledge – Gadamer's discussion of 'historical consciousness'[7] explicitly demonstrates that such knowledge is unattainable – and instead concerns itself with the understanding we arrive at by being-*there*. Given this situated, historical understanding, we must, as Grondin writes, 'ceaseless[ly] endeavour to understand and say what we understand'.[8] The task of hermeneutics is infinite, by virtue of our finitude.

That hermeneutics is a philosophy of finitude is perhaps most clearly framed when Gadamer, in the final pages of *Truth and Method*, includes the following quote from Plato: 'None of the gods philosophizes.'[9] Infinite beings with access to absolute, indubitable knowledge have no need for philosophy. Gadamer asserts that 'the universality of the hermeneutical experience would not be available to an infinite mind, for it develops out of itself all meaning, all noeton, and thinks all that can be thought in the perfect contemplation of itself'.[10] Precisely what conclusions we may draw with respect to the 'knowledge' (or lack thereof) possessed by infinite beings is not our concern. What is of interest is the way in which, by highlighting the finitude of human knowledge, Gadamer, following Heidegger, casts into doubt the task of metaphysics to uncover certain and enduring truths about the world. By acknowledging our historical situatedness – the way in which we always already find ourselves in a certain tradition, culture and language that structures the way we understand the world, which, as we learn from history, is always different to those from other traditions and epochs – Gadamer presents hermeneutics as a philosophy of finitude. It is because we cannot think all that can be thought and attain absolute truth that hermeneutical experience is available to us.

As a philosophy of finitude, hermeneutics becomes improvisational. Hermeneutics demands improvisational variation upon a theme – finding the right words to say something to others, experiencing works of art, to 'say again' or 'say further' the messages of texts (particularly those written in and for a different tradition and/or epoch) necessarily requires a certain improvisational engagement. Gadamer writes, 'precisely through our finitude, the particularity of our being... the infinite dialogue is opened in the direction of the truth that we are'.[11] This infinite dialogue is equally infinite improvisation: we do not know the world, we interpret it, and this mode of interpretation, as will be discussed later, is distinctly improvisational. Truth is improvised; truth emerges on the basis of improvisational engagement. Substantiating this assertion involves attending to the circularity of understanding, the historicity of understanding and Gadamer's conception of the task of hermeneutics.

The hermeneutic circle

As touched upon before, prior to Heidegger, hermeneutics was considered a methodological tool for interpretation, particularly the interpretation of text. This form of hermeneutics lacked the universalism of Gadamer's ontological hermeneutics (the move towards the ontological draws out an improvisational character of hermeneutics, which will be discussed further). Despite the clear differences between 'romantic' and 'philosophical' hermeneutics, as Gadamer labels them,[12] the improvisational character of Gadamer's hermeneutics shines most brightly when viewed from a historical perspective. It is from the vantage point of the hermeneutic tradition that extends from Ast, August Boeckh and Schleiermacher, to Count Yorck and Dilthey, and reaches Gadamer, coupled to phenomenology, via Heidegger, that gives the most weight to the improvisational nature of Gadamer's hermeneutics. Briefly tracing this tradition, with a particular focus on Heidegger's transformation of hermeneutics from a methodological/epistemological concern to an ontological concern, up to the point at which Gadamer takes it up and makes it his own, provides the necessary background to appreciate the improvisational nature of hermeneutics.

The relevant story that leads to Gadamer can be read by focussing on the nature of truth at issue in hermeneutics, into which a certain insight is gained by attending to the circularity of understanding, commonly referred to as the 'hermeneutic circle'. The hermeneutic circle forms the basis of hermeneutic inquiry. The way in which this structure has been taken up by different thinkers as a means (or obstacle to be overcome) to arrive at truth and understanding, however, has not been consistent. The hermeneutic circle broadly refers to the way in which one's prior understanding is always present with respect to the knowledge of the human sciences. While from a scientific methodological perspective the hermeneutic circle was thought to pose a problem for the human sciences – how can one arrive at objective truth about the world if one's prejudices cannot be eliminated from the inquiry? – Heidegger's ontological characterization of hermeneutics determined the hermeneutic circle as something positive. For Heidegger, and indeed for Gadamer, it is precisely *because of* one's prior understanding or prejudice that one becomes interested in and pursues knowledge in the first place. Thus, as Heidegger puts it, 'what is decisive is not to get out of the circle but to come into it in the right way'.[13]

The 'hermeneutic circle' became a prominent theme in hermeneutics after Ast identified the circularity of understanding and knowledge in 1808;[14] although it was likely Boeckh, a year later in 1809, who first spoke explicitly of a 'hermeneutic circle'.[15] The hermeneutic circle, irrespective of whether it is named as such, emerges in varying ways throughout the history of hermeneutics. The circular structure at issue, in its most basic form, relates to the way in which one cannot understand the whole without first possessing some understanding of the parts of that whole, but equally, one cannot understand the parts without some understanding of the whole. For instance, in terms of music, a melody is a unity. The significance of individual notes is a result of their organization within the structure of the melody. Reciprocally, however, the character of the melody itself is dependent on the pitch and rhythm of the individual notes. Such a relationship equally exists between individual words and the unity of the sentence of which those words are a part. It is this basic, ineliminable relationship between the parts and the whole with respect to the nature of understanding that is at issue in hermeneutics.

The way in which the hermeneutic circle may be thought to function in the respective work of those who have concerned themselves with the hermeneutical broadly correlates with their account of truth. While the idea that the hermeneutic circle essentially refers to a part-whole structure has largely been consistent in hermeneutic scholarship, the way this structure supposedly operates differs depending on one's conception of the task of hermeneutics. Richard E. Palmer notes that for Schleiermacher 'understanding as an art is the reexperiencing of the mental processes of the text's author. It is the reverse of composition, for it starts with the fixed and finished expression and goes back to the mental life from which it arose'.[16] Broadly speaking, for Schleiermacher the hermeneutic circle is the foundation or principle upon which one's reconstructive process is grounded. The interpreter circles between the parts and whole, and between the grammatical and the psychological,[17] to reconstruct the viewpoint of the original author of a text. Put simply, a text, for Schleiermacher, is inseparable from the subjectivity of its author. Therefore, unlike Gadamer who considers the truth of a text to be wholly contained in the text itself, Schleiermacher thinks that claims regarding the truth of a text should be verifiable against the reconstructed viewpoint of the author. For Schleiermacher, as for Dilthey, for instance, the hermeneutic circle refers to a methodological foundation not so far removed from the scientific ideals from which they attempted to distance themselves. Heidegger, however, transforms the '*hermeneutic* circle' into what could be described as an '*ontological* circle',[18] which constitutes a radical break from the work of those who came before him.

While Heidegger does not explicitly discuss a part-whole structure, this structure of the circularity of hermeneutics is clearly evident in his early work. But instead of viewing the circularity of understanding as a methodological tool, or something to be avoided, Heidegger identifies the ontological significance of the hermeneutic circle, where ontology, Heidegger says, 'means doctrine of being'.[19] Ontology, for Heidegger, does not designate a particular discipline or field of inquiry but refers to an 'indefinite and vague directive that . . . being should in some thematic way come to be investigated and come to language'.[20]

As an inquiry into the question of being, the mode of analysis required cannot be predetermined. In this sense, any genuine questioning of being must equally be a questioning of ontology – no prior determinations can be made of the object of one's inquiry, thus no prior determinations can be made of the nature of that inquiry.[21] Ontological inquiry becomes an attending and responding to being such that being is made thematic; every inquiry is singular and follows its own path. The indeterminacy of this engagement – its irreducibility to prior determinations and the necessity for genuine participatory engagement – situates the ontological concerns of hermeneutics squarely in the domain of the improvisational.

Rather than provide a methodological foundation for interpretation, the circularity of understanding offers a 'way in' to question and engage with being – attending and responding to the situation in which one finds oneself – in this improvisational manner. One's prejudice, which had otherwise been considered something to be overcome, becomes essential to the questioning of being. Heidegger claims the fundamental question of Western philosophy is the question of being. He writes, 'everything we talk about, everything we have in view, everything towards which we comport ourselves in anyway, is being'.[22] That we inquire into the character of being arises from what might be described as a 'circling back' where one questions being because the notion of being – something that we already have and to some extent understand – is 'an *issue*'[23] for us. It is only because we can *already* identify being that we attempt to gain further understanding of it. Thus, it is precisely one's presuppositions about the object of one's inquiry that directs one's encounter with that object or thing.[24]

Importantly, Heidegger is not seeking some logical or analytic 'proof' of being. Instead, he notes that 'if Dasein is understood correctly, it defies such proofs, because, in its Being, it already *is* what subsequent proofs deem necessary to demonstrate for it'.[25] The point is not to prove the reality of the world. As Malpas notes, 'the attempt to prove Dasein as being-in-the-world is doomed to failure since Dasein must already be-in-the-world before such a proof can be attempted'.[26] The point is rather to 'lay bare', as Heidegger would say,[27] the structure within which experience is possible, which is a structure where the very possibility of laying bare that structure is already given. Thus,

Heidegger writes that 'the "circle" in understanding belongs to the structure of meaning, and the latter phenomenon is rooted in the existential constitution of Dasein – that is, in the understanding which interprets'.[28] Understanding, for Heidegger, emerges because one is always *already* standing in relation to the being of other beings with which one is acquainted. All questioning and understanding of being arises because we are already somewhat familiar with the phenomenon of being, and thus we seek to articulate the structure within which those elements (including ourselves) are already situated.

The historicity of understanding

The historicity of human being-in-the-world central to Heidegger's positive conception of the hermeneutic circle echoes the thought of Dilthey, who argued that all experience depends upon an implicit temporal or historical structure, such that experience depends on both recollection and anticipation. Dilthey writes, 'not through introspection but only through history do we come to know ourselves'.[29] Palmer notes that for Dilthey all understanding is historical – one understands the present 'only in the horizon of past and future; this is not a matter of conscious effort but is built into the structure of experience itself'.[30] Historicity, like the circularity of understanding more generally, is not a hurdle to be overcome but constitutes the principle of understanding.

The significance of the historicity of being for Heidegger is made evident when, in *Being and Time*, he describes his approach to phenomenological description as 'interpretation'. He writes that 'the phenomenology of Dasein is a *hermeneutic* in the primordial signification of this word, where it designates this business of interpreting'.[31] Rather than follow Husserl's path of 'founding a theory of transcendental subjectivity and intersubjectivity',[32] Heidegger took phenomenology as a mode of apprehending phenomena and brought it together with a historically mediated circle of understanding. Heidegger was not satisfied with Husserl's basically 'Cartesian subjective starting point', which for Heidegger, Daniel Dahlstrom writes, 'betrays the ontological promise of phenomenology'.[33] In his quest to unveil the nature of being, Heidegger thought it vital to consider the historicity of being-in-the-world. One may say that the 'hermeneutic' in Heidegger's 'hermeneutic phenomenology' refers to the historicity of thought, in contrast to Husserl whose phenomenological approach remained basically scientific.

By acknowledging the way in which we are always already the inheritors of tradition and culture, Heidegger guides philosophy away from Cartesian 'subjectism', where things are not ontologically independent but are instead objects apprehended by human subjects.[34] A subjectism worldview severs interpretation from practical philosophy; interpretation becomes a methodological process of selecting the correct interpretation that fits with the object of one's inquiry. Indeed, romantic hermeneutics saw one's historicity as something to be overcome or displaced by method so as to arrive at objective truth. By acknowledging the historicity of being, Heidegger recognizes that we can never remove ourselves from the world, as it were, to gain an objective, bird's-eye view of the world and therefore acquire absolute or certain knowledge. Heidegger recognizes the futility of the pursuit of objective and stable knowledge and rather presents truth as unveiling or revealing that which is concealed (as touched on in Part I and discussed further later), where what is concealed will be intimately tied to one's historical situatedness and, as the American philosopher of science Thomas Kuhn would say,[35] the 'paradigm' within which one is operating. For Heidegger, understanding is both fundamentally interpretive and practical – it is always in response to and emerges from the situation in which one *is*. Hermeneutical interpretation is never an objective apprehending or describing. Rather, one's being-there and being oriented towards a thing not only calls into question the thing itself but, more importantly, it also calls into question one's self-understanding – one has always already oriented oneself towards something and not another. Thus, if one is reflective, one encounters oneself in one's encounter with the world.

What draws Heidegger to hermeneutics is the way in which hermeneutics refers to a mode of self-disclosure or self-transparency. Of Heidegger's conception of hermeneutics Grondin writes, 'conceived with a view to Dasein's possible *self*-transparency, hermeneutics does not itself carve out a trail to this awareness or propose models for doing so. It must remain the task of each individual Dasein to open up its own path to self-transparency.'[36] Hermeneutics calls for us to reflect upon and interpret ourselves but, given the singularity of experience, acknowledges that there can be no predetermined model for such reflection – the path to hermeneutic interpretation must be worked out 'in the moment'. The importance of hermeneutics for Heidegger, Grondin tells us, is to guard against *Dasein's* 'propensity to overlook itself',[37] where, 'instead of undertaking their own interpretations of themselves, [human beings] take up interpretations that are already available and so relieve themselves of the burden of self-elucidation'.[38] Hermeneutics, as Heidegger conceives it, calls *Dasein* back to itself, back to the facticity of its self-existence. Heidegger's radical transformation of hermeneutics is that instead of being merely a technique or method to interpret texts, for instance, hermeneutics is that which allows one to encounter oneself; it is a practical mode of thinking and being where one strives to make transparent a character of being.

Gadamer and the task of hermeneutics

Gadamer takes Heidegger's ontological conception of hermeneutics as his starting point. Indeed, for the most part, we may say that the account of truth Gadamer attests is at issue in the human sciences is Heidegger's. Heidegger's primary interest in hermeneutics, however, is to return us to our facticity. Hermeneutics allows Heidegger to overcome historicism's concern with epistemology, as well as highlight the untenability of universally valid truths traditionally sought by metaphysics. While Heidegger was certainly aware of the problem of method with respect to the human sciences, attending to the human sciences themselves was not a priority for him. Gadamer, on the other hand, takes up the problem of knowledge in the human sciences as his primary concern.

Of Heidegger's positive re-conception of the hermeneutic circle, Gadamer writes, 'I have given the following formulation to this [Heidegger's] insight: It is not so much our judgments as it is our prejudices that constitute our being.'[39] For Gadamer, the curiosity afforded by prejudice is the foundation of knowledge and understanding. All questions, be they of the human or natural sciences, emerge from a basic curiosity to understand something that is familiar enough that one can consider its existence and therefore ask questions about it and yet alien enough that one inquires after it and seeks further understanding. That prejudice is integral to understanding is highlighted well by Grondin in the following (negative) example: 'Whenever we cannot understand a text, the reason is that it says nothing to *us* or has nothing to say.'[40] For Gadamer, understanding, a text for instance, 'is not merely a reproductive but always a productive activity as well'.[41] In contradistinction to Schleiermacher whose hermeneutics strove to reproduce the original understanding of the author, for Gadamer, the task is not to understand the intent of the author or to understand the text as the author did but to understand the text itself as a distinct and autonomous entity or whole. Whether or not an understanding is produced through one's reading of a text relies upon whether one is able to receive what the text is trying to say.

That the author of a text does not have the final word on the meaning of their work does not merely have to do with the fact that texts commonly outlive their authors. Gadamer asserts, 'not just occasionally but always, the meaning of a text goes beyond its author'.[42] According to Gadamer there is no final or absolute understanding of a text, and there is not necessarily any 'better' understanding; the author does not by default possess any more authority than anyone else with respect to the meaning of a text. Thus, as noted, understanding is not about reproducing the understanding of another, but producing an understanding for oneself. Understanding is that which emerges through one's hermeneutical conversation with a subject matter. What makes the conversation truly productive, and therefore hermeneutical, relies upon two things: First, an understanding of the subject matter must emerge, and second, that understanding must bring about *self*-understanding; interpretation is only hermeneutical insofar as that interpretation influences self-understanding. That is, through one's hermeneutical conversation one encounters and comes to recognize inadequacies or inconsistencies in one's prior understanding and subsequently comes to better understand oneself – one engages in the process of 'becoming cultured'.

As noted, for Gadamer it is one's prejudices that form the basis for one's inquiry into a particular subject matter. One possesses a particular, limited understanding of a thing and one asks questions of that thing to gain further understanding. It is when one's prejudices are challenged that the person may begin to think differently about the subject matter at issue; one's questioning has led to a *different* understanding. Gadamer writes, 'we understand in a *different* way, *if we understand at all*.⁴³ Understanding is both an understanding of the thing and an understanding of oneself – for to understand differently is to acknowledge the shortcomings of one's prior understanding.

While Gadamer's primary concern is an ontological one, unlike Heidegger who did not primarily concern himself with the human sciences, Gadamer demonstrates the universal application of hermeneutics. Not only is hermeneutics a means to encounter oneself in factical existence, but Gadamer also gives room to the way in which his conception of hermeneutics plays out in specific interpretive contexts. Given his concern for the way in which hermeneutics may be taken up by the human sciences more broadly, Gadamer offers insight into the way in which hermeneutical understanding unfolds in particular contexts, such as in understanding a text, aesthetic experience, verbal conversation or interpreting scientific data.

Gadamer writes that 'understanding begins . . . when something addresses us'.⁴⁴ Hermeneutics begins with a certain encounter – with an artwork, a text, an interlocutor and so forth – that occurs nowhere if not in factical existence. In this sense, hermeneutics has its origins in the event or situation – Heidegger's Event – as the happening of truth as disclosedness or unconcealment (*aletheia*), discussed in more detail later. What is at stake in hermeneutics is the way in which one's participation in the event brings about truth and understanding – an interpretation. For Gadamer, what is essential to truth and understanding is their essentially participatory nature. Truth is not disclosed to those who merely wait; truth comes forth in active engagement, which is not to suggest that people cannot find themselves in situations where they are 'forced' to come to terms with a truth they were reluctant to face. But for the philosopher as for the musician, this engagement is not merely subjective or intentional conduct. Indeed, Gadamer asserts that 'theoria is a true participation, not something active but something passive (pathos), namely being totally involved in and carried away by what one sees'.⁴⁵ The passivity at issue here refers us back to an essential character of Heidegger's Event where 'true participation' is an 'event of appropriation', which may also be understood in terms of the attentiveness and responsiveness at issue in the *improvisational situation*. Gadamer directs us away from hermeneutics as being something 'active' only in the sense that hermeneutic engagement is not concerned with subjective action towards an object. The pathos Gadamer speaks of refers to one's surrendering oneself to the event, to the situation that one *belongs* to, contributes to, and is *led* by. Pathos refers to the event of appropriation that is genuine participation – improvisational engagement.

Just as to improvise is to be *of* the moment in the sense of *extempore*, so too is hermeneutics *of* the moment or situation. If understanding begins when something addresses us, there is necessarily a happening – conversational engagement – that works towards 'reaching agreement'.[46] For Gadamer, 'understanding is, primarily, agreement'.[47] We gain a certain insight into Gadamer's idea of hermeneutic engagement via the components of conversation, which Gadamer describes as 'argument, question and answer, objection and refutation, which are undertaken in regard to a text as an inner dialogue of the soul seeking understanding'.[48] 'Conversation' refers to an ontological, improvisational engagement. The to-and-fro of question and answer, for instance, is tied to the pathos described before, in the sense of play, where one is taken up or carried away by one's participation in the happening of the event, which is, it has been elucidated, precisely what is at issue in improvisation, particularly with respect to the idea of being 'in the moment', discussed in Chapter 3.

Gadamer himself ties being and truth to the event,[49] writing, 'being is self-presentation and . . . all understanding is an event', and 'the mode of being of understanding [has] the character of an event'. That truth is an event of self-presentation highlights the way in which Heidegger's idea of truth as disclosedness is deeply manifest in Gadamer's thinking. Indeed, the idea of truth at issue in Gadamer's thinking is indebted to Heidegger's 1935–6 lectures on 'The Origin of the Work of Art' to the extent that Gadamer writes,

> These three lectures so closely addressed my own questions and my own experience of the proximity of art and philosophy that they awakened an immediate response in me. My philosophical hermeneutics seeks precisely to adhere to the line of questioning of this essay *and the later Heidegger*.[50]

For Gadamer, a key influence of Heidegger's 'The Origin of the Work of Art' has to do with the way in which Heidegger connects art and truth.

Of the relationship between truth and the work of art, Heidegger writes, 'in the work's work-being the happening of truth, the opening up or disclosure of what is, is at work'.[51] Heidegger's conception of truth is not synonymous with the common understanding of the term as 'correctness'. Rather Heidegger thinks of truth as 'unconcealedness', which he says aligns with the ancient Greek word for truth, '*aletheia*'.[52] Truth as unconcealment has much broader implications than truth as mere correctness, which is not to suggest we should do away with truth as correctness; unconcealment is not proposed as replacing truth as correctness, instead, unconcealment should be understood as the ontological ground of truth as correctness. Indeed, Heidegger argues that truth as correctness has its origins in truth as unconcealment. He writes,

> How can fact show itself if it cannot itself stand forth out of concealedness, if it does not itself stand in the unconcealed? A proposition is true by conforming to the unconcealed, to what is true. . . . This nature of truth which is familiar to us – correctness in representation – stands and falls with truth as unconcealedness of beings.[53]

Truth, for Heidegger, is the play between concealment and unconcealment, discussed earlier in Part I. Unconcealment is itself a form of concealment in the sense that for something to come forth, something else must be closed off; one cannot experience everything at once. By orienting oneself towards one thing, or one aspect of a thing, one must necessarily turn oneself away from another, as we saw earlier in Chapter 2 with respect to the orientation of the player attending to the familiar and the strange. The truth of the work of art is that which *stands out* from the event or situation of its happening.

At issue in 'The Origin of the Work of Art' is also a conception of truth as *Lichtung*, that is, momentary and sudden. *Lichtung* is commonly translated as 'lighting', but also, as Heidegger employs it, refers to 'clearing', where 'in the midst of being as a whole an open place occurs. There is a clearing, a lighting.'[54] *Lichtung*, Heidegger writes, refers to 'the lightning-flash of the truth of Being.'[55] *Lichtung*, like the *Augenblick* of the early Heidegger, which refers to the 'moment of vision',[56] presents truth as something sudden that comes forth in a flash where a certain character of place is illuminated or disclosed. This 'moment', consistent with the discussion from Chapter 3, is best thought of as an event in which one comes to grasp the situation in which one finds oneself.

This character of truth is apparent in Gadamer's account when he writes that 'truth dawns on them like an alternate world in the suddenness of a rupture or a flash. When a new word forces a new thought, it is like an event [*Ereignis*].'[57] However, Gadamer's concern with the disparate ways in which hermeneutics may be taken up in human sciences means he spends more time than Heidegger detailing the inner working of hermeneutic engagement, the participatory to-and-fro of conversation, that enables one to arrive at an interpretation in everyday hermeneutic engagement. Gadamer writes,

> Theoria is not so much the individual momentary [*augenblickliche*] act as a way of comporting [*Haltung*, literally, a way of holding or carrying oneself] oneself, a position and condition. It is 'being present' in the lovely double sense that means that the person is not only present but completely present.[58]

Although their account of truth is for the most part one and the same, Gadamer, more so than Heidegger, attends to the way in which hermeneutical engagement in everyday interpretation involves a certain 'tarrying' or 'lingering' (*Verweilen*), which denotes 'working things out' or improvisational engagement, if you will, which prepares the way of the lighting of truth, in the sense of *Lichtung* or a 'rupture'.

The call to improvise

Given that Gadamer's hermeneutics is concerned with the nature of interpretation and therefore questions that are fundamental to philosophy, we might say that philosophy, as well as understanding more generally, is essentially hermeneutical.[59] And we may be so bold as to suggest that philosophy is essentially improvisational, insofar as hermeneutic inquiry involves improvisation, the argument for which is the focus of this and the following chapter. The call to improvise in hermeneutical engagement emerges most clearly when we attend to three aspects of Gadamer's hermeneutics:

1. Hermeneutics is a philosophy of finitude: By attending to the historicity of human understanding both Heidegger and Gadamer illuminate the misconception of seeking an absolute truth of being. Moreover, by highlighting, for instance, the way in which the meaning of a text always goes beyond the meaning given to it by the author, Gadamer argues that not only is understanding structured by history and tradition, such that when one views a work of art from a different epoch one 'not only sees things in a different way, [one] sees different things',[60] but also there can be no final or 'best' understanding even between those living in the same tradition and epoch. Thus, understanding is *always* interpretation, and interpretation is always an interpretation *for us*; every interpretation is always open to re-interpretation. Such a worldview can be equated with the phrase, 'improvising on a theme'. Human finitude necessarily means we must take up, again and again, certain themes and improvise anew.

2. The task of hermeneutics is essentially ontological: When the early Heidegger discusses ontology with respect to the hermeneutics of facticity, ontology becomes the questioning of being. As noted, ontology refers to an indeterminate circularity where the inquiry into being is itself given in the facticity of our own being. That hermeneutics is concerned with the interpretation of being and not merely the description of an object, such that the being of beings comes forth in one's encountering oneself in one's own factical situation, means that manifest in ontology is *improviso* – an engagement with the unforeseen and unexpected that is illuminating in the sense of awareness; one comes to find oneself situated and oriented in the world.[61] The *improviso* of ontology is the indeterminate and spontaneous engagement with and questioning of being that brings about self-understanding. That ontology calls for engagement with being in active-presence, rather than merely a stable representation of being, places improvisation at the very heart of the ontology at issue in hermeneutics.

3. Hermeneutic interpretation involves participatory engagement: When Gadamer discusses the hermeneutics at issue in aesthetic experience, reading a text, or verbal conversation he devotes considerable effort explicating the non-subjectivist engagement at issue in arriving at truth. Through concepts such as 'play' and 'conversation', for instance, Gadamer draws out the *extempore* of hermeneutic engagement – the improvisational happening of the event or situation. Gadamer highlights the improvisational attending and responding to the subject matter that is necessary to arrive at an interpretation. One's participation in the disclosure or lighting of truth is analogous to the play of improvisation at issue in improvised musical performance.

The happening of the event of truth is an improvisational happening that involves both *improviso* – the unforeseen and unexpected – and *extempore* – being *of* the moment, where one's engagement or tarrying with a subject matter is an improvisational attending and responding to the situation in which one finds oneself.

The improvisation of hermeneutic engagement

While it is our finitude that makes salient the essentially improvisational character of hermeneutics – our historicity calls for us to improvise – the act of improvisation, seen here as an ontological mode of inquiry, is manifest in hermeneutics with respect to one's engagement with a subject matter. It is this engagement – one's participation in the situation – that will be our focus for the remainder of this chapter. Attending to the three basic elements of Gadamer's account of hermeneutics noted at the beginning of this chapter (the encounter, engagement or participation and the self-presentation of truth), the relationship each of these has with improvisation will be outlined.

Improviso *and the hermeneutic encounter*

Gadamer's philosophical hermeneutics is distinctly phenomenological in the sense that the hermeneutic encounter necessarily occurs in factual existence/

experience. Understanding, Gadamer writes, 'belongs to the encounter'.[62] All understanding is essentially situated. It is *in* the situation that we encounter that which is not in accord with our prior understanding of the world – that which calls us to participatory engagement and to understand differently. The situation in which one finds oneself gives rise to understanding if one comports oneself towards the situation appropriately and engages with the subject matter of the encounter; one must allow oneself to be *led* by the subject matter and *receive* understanding. The understanding one arrives at is always dependent upon prior understanding, for one never has access to the broader situation *as it is*, only as it is *for them*. But it is still the situation as such, a situation that goes beyond the subjectivity of the individual, that gives rise to understanding. Malpas writes, 'it is only in virtue of where and how we find ourselves that anything is able to present itself to us as something that calls for understanding, and it is only on that basis that we are moved to understand'.[63] The relationship between situation and understanding is a circular one that constitutes the basic form of hermeneutic understanding.

This fundamental character of understanding – being called to understand by one's encounter with the world – is tied to the indeterminacy and spontaneity – the *improviso* – of place and situation. One is always already situated in the midst of things, already there with that which does not accord with one's prior expectations – the unforeseen and unexpected – that demands one to understand differently. Just as in improvised musical performance where the player encounters the work in the improvisational situation and attends and responds to that work, understanding emerges through one's improvisational participation with a subject matter in the situation in which one finds oneself.

To conceptualize the encounter that calls one to improvise we might consider Gadamer's description of conversation. He writes, 'a genuine conversation is never the one that we wanted to conduct. Rather, it is generally more correct to say that we fall into conversation.'[64] Let us pursue this notion of 'falling into', which refers to the spontaneous and indeterminate way in which one comes to be in a genuine conversation or improvisational situation. For example, while someone may deliberately intend to converse with someone else – one may intentionally walk to the office of another person to discuss a certain subject matter – the actual point at which the conversation 'takes hold', as it were, *happens* beyond one's intending it. It is in this sense that one 'falls into' a conversation, and it is in this sense that it is suggested that conversation requires a fundamentally improvisational comportment – one encounters something in the world *improviso* that does not accord with one's prior understanding of the world that calls for engagement that initiates a 'falling into' hermeneutic conversation. It is the very happening of one's falling into, as can be noticed in the literal sense of tripping and beginning to fall, that calls for improvisation. The way in which the person was originally proceeding is taken away from them, their subjective intentions towards the world suspended in the sense that Gadamer describes as a 'loss of self'.[65] and they are taken up by the conversation as musicians are taken up by and participate in the happening of the situation in which they find themselves.

Falling is something that simply happens to us. When we genuinely fall, we have no choice but to *be* in *that* situation. In being called to understand the world differently, the world is framed by a particular horizontal field that constitutes the place or region in which one participates in a hermeneutical/improvisational conversation. By falling into, one finds oneself in a certain improvisational situation which frames and structures one's engagement with the subject matter that provoked one's falling into. Consistent with Part I, we may say that the improvisational situation is the 'focus', 'origin' and 'horizon' of hermeneutic engagement. The 'situation' in which one finds oneself is consistent with the 'world' in which Gadamer says one finds oneself when one experiences a work of art. He writes of drama, 'what no longer exists is the world in which we live as our own . . . . [T]he action of a drama . . . exists as something that rests absolutely within itself.'[66] So too is falling into the improvisational situation an extraction of oneself from the ordinary world and finding oneself already placed in an *improvisational situation* that exists as a distinct region of improvisational engagement.

As we saw with respect to Denley's improvising in the Budawang Mountains in Chapter 3, a certain horizontal field emerges with respect to that which is a matter of concern that frames the improvisational situation, limiting that which is of concern and structuring one's engagement. It is from within this field or boundary that the work comes forth. Equally, with respect to hermeneutics, understanding emerges from or is disclosed in the situation in which one finds oneself. What is understood is always already there with those who come to understand it, but what they come to understand is always an understanding *for them* disclosed in *that* situation.

The situation into which one falls is no mere blank canvas upon which one may present the genius of one's response. Instead, just as unexpectedly tripping and beginning to fall when one is walking, the situation presents a set of circumstances to the person who falls. The situation demands that the person attend and respond to the circumstances suddenly facing them, and they do that, not by appealing to some predetermined method but by improvising – which is not to suggest that hermeneutic engagement is void of habits, rules or conventions (discussed in the following chapter). Just like in improvised musical performance, prejudice or prior understanding accompanies the individual into any given situation and forms the basis for the individual to generate 'passing theories' or 'appropriate' spontaneous responses to the unexpected and unforeseen elements of the situation. The 'call' to improvise is something that simply happens and thus one can never be entirely prepared to understand. The discord that one experiences that initiates one's falling into arrives *improviso* and relieves the individual of their subjective intentionality. One's participation in hermeneutic conversation occurs by virtue of one's unexpected and spontaneous *falling into*, a happening initiated by one's encounter with difference.

Hermeneutical engagement as an improvisational traverse

That understanding emerges from the productive happening of one's improvising in the situation into which one has fallen suggests a situated conception of understanding. As mentioned, that which is to be understood is *there* in the situation. It is important to remember, however, that the subject who has fallen is equally *a part* of the situation – they are always already *there* in the situation, for it is only by being in the midst of the situation that they receive what is illuminated. Thus, the understanding that is *there* should not be thought of in terms of an enduring metaphysical object. Neither should the situation or place into which one has fallen be considered to possess an enduring metaphysical 'essence', in the sense that *every* possibility for interpretation is inherent in that place, now and forever, independent of who they encounter in that place and is therefore *discovered* by the subject in a Platonist sense. Such an understanding renders the subject separate or detached from the situation, rather than an integral part of it.

The truth or understanding at stake that is *there* in the situation is in its totality – a totality that goes beyond any individual experience – the *unity* of the situation. It extends across the situation and constitutes the limit or boundary of the place, just as the work extends to the limits of the horizonal field in improvised musical performance. Consider an example of a house. The truth of the house is not confined to any individual aspect or component of the house, instead, it extends through the house as a whole. Likewise, the truth of a text cannot be reduced to a single word, sentence or page. Moreover, the truth of the house, text or work of art is not independent of the subject interpreting that house, text or work of art. Having fallen into the improvisational situation, the improviser who seeks understanding traverses, explores and experiences the situation as it is *for them*.

The 'traverse' is one's spontaneous attending and responding to the situation to which one *belongs* by virtue of one's falling into an improvisational engagement. Indeed, the 'traverse' at issue here is consistent with how it was touched upon in Chapter 3, where the player is *led* through the improvisational situation by attending and responding to possibilities that emerge from the happening of the situation. The region offers possibilities to be understood in a certain way and it is the task of the interpreter to engage with those possibilities to arrive at an understanding. This is consistent with the way in which Denley was described as attending and responding to the improvisational situation, which in his case was nested within the Budawang Mountains. Denley orients himself within the horizonal field of the improvisational situation, his traverse is his attending and responding to the possibilities offered to him by virtue of his improvisational engagement.

Gadamer speaks of finding and following a 'trace' in much the same way I am suggesting one embarks upon an improvisational traverse. He writes, 'when a trace is found, we acquire a first direction and it opens onto something. Yet, where the trace will lead is open. We let ourselves be led.'[67]

This is the participatory nature of pathos mentioned earlier. We may say one's improvisational engagement – one's traverse of the improvisational situation – is guided by the trace. The way in which one engages with the trace is both *improviso* and *innovare*, for Gadamer writes that 'there develops around the trace . . . a field of actions of a completely unique kind'.[68] The originary situation into which one has fallen calls for improvisational engagement that is without precedent, for it is particular to the situation or event of its occurrence. Moreover, the indeterminate nature of this engagement, as Gadamer recognizes, means that being led by the trace requires participation. He writes, 'we strive not to lose the trace and to stay the course. If we lose the trace we lose our way. Then, we have gone astray and do not know how to continue. As a result, we must search anew for the trace and find it again.'[69] One attempts to maintain an essential orientation so that one might stay the course of the trace. Indeed, the improvisation at issue here is not merely a blind following, but genuine engagement with both the strange and familiar to understand *differently* by virtue of what is illuminated in the situation.

What comes forth does so only insofar as there is improvisational engagement. Gadamer writes,[70] 'the text is indeed encountered by us as another person and we try to get closer to it. We try this or that. We have new ideas.' 'The dialogue', he continues, 'is indeed no well-crafted treatise.' With respect to interpreting texts, the reader follows traces as they read. They engage with the text by posing questions and answers and by attempting to give direction to the dialogue. Gadamer is explicit that what does *not* exist is 'the reader who, when he has his text before him, simply reads what is there'.[71] In hermeneutic engagement, the reader has 'fallen into' the improvisational situation and is *there* engaging with the text in an improvisational manner in the sense of a traverse. The reader criss-crosses the terrain, re-sighting lost traces, picking up and being led by new ones, reaching dead ends and doubling back, working within the boundary or horizonal field of the situation, piecing together a certain topological ordering of the situation so that truth and understanding might dawn on them. What comes forth emerges from the situation that is the happening of improvisational/hermeneutic engagement.

As noted, it is because we *are* in culture, because we inherit tradition, and because we are finite beings that we can never know the world in any complete or absolute sense. It is because we are always already *in* history that we can never step outside it, as it were, and view it in any objective sense. And because we can never know the world completely, the tarrying that gives rise to understanding is always a performance of a *particular* understanding tied to history, discourse and practice – a historical improvisational response to the situation into which one has fallen. Understanding is always the enactment of the historicity of the interpreter and the subject matter colliding. It is the movement of the hermeneutic engagement – the improvisation – such that one comes to recognize a certain topological ordering of things, an ordering of the parts with respect to the whole, that yields understanding, if understanding occurs at all.

While the improvisational traverse is certainly indeterminate in the sense that, as Gadamer writes of conversation, 'no one knows in advance what will "come out" of a conversation',[72] it is not arbitrary. There is always an orientation to one's falling into, an orientation directly tied to one's prejudice that directs the improviser towards a certain aspect of the subject matter. The way in which one traverses the improvisational situation is structured by this circularity. One's orientation towards certain aspects of the 'house', to continue that example, is always already structured by one's prejudice, despite an aspect of one's prejudice being called into question by a certain character of the house, such that a falling into was provoked. Further, consistent with the discussion from Chapter 2, the improvisational situation itself is suggestive of a certain *topos*, as we saw with respect to the way in which musical instruments 'play' the musician as much as the musician 'plays' the instrument. The traverse that one embarks upon to receive an understanding or reach an agreement is largely structured by the topological ordering of the improvisational situation itself.

Traversing the improvisational situation, one gradually maps out, as it were, a particular interpretation or understanding of the subject matter at issue. It is in this manner that one orders certain themes, and a certain character of the situation comes forth. This improvisational engagement is not pre-planned or organized. It is a traverse that has a spirit of its own, akin to Gadamer's 'play' and Heidegger's characterization of ontological inquiry; one's traverse, like 'play', bears its own structure within it. As Gadamer writes, 'in playing, all those purposive relations that determine active and caring existence have not simply disappeared, but are curiously suspended'.[73] The understanding that emerges through one's attending and responding to those aspects of the situation one encounters emerge by virtue of one's comportment towards the situation; one's tactful openness to receive and engage with those traces encountered within the horizonal field of one's improvisational engagement.

It is understanding, as a traverse through the situation opened up by the happening of improvisation, that transforms the improviser and allows them to experience what Gadamer refers to as a 'fusion of horizons'.[74] To return to the example of the house, where improvisation is the traversing of the house, and the 'map' of the house one acquires through their traverse is the productive 'outcome' of that traverse, one can think of the fusion of horizons in terms of the 'outcome' – the productive element that emerges and comes forth from improvisation. In this way, the fusion is not a 'becoming one' of one horizon and another such that all difference disappears without remainder. The fusion of horizons is better thought of in terms of experience, in line with the concept of *Bildung*, mentioned earlier. Indeed, commenting on Gadamer's thought, James Risser explains it is better to think of 'fusion' not as a 'joining' in the sense that 'what is two becomes one'[75] but as a '*holding together*, which is not equivalent to unification'.[76] The 'map', from the earlier example, is this holding together of different elements such that one may understand the relationships between particular elements, and yet one does not possess an absolute understanding of the house. The fusion of horizons – the agreement one reaches by virtue of one's improvisational engagement with the subject matter – is one's coming to understand a certain topological ordering or relationality of things.

Improvising in language

The understanding that emerges from the improvisational traverse is tied to what Gadamer refers to as the 'linguisticality of understanding', where 'the essential relation between language and understanding is seen primarily in the fact that the essence of tradition is to exist in the medium of language'.[77] Language, according to Gadamer (as discussed in Chapter 1), does not merely refer to linguistics or semantics, insofar as these disciplines refer to the structure, grammar and syntax of language. Rather Gadamer is interested in language as *conversation*; he is concerned with the application or practice of language. He writes, 'we should follow the semantic life of language and this means: go back to the point where the concept emerges out of speaking itself, out of the "situatedness in life".[78] For Gadamer, 'the real being of language is that into which we are taken up when we hear it – what is said'.[79] The language of truth and understanding is the language that one encounters in one's improvisational traverse. When one is 'taken up by' what is said and is genuinely attentive and responsive to the other, one falls into the improvisational situation. By attending to the other, one comes to *belong* to the situation, but one maintains one's essential orientation in the improvisational situation through language. It is language that guides one's traverse of the situation in search of agreement – a fusion of horizons.

For Gadamer, 'the world is the common ground, trodden by none and recognised by all, uniting all who talk to one another'.[80] The 'world', as distinct from habitat or environment, which animals have, too, is that which one accesses through language. According to Gadamer, one accesses the world and interprets it hermeneutically through, or, better, *in*, language – interpreting is a mode of participating in the world; a world common to all who speak. Language and world cannot be separated, for the world is in language. Grondin writes, 'for Gadamer, language is not a "take" on reality, nor its putting into linguistic form; it is the world which is most world'.[81] One's engagement with the world is always in language, not in the sense that one possesses pre-linguistic thoughts about things that one then attaches to language in order to communicate about those things but in the very real sense that, as Heidegger says, 'language speaks'.[82] That is, we may utter sounds or words but it is language, not us, that names a thing, and it is by being named by language that a thing is of concern to us – we do not concern ourselves with that for which we have no language. Heidegger writes, 'something *is* only where . . . word names a thing as being, and so establishes the given being as a being'.[83] It is precisely language that allows entities and the world to appear. One's experience of the world is fundamentally linguistic; all understanding occurs in the medium of language.

Language, for Gadamer, is not representational but presentational. Risser states that 'what comes to be understood is not something that has already been understood and which has not been put into words, but is the very working out of the moment of understanding'.[84] To understand is to encounter and interpret the *self-presentation* of the word or language of a thing (discussed further later). This is why Gadamer puts so much emphasis on the conversational model of understanding. To converse is to presuppose or create a common language.[85] It is in this sense that one can understand Gadamer's assertion that texts and artworks, for instance, speak to us or address us.[86] In our coming to understand the text we find a common language through which the text may present itself to us in language.

The way in which Gadamer's account of conversation and the linguisticality of understanding at issue here might be said to involve a certain improvisational character has to do with Gadamer's understanding of language as essentially practical. He writes, 'we are continually shaping a common perspective when we speak a common language and so are active participants in the communality of our experience of the world.'[87] Language is that through which we participate in the world. Moreover, there is an indeterminate character of language where words have no simple correlative function, no basic structure of sign and are signified to the extent that Gadamer writes, 'expressive signs . . . remain variable . . . in the sense that within the same language the same expression can designate different things and different expressions the same thing'.[88] The word is less like a sign and more like an image; words have a certain depth, complexity and alterity about them. As Davey writes, 'words and images point beyond themselves by inferring without putting into words the infinity of meaning (the whole) which shades and nuances every particular meaning.'[89] One must engage with, interpret and participate in language, that is, improvise.

By conceptualizing language and understanding as conversational, Gadamer highlights the openness and indeterminacy of language. He writes,

> Every word breaks forth as if from a centre and is related to a whole, through which alone it is a word. Every word causes the whole of the language to which it belongs to resonate and the whole world-view that underlies it to appear. Thus every word, as the event of a moment, carries with it the unsaid, to which it is related by responding and summoning.[90]

Human speech and dialogue do not emerge from, nor are they tied to, rules or theories of grammar and syntax but rather come forth from the occasionality of the encounter – the 'event of a moment'. That each word, by virtue of it being part of the whole of language, is tied to the 'unsaid' means that human speech possesses an 'infinity of meaning'.[91] Because there is always this dialectic between the said and the unsaid, artworks and texts, for instance, always bear within them more than just the meaning they have for the individual – the self-presentation of the thing always goes beyond any particular interpretation or understanding. Thus, as noted, understanding is not merely the reproduction of meaning. Understanding always comes forth anew as something *produced* from improvisational engagement.

The indeterminacy of language

Gadamer writes that 'the general process of reaching an understanding between persons and the process of understanding *per se* are both language-events'.[92] Insofar as there is an accord between one's thinking, saying or doing and one's understanding of that thinking, saying or doing, it suggests linguistic understanding; there is always a correlation between language and understanding. Perhaps the most common counter to such a claim is the silent gesture. However, Gadamer would argue that this, too, occurs in the medium of language. The following quote from Augustine, whose thinking on the matter was influential for Gadamer,[93] illuminates the primacy of language with respect to silent gestures:

> For even to nod, what else is it but to speak, as it were, in a visible manner? . . . he spoke by beckoning what he did not venture to speak aloud. But we make use of these and other corporeal signs of this kind when we speak to the eyes or the ears of those who are present.[94]

Gesture of this kind is naught but the attempt to convey meaning. That a gesture such as a nod does indeed convey meaning to another indicates that the other is already in possession of some prior understanding – a common language – that allows them to interpret such a gesture in an appropriate way.

Moreover, Gadamer asserts that even being 'lost for words' is tied to language. He writes that 'when speech deserts us, what this really means is that one would like to say so much that one does not know where to begin'.⁹⁵ Being 'lost for words' is more accurately 'searching for words'; one seeks those words that might do justice to one's experience. Being so moved by an artwork that one is lost for words, for instance, does not signal that language has come to an end but, as Gadamer asserts, 'to a beginning'.⁹⁶ Further, noting the conversational character of *all* understanding, we might note that often when we find ourselves lost for words, it is less that we do not understand the other, but that we do not understand ourselves.⁹⁷ Understanding is as much an internal conversation with oneself as it is an external conversation with an interlocutor or thing.

Understanding always occurs in language, as a language-event. This relationship to language constitutes a salient part-whole structure. It is precisely because we are always already *in* language (the whole) that we are able to understand distinct aspects of the world (the parts). But equally, it is only by virtue of our concrete experience as the inheritors of language (the parts) that we grasp the universality of language (the whole). Two assertions can be deduced:

1. All understanding emerges within the horizon of language.
2. All understanding arises from a particular situated encounter – an event of truth.

As noted, what precedes understanding is always some sort of perceived discord between oneself and the world. One does not seek understanding when one's experience of the world is in accord with one's prior understanding and expectations. It is only when one encounters and is addressed by something strange or challenging that one experiences a falling into. That one's experience was not in accord with one's prior understanding calls for a reconsideration of that understanding. If one rises to that call and engages with the circumstances encountered in the improvisational situation, one may come to understand the world, and oneself, differently.

The agreement or understanding always arrives in the form of language. In this sense, language, as something that is said or thought, is always *for someone*. One does not just speak any words in any context. That language is indeed a language, that is, it conveys meaning and can be understood by others, assumes that when one speaks, one speaks (or at least tries to speak) the right words. Such speaking, Gadamer writes, 'places [that which is said] before the eyes of the other person to whom I speak'.[98] It is through language that one accesses the world, it is through language that one accesses the other, and indeed oneself; that for which one has no language does not exist. Language is always geared to the occasion. It is always encountered as something that conveys meaning, and such that one receives a resolution to one's experience of discord highlights how language is geared towards consonance in *that* situation, which is not to suggest that the understanding arrived at does not have implications beyond the individual encounter.

The understanding that emerges does so as a spontaneous 'happening' of language. Despite any intent or purposiveness, the arrival of understanding is always indeterminate, occasional and, to a degree, unforeseen and unexpected. Just as one cannot predict precisely how or when a conversation will 'take hold', neither can one know with any real certainty how or when a fusion of horizons might occur. The spontaneity of understanding is alluded to in the language we use to describe it: 'it dawned on me', '... and then it hit me', 'I had a lightbulb moment', 'ah-ha!' In every instance we encounter a scene where someone does not understand and then suddenly, they begin to grasp what is at issue for them. The person left 'speechless' from an encounter, when asked to describe their experience, will quite commonly, and all of a sudden, find many words in an attempt to articulate their experience. There is a sense in which the spontaneous emergence of understanding is beyond one's conscious control; the occurrence of language is something that happens.

Our being in language, whether through speaking, searching for words or experiencing the beginning of language, always emerges in a certain situation in response to a particular encounter. It is always an improvisational being in language where it is a traverse of – an attending and responding to – the situation in which one finds oneself that is the letting be of the language of the situation. Understanding, like the work in improvised musical performance, emerges from the improvisational situation where what 'comes forth' is cultivated by one's improvisational traverse. Improvisation, we may say, and explore in the next section, is the letting speak of the thing itself.

The language of the thing itself

For Gadamer, all conversation is concerned with a subject matter. As noted, it is in this way that one can genuinely converse with an interlocutor, a text or with oneself. Gadamer writes,

> This understanding of the subject matter must take the form of language. It is not that the understanding is subsequently put into words; rather, the way understanding occurs – whether in the case of a text or a dialogue with another person who raises an issue with us – is the coming-into-language of the thing itself.[99]

In a genuine conversation, and this is made particularly salient when we consider one's encounter with what is generally considered a non-linguistic thing such as instrumental music or a painting, the interpreter is not 'told' anything in an explanatory sense – indeed how could an artwork 'explain' the truth of itself? Rather, as Gadamer writes, 'in a successful conversation [one comes] under the influence of the truth of the object'.[100] Understanding comes about by the interpreter's participation in the situation and by *receiving* a particular understanding disclosed to them by virtue of their improvisational engagement with a subject matter, not dissimilar to the way in which musicians receive possibilities for action in the improvisational situation by virtue of their attending and responding to a common matter of concern.[101]

To speak of the language of things is to reaffirm the mode of being-in-the-world that is the spontaneous falling into the improvisational situation. The improvisational situation is the place in which one encounters and is responsive to the world as such, for, as was discussed in Chapter 2, much of one's improvising is structured by the way in which the world itself acts upon and draws out certain responses from the player. One's spontaneous attending and responding to the improvisational situation largely occurs before the subject can objectify the world or project their subjective understanding of the world onto that which they encounter. The improvisational situation is the place where one encounters and receives the world as it *presents itself*, it is the place where one encounters the language of things.

Gadamer writes,

This expression ['the language of things'] has a kind of polemical accent. It expresses the fact that, in general, we are not at all ready to hear things in their own being, that they are subjected to man's calculus and to his domination of nature through the rationality of science. . . . But we can still speak of a language of things when we remember what things really are, namely, not the material that is used and consumed, not a tool that is used and set aside, but something instead that has existence in itself and is 'not forced to do anything,' as Heidegger says. . . . This common expression rouses the memory (slumbering in us all) of the being of things that are still able to be what they are.[102]

A technical view of the world as described here by Gadamer struggles to genuinely engage with the world by virtue of the fact that one must view oneself as standing apart from the world so that one may attempt to control or manipulate it – the antithesis of allowing oneself to be *appropriated* by the situation. It is a view that embraces a subject-object distinction where things in the world are seen by the subject as objects to be 'used and consumed', as Gadamer says. Thus, it is a view that is ignorant to the improvisation of being, which, as will become clear, is an engagement with the world where one comes to *be-in*-the-world and allows oneself to be appropriated by the world, as opposed to attempting to view oneself as standing apart from the world. The improviser is *in* and *of* the world just as everything else is. In their being-*in*-the-world, the improviser does not encounter the world as something to dominate or consume. Rather, the improviser encounters the world as such, listening for the possibilities and searching for the traces offered by the world in an attempt to arrive at a fusion of horizons.

The experience of music provides a particularly salient example of this mode of being: When a performance affects an audience member in such a way that it evokes a strong emotional connection or leaves them 'speechless', it is the *work* rather than the players that has this affective quality. In such cases the player truly *belongs* to the situation and they, in a sense, withdraw behind the work. Indeed, one of the pioneers of free improvisation in Australia, visual artist, bassist and electronic musician David Tolley alludes to such self-forgetfulness in his reflections on the relationship between the audience and the musician.

He describes three options for the solo improviser (from least experienced to most): 'Listen to me', 'listen to me playing' and 'listen to this'.[103] While Tolley maintains a certain subjectivity with respect to the player intentionally gifting something to the audience, the general sentiment of his statement – that in foregrounding the work, the player increasingly steps back – is accurate. When performers genuinely improvise, they surrender themselves to the situation and encounter the world of which they are a part, allowing the work to come forth as the happening of place. It is the work itself that affects the concertgoer.

When one is met with a certain feeling or quality in aesthetic experience, this is a direct result of the encounter. One does not merely conjure these feelings independently of the artwork; one cannot receive beauty from that which does not possess beauty. Thus, the character of the thing that one encounters truly belongs to the thing itself; it is the *presentation* of itself. As Gadamer writes, 'what presents itself in this way is not different from itself in presenting itself'.[104] With respect to non-artistic things, truth manifests itself in the same way. The truth of one's experience emerges from the experience itself; truth is self-presentation. When one encounters the truth of a text, for example, they encounter the self-presentation of the truth of the text itself, 'it asserts itself as truth',[105] Gadamer says. Encountering the language of the thing is the disclosure of truth itself. The improvisational situation creates a certain space where *more* of the truth comes forth in this self-presentational manner.

The dialectical movement of conversation should not be thought of in a methodological sense, as the conscious intentional movement of thought *about* a thing. Gadamer says that 'what thought experiences is the *movement of the thing itself*' [emphasis added].[106] The movement of thought, which occurs linguistically as one improvises with the traces encountered in the situation – the traces are *of* the situation – can only be the movement of the thing itself. The interpretation of a thing that emerges from one's traverse of the improvisational situation is the self-presentation of the thing in language. German phenomenologist Günter Figal writes, with reference to Gadamer,

> Because every saying is to be conceived as an answer, whatever is brought to speech must already have been linguistically disclosed, and, at the same time, it must be said again. In this 'dialectic of question and answer'..., the

question refers to the possible answer and the answer refers back to the question.[107]

Question *and* answer are bound together with the thing itself. Gadamer writes that 'questions impose themselves',[108] in the sense that to ask a question one must have already picked up on a certain trace that belongs to the thing itself, and to ask *that* question is already to be working towards a certain answer, in the sense of following the path given by the trace. Because this movement of thought is not separate to the thing but necessarily involves one's improvising *with* the thing, one's subsequent understanding of the thing that emerges in the form of a fusion of horizons has a claim to truth. Any event of truth, then, relies upon encountering the thing in the right way, that is, improvisationally.

Upon experiencing discord and being addressed by a subject matter, one falls into an improvisational situation. By attending and responding to the possibilities and traces offered by the subject matter, one may encounter the language of the thing itself. The truth of disclosure is an event where the interpreter receives and experiences the truth of the word. Truth emerges by virtue of the happening of improvisation. In this way truth *presents itself*; the interpreter *receives* truth. To understand is to receive the language of the thing itself in the improvisational situation. To receive truth, we may say, is to improvise.

Improvising in language

The way in which we are in the world is an improvisational mode of being insofar as Gadamer's conception of conversation and the structure of improvisation seem to be in accord with one another. This improvisational being-in-the-world is not a mode of being structured by predetermined or static rules or methods but is instead a dynamic happening where one, by virtue of one's being *in* language, attends and responds to the peculiarities of the improvisational situation into which one has fallen. This attending and responding to the world necessarily involves orienting oneself towards certain aspects of the world, attending to the familiar and the strange. One's engagement with the situation is an improvisational happening where one encounters, or receives, the language of a thing.

That the nature of language is conversational means one can never exhaust the meaning of a thing. In this way, everything that has been said can be said differently. It is our being-in language that means we can arrive at different sayings for the same subject matter. 'The first pronouncement' writes Grondin, 'is only the first expression.' He continues, 'to possess a language is in a way to be able to rise above it, to enlarge our horizons whilst remaining in the horizon of possible sayings'.[109] Every saying goes beyond itself and thus one questions oneself through language to expand one's horizon. As a result of the infinite meaning within what is said, one can transcend one's prior saying and through improvisational engagement with that prior saying question oneself to arrive at a new saying, a new interpretation of what was originally said. One can improvise on the same themes over and again. Thus, one can always understand oneself in another way, but in this way, too, one can never transcend the horizon of understanding itself.[110] Understanding bears an affinity with improvisation as it is commonly manifest in jazz. Just as a jazz musician can interpret the melody of a tune differently whenever they play that tune, so too are there multiple – infinite – interpretations of texts or artworks due to the indeterminate character of language and the finitude of human being-in-the-world. The circularity of improvisation is not an endless repetition of the same but endless repetitions of accumulative differences, where non-identical repetitions allow for the development of a practice.[111]

Thus, understanding involves the coming into language of a thing in the improvisational situation. One's understanding of a thing in language is intimately tied to an improvisational mode of being-in-the-world. The improvisation of understanding is improvising *in* language. But equally, due to the dynamic, occasional and indeterminate nature of language, one's *being-in* language is necessarily improvisational. If language could be understood as merely a syntactic system or a representational structure, there would be an understanding that was essentially separate from or prior to language. A separatedness that would allow one to objectify – stand apart – from language and theorize from beyond it. According to Gadamer, there can be no such removal from or going beyond language. Language is that within which understanding comes forth.[112] But that coming forth is always an improvisational coming forth. The priority of language is tied to the priority of improvisation; one cannot receive the gift of language without adopting a certain improvisational comportment. The improvisational structure of language is that which opens one up to ever new experiences, truth and world; it is that which allows one to encounter the language of the world. The movement of language, of hermeneutics, and so we may say philosophy itself, is a movement that is in accord with the structure of improvisation.

The happening of truth

As mentioned, it was Heidegger who reformulated hermeneutics from a methodological concern to an ontological one – the 'hermeneutics of facticity'.[113] For Heidegger, writes Gadamer, 'understanding is the way in which the historicity of Dasein is itself carried out'.[114] This carrying out of the historicity of *Dasein* is realized through the way in which one's prejudices are called into question as not only orienting *Dasein* in the hermeneutic encounter but also illuminating that orientation during the traverse of the improvisational situation. The improvisation of understanding occurs by virtue of one's falling into the situation, that is, prior to the subject-object split and therefore prior to one's reflecting on the situation. Even to reflect, if it is to result in understanding *differently*, is to encounter and thematize certain thoughts and improvise with them such that an interpretation emerges. Indeed, as Gadamer writes of Heidegger, 'the question is not in what way being can be understood but in what way understanding *is* being'.[115] Hermeneutics does not describe a way in which one comes to understand being but rather characterizes being as essentially improvisational.

Expanding on the tradition initiated by Heidegger who concerned himself with overcoming the forgetfulness of being through the hermeneutics of facticity, the event of being (*Ereignis*) and the 'there' as the clearing of being (*Lichtung*),[116] which extended into Gadamer's work with respect to his articulation of the conversation of being, we may further extend Gadamer's formulation of the conversation to include the improvisation of being. What is at issue in each of the aforementioned formulations, Gadamer explains, is that understanding 'cannot be grasped as a simple activity of the consciousness that understands but is itself a mode of the event of being'.[117] Being is an event, a happening. Being is performative and comes forth in active-presence or as self-presentation. Understanding comes forth in the happening of improvisation.

One may observe what may at first appear to be a certain aporia in the nature of truth and understanding presented in this chapter. On the one hand, as noted, Gadamer describes understanding in terms of a 'rupture' or 'flash', which echoes Heidegger's *Augenblick*,[118] the authentic momentary 'flash' or 'lighting' of truth. On the other hand, Gadamer also speaks of a certain 'tarrying' (*Verweilen*), where understanding takes time, such as in the sense of a conversation or an improvisational traverse, which is sometimes thought to stand in opposition to Heidegger's *Augenblick*.[119] That Gadamer speaks of truth and understanding in terms of both a 'flash' and a 'conversation', however, is not indicative of a tension or confusion in his thinking, as is made particularly clear when one considers truth and understanding as improvisational.

To understand the way in which truth and understanding happens in Gadamer's hermeneutics one need only look to the way in which the work happens in improvised musical performance. The work as such does not suddenly appear, rather it comes about by virtue of the happening of the improvisational situation. The happening at issue here is the 'working out' or the play of improvisation; it is one's traversing the improvisational situation into which one has fallen. One's falling into is indeed sudden and to a certain extent unforeseen and unexpected. But understanding, for Gadamer, only occurs insofar as one embarks on the traverse or engages in conversation. The 'flash' or 'rupture' of understanding happens by virtue of that traverse – of having pieced together or mapped out a certain topological ordering of the situation. That is, the traverse prepares the way for the flash or rupture.

Indeed, one notices such a 'flash' with respect to the improvisation of musical works, too. One cannot pinpoint the instant where the work comes into fruition as something 'finished'. To treat the work as a series of divisible moments in time such that one may plot the moment at which the work transitions from incomplete to complete is to appeal to temporal rather than a topological conception of the event such that performance is understood in terms of succession rather than as an event or situation. A work suddenly *is* but that suddenness is the result of an improvisational happening. It is in this manner that the flash of truth and understanding happens to those who improvise. The understanding that dawns on the interpreter 'in the suddenness of a rupture or a flash', to re-quote Gadamer, cannot be separated from their falling into and their traverse, which prepares the way for that flash. Thus, truth and understanding in Gadamer's philosophical hermeneutics emerges from the improvisational situation. The truth of disclosure, we may say, occurs by virtue of improvisation.

6

Improvisation, ethics and factical Life

Having considered the improvisational character of truth and understanding, as well as the way in which we receive the language of things, we might now turn to an arguably less explicit but no less fundamental theme of philosophical hermeneutics: ethics. Addressing the ethical character of hermeneutics is important on two counts. First, as will become clear, a concern with the ethical is central to Gadamer's hermeneutics. Second, insofar as ethics is fundamentally practical, illuminating the improvisational character of ethics not only highlights further the ubiquitous nature of improvisation but also gives a prescriptive force to this otherwise descriptive study. It is argued that the way we improvise is directly connected to what we are becoming; improvisation is fundamental to who we are.

The call to hermeneutics

In the work of both Heidegger and Gadamer one encounters a certain call. In Heidegger it is a call to think 'meditatively' in what is otherwise characterized as a 'thoughtless' time.[1] In Gadamer it emerges as a call to hermeneutics.[2] In both instances, it is a call for the restoration of balance between hermeneutic or ontological thought and scientific or technological thought. Gadamer, expanding on a topic already common to phenomenology,[3] warns of succumbing to scientific thinking at the expense of the hermeneutical. Indeed, he explicitly calls for the acquisition of a certain 'hermeneutic virtue',[4] where the first step towards achieving the 'solidarity of humanity' is *understanding other people*. Both Heidegger and Gadamer have approached this 'call' in the context of atomic warfare, noting the ease with which humankind is now capable of destroying itself. But while the threat of atomic devastation is clearly in the mind of both thinkers, it is not the looming threat of this form of annihilation that is their focus. Rather they are concerned with the *absence of emergency* in the presence of such annihilation. Their primary concern is that advancements in technology, such as the development of atomic weapons, might so 'captivate, bewitch, dazzle, . . . beguile'[5] and ultimately blind us to what Gadamer understands to be the essential tasks of humanity: 'living together and surviving together'.[6]

The issue for both Heidegger and Gadamer, as mentioned, is the dominance of scientific thinking at the expense of the hermeneutical. While Heidegger nowhere refers to a call to 'hermeneutics' as such, in the present context grouping Heidegger and Gadamer together under the banner of 'hermeneutics' does not misrepresent Heidegger's thinking on the matter. Indeed, while it is true that Heidegger abandons any explicit hermeneutical focus in his later thinking, his interest in language and understanding in the sense of one's relationship to the world 'keeps his late philosophy', Ingo Farin writes, 'at the very least in the *neighbourhood* of hermeneutics'.[7] Moreover, if we consider Gadamer's work, which explicitly pursued the line of thinking of the later Heidegger,[8] it is clear that Heidegger's later work gives rise to, and is consistent with, Gadamer's hermeneutics. Thus, the basic premise of both Heidegger's and Gadamer's call to a fundamental ontology may be accurately understood as a hermeneutical concern.

As noted, Gadamer's call for hermeneutic virtue is a call to restore *balance* within the discipline of thinking. Gadamer's argument is not that scientific thinking has no place in the modern world, instead, he is concerned that science has come to dominate thinking and has problematically asserted itself as the *only* mode of thinking that can lead to truth and knowledge. Such a dominance is as apparent in music studies as anywhere else, with analytical, quantitative and epistemological studies largely dominating the field. For

Gadamer, one's acquisition of hermeneutic virtue offers a way forward to correct this imbalance and restore to their rightful place different and distinct modes of thinking.

To differentiate between what one might refer to as 'scientific thinking' and 'hermeneutic thinking', Gadamer provides an example from Plato's *Statesman*,[9] where Plato distinguishes between two different ways of measuring. On the one hand, according to Plato, measuring refers to 'all those kinds of expertise that measure the number, lengths, depths, breadths and speeds of things in relation to the opposite'.[10] Here, measuring takes on a distinctly quantitative meaning. On the other hand, Plato observes that measuring also refers to 'what is in due measure, what is fitting, the right moment, what is as it ought to be'.[11] That is, measuring also possesses a qualitative meaning. The implications of Gadamer's invocation of this example rest in Plato's assertion that *both* understandings of measuring – quantitative *and* qualitative – are indispensable and should be held in balance. Gadamer's observation of humanity is that we have lost this balance.

In Heidegger's thought this tension emerges with respect to *ge-stell* and calculative thinking on the one hand, and *ge-lassenheit* and meditative thinking on the other. Calculative thinking refers to a mode of thinking employed to understand objects, where one objectifies phenomena to control, manipulate and, ultimately, dominate the phenomena. In the system of *ge-stell*, Heidegger scholar Miguel de Beistegui asserts that 'technology signals the contemporary hold of man over nature'.[12] Meditative thinking, in contrast, is the thought that stops and ponders. Meditative thinking directs thought back to that which calculative thinking, in its haste to move ever forward, skips over and pays little or no attention to. Meditative thinking is a mode of thinking about the world that does not attempt to dominate or control the world, nor is it a mode of thinking that considers the world subjectively, that is, as something that is an issue for humans. Meditative thinking, and *ge-lassenheit*, signals a mode of 'letting-be', where we do not attempt to dominate the world or explain it objectively, instead we *encounter* the world and listen to it to receive the language of things.

Twentieth-century Italian philosopher Luigi Pareyson expresses a similar observation to Heidegger and Gadamer when he warns of the 'culture of surrogates', of which he writes, 'in every field, a specific activity is replaced by an inferior or different activity that, forced to take the place of the original with diminished and inadequate powers, corrupts its primary intent'.[13] He elaborates:

> Technics becomes, in every field, the surrogate for excellence: in art, where the deft manipulation of artistic means gives the appearance of art without giving the substance of it; in science where the technical moment is emphasised over the cognitive and creative moment; in ethics, where the technics of behaviours replaces the inventive process through which the originary moral appeal translates itself into norms; and in philosophy itself, reduced to a procedural rationality of techniques variously adapted to specific fields of inquiry.[14]

It is precisely this culture of surrogates that is at issue here. Scientific thinking has become the surrogate for the hermeneutical, which, as we learn from Pareyson's example, is to the detriment of all fields, science included. What is problematic with this surrogate culture is that science, for example, cannot encompass philosophy without significantly narrowing philosophical inquiry and resorting to scientism.

Gadamer and Pareyson both make a similar claim: Scientific thinking is not separate from the hermeneutical but rather emerges from within it. Scientific method alone offers no guarantee of productivity or insight, as in the case of statistics where the *questions* the 'facts' of statistics address and the *consequences* that follow are essentially hermeneutical concerns.[15] For science to offer meaningful insight into the world, scientific inquiry must be founded upon a genuine hermeneutical question. Indeed, the art of questioning, of having the prejudice of being interested in a particular subject matter to be meaningfully pursued, is the domain of hermeneutics.

Thus, we return to the notion of *balance*. Both philosophy and science need to understand the limits of their field and must resist any notion of becoming a surrogate for one another. In the wake of modernity's fascination with science and the subsequent devaluation of other forms of knowledge, one encounters what might be considered a homogenization of thinking. With the domination of science, we fail to recognize science, philosophy, art, religion and politics as distinct fields offering particular insights. Instead, science holds the dominant position, and what cannot be assumed under its umbrella is cast aside and lumped together as a field that no longer has anything to say. The plane of thinking – the questions we ask and the answers we provide – becomes narrow and lacking in depth.

A consequence of the dominance of scientific thinking is evident in the way art, which, Heidegger asserts, was once an essential way in which we received truth about the world,[16] is relegated to 'aesthetics'. That is, considered from the perspective of aesthetics, art is denied an ethical character; it is merely beautiful or in possession of aesthetic appeal. Echoing a similar sentiment, Pareyson writes,

> Having become pure play, mere technique, simple experimentation, extreme specialisation, art almost returns to its infancy but without the support of myth and magic, which in primitive societies fill those empty artistic manifestations with meaning.[17]

When science is considered the sole arbiter of truth and knowledge the importance of other fields is reduced. When art is no longer thought to disclose truth and becomes mere aesthetics, art is valued and appreciated only because, as the philosopher Julian Young observes, 'it is a form of stress relief, a moment of lyric *stasis* in the midst of busyness, a holiday from the anxious world of willing and working'.[18] As a consequence, art is reduced to something of 'peripheral importance'.[19]

In contrast to the 'scientific' view of art, for example, Yolŋu, an aggregation of Indigenous Australian people from north-eastern Arnhem Land in the Northern Territory of Australia, tell stories about the Dreamtime in their songs. Aboriginal writer and educator Bruce Pascoe writes that the Dreaming 'refers to the creation period (a time beyond human memory) when ancestral being are said to have spread across the continent, creating human society and its rules for living, language customs and laws as they went'.[20] These ancestral progenitors transformed a flat, featureless plain into the topography inhabited by the indigenous peoples of Australia past and present. It is believed the spiritual essence of the ancestral beings remains 'in the landscape, the heavens, and the waters'.[21] These songs are passed down orally from generation to generation.

The songs not only contain knowledge about the land, but performers are also said to embody the land itself during performance. Anthropologist and ethnomusicologist Fiona Magowan writes:

> Singers must learn to 'feel' the environment as sensory experience within the body.... Aural, visual and kinaesthetic fields are completely intertwined ... Yolŋu singers and dancers allude to their bodies as 'feelingful extensions' ... of the ancestral seascape and landscapes as the ritual context invites men to dance *as the ancestors.*[22]

For Yolŋu singers and dancers' music does not imitate or represent the land or the ancestral creators, rather they sing and dance *as* the land, *as* the ancestors. Through song and dance they do not merely represent place; they *are* place and country. Such a music practice retains essentially the 'myth and magic' expressed by Pareyson – it has not been corrupted by technics, or scientific thinking.

Not only are non-scientific fields reduced in importance as a result of science's dominance, but as touched on earlier, the value of science itself is also called into question when balance is lost. When science absolutizes itself and claims the totality of knowledge production and becomes scientism, it fails to meet its own aims. Pareyson elucidates,

> It therefore follows that just as scientism does not destroy philosophy because, however indirectly and incoherently, it affirms it, likewise denying scientism does not mean killing science, but recognising it within the limits that belong to it and within which it is sovereign. Without philosophy, science exceeds its proper sphere and degenerates into scientism: Only philosophy can protect it from the transgression and preserve it as science.[23]

It is only when the limits, independence and interdependence of science, philosophy, art, religion and politics are restored that each field can take up its own tasks and operate most effectively. It is only when the appropriate *balance* between distinct fields of knowledge has been found that we can protect ourselves from unnecessary error. The central concern of this chapter is to provide an account of the ethical that highlights the fundamental importance of attending to the hermeneutical and improvisational that has largely been pushed aside by technological and scientific thinking.

For Heidegger, what both science and metaphysics fail to achieve is to relate us back to factical existence. They fail to attend to the situated character of our being-in-the-world as always already oriented and standing in relation to other entities. Thus, intentionally or not, science and metaphysics advocate for a certain detachment or dislocation from factical life, which has immediate consequences for our understanding of ethics. Attempting to prescribe enduring rules, principles or precepts for the way in which we understand and act in the world perpetuates a certain technical or methodological approach to understanding at the expense of a genuinely ontological approach. We notice this detachment from factical life in the way in which contemporary ethics (particularly in the English language philosophical tradition), especially 'applied ethics', tends to focus on the prescription of rules or guidelines. It is the *system* or *method* that prescribes *in advance* the best course of action that takes precedence. And thus, a certain (objective) distance is introduced between the person who must act and the situation from which the imperative to act emerges, effectively divorcing the person from the conditions from which the ethical imperative comes forth. In contrast, by acting in accord with the structure of improvisation, one genuinely encounters the ethical imperative and intimately engages with it, and is thus related back to factical life itself, in a manner advocated for by both Heidegger and Gadamer.

Awakening to the situation

The improvisational character of hermeneutics, where to improvise is to attend and respond to the situation, draws into focus the relationship between the universal and the particular. To improvise is to assume a certain universal *topos* in the situation to respond to the particularities of the situation. Indeed, as Gadamer writes with respect to hermeneutics, 'understanding . . . is a special case of applying something universal to a particular situation'.[24] Understanding, like improvising, is something practical, it is tied to one's participation in a particular situation. What became clear in the preceding chapter is that the 'act' of hermeneutical and improvisational engagement cannot be governed by predetermined rules or methods. Rather, one's acting is contingent on the peculiarities of the situation one has fallen into. That is, to echo Part I, the context and content of hermeneutical engagement are given by the improvisational situation. The way in which one should act in any given situation cannot be prescribed in advance, instead one's acting is necessarily in response to the situation.

The spontaneity and indeterminacy of 'falling into' may appear to preclude improvisation from bearing within it an ethical dimension on the basis that one's actions cannot be said to be premeditated. The improviser cannot be entirely prepared for that which they may encounter and thus they are not in a position to contemplate the most appropriate course of action. One might argue, however, that improvisation, insofar as it is an attending and responding to the situation such that something productive might emerge, *presupposes* an ethical encounter. Improvisation, like hermeneutics, *requires* an encounter instigated by difference. The improvisational traverse is a being led by something beyond oneself in the sense that one responds to possibilities given by the situation; one must be open and receptive to difference, effectively decentring subjective experience. An attitude that allows one's acting to be structured by difference does not relieve ethical responsibility but engenders a certain civility.[25] Improvisation, we may say, advocates for a civility of difference. Thus, ethics is central to improvisation such that the imperative to act ethically emerges from the very place of improvisational engagement. It is the improviser's attending and responding to the improvisational situation into which they have fallen that is consistent with what Heidegger refers to as an 'original ethics'.[26]

In contradistinction to the dominant conception of ethics that focusses on systems or guidelines for action divorced from the circumstances that call for that action, Heidegger, somewhat cryptically, asserts that ethics needs to become 'original' again. That is, ethics needs to be born anew from out of factical life. While Heidegger himself offers little direct insight into what an 'original ethics' might look like, Dennis J. Schmidt argues that Gadamer's hermeneutics is '*fundamentally* . . . concerned with the task of thinking about that which Heidegger referred to as an "original ethics"'.[27] Schmidt notes that an original ethics must be thought from out of ethical or factical life itself.[28] As such, ethics should not be conceived as something applied to a particular situation as if one could predetermine the right course of action in each situation prior to that situation's occurrence. Rather, an original ethics needs to be thought of as emerging from and being intimately tied to the singular situation. Ethics is not something learnt or taught, like math or some technical ability. Instead, as Schmidt writes, 'one might do well simply to say that ethical knowing is *understanding*',[29] where we may equate Schmidt's use of 'understanding' with the notion of *Bildung*, where we engage in the life task of gaining experience and cultivating our capacities and knowledge.

The understanding at issue here is the same understanding one exhibits when they embark upon an improvisational traverse. The example of free improvisation in music provides insight: One cannot determine what is (musically) 'right' or 'wrong' independently of the musical event. Recall Denley's performances in the Budawang Mountains, discussed in Chapter 3. The indeterminacy of the situation in which Denley finds himself precludes any preconceived script or structure of how the work should take shape. To be sure, some actions could be judged as 'wrong' but there is no singular or objective 'right', either – indeed it is rather awkward to talk in terms of 'right' and 'wrong' in the first place. The task, simply put, is to not approach the situation dogmatically. If Denley were to apply a preconceived script for performance, we would likely deem his performances contrived or lacking nuance and substance. It is precisely because Denley takes seriously his improvisational responsibilities that his work is 'successful'. Denley's playing offers an exemplar of what it is to genuinely attend and respond to the situation in which one finds oneself.

Gadamer writes, 'the opposite of seeing what is right is not error or deception but blindness'.[30] To act ethically, musically or otherwise, is, following Denley, to *see*,[31] in the sense of attending and responding. It is when one becomes overwhelmed and loses sight of the situation such that they dogmatically rely upon pre-established rules or guidelines, or retreat into themselves and turn away from the situation towards their passions, for instance, that they are blinded. Blindness effectively disorients the subject, divorcing them from a genuinely meaningful engagement with the improvisational situation. 'Moral knowledge', writes Gadamer, 'is clearly not objective knowledge – i.e., the knower is not standing over against a situation that he merely observes; he is directly confronted with what he sees. It is something that he has to do.'[32] In being confronted by difference one is called to action, in the sense that one's encounter initiates a falling into the improvisational situation. That means, however, in light of the indeterminacy and spontaneity of falling into, that one is always already in the situation of having to act. One must already possess some moral knowledge that, in the sense of Gadamer's concept of 'tact', discussed in Chapter 2, guides one's engagement in the improvisational situation. What is important is *seeing*, for it ensures an engagement with the situation as such, rather than merely with oneself, or something external to the situation, such as preconceived rules or guidelines. One must attend to the ethical imperative that emerges from the situation itself. We may say, then, that to enact an original ethics, one must not stand apart from but, as Grondin suggests,[33] turn towards and 'awaken to' – *see* – the situation.

If there is a prescriptive force to emerge from this book, it is the basic idea that one should attempt to be informed and consistent in what they do. That is, with respect to the ontology of improvisation, the question that one may ask oneself is not, 'am I or am I not improvising?' Rather the question is, '*how* am I improvising?', or 'am I improvising in a manner that is reflective and informed, or am I doing it in ignorance?' The prescriptive consequence of the ontological account of improvisation at issue here is the *imperative of consistency*. This imperative to consistently act in accord with the structure of improvisation draws out an ethical dimension; it highlights the way in which action involves an engagement with that which is beyond oneself. All action requires ethical consideration. Once it is acknowledged that musical works and hermeneutic understanding, among other things, are far from individual achievements and are tied to the dialecticity of the situation, the imperative of consistency compels us to awaken to the situation. It compels us to take seriously the idea that ethical discernment is not a matter of objectification or application but is the enactment of understanding that emerges from the improvisational situation. One must attend and respond to the situation. For an original ethics to emerge, one must awaken to the situation.

Falling into the ethical

When ethics is approached from the perspective of pre-established rules or guidelines, such as when the method becomes the focus at the expense of the situation, the ethical itself withdraws, or is obscured. By uniformly and dogmatically approaching all situations from the perspective of utilitarianism, for instance, one does not attend to the situation from which the ethical imperative emerges. Instead, one attends primarily to a preconceived system of calculation. Such an approach effectively divorces the person from the situation and therefore from the ethics at issue in *that* situation. Consequently, ethics is replaced by a preconceived system. Such a view is akin to the musician who seeks rules and guidelines to govern their improvising, which demonstrates a fundamental misunderstanding of what it is to improvise. When one approaches ethics or improvisation from such a position, one does not *see* the situation but is blind to it.

This is not to suggest that any and every appeal to rules or guidelines is inherently flawed. The argument is, rather, that ethical action must be in response to the situation in which one finds oneself – rules or conventions should not be applied dogmatically. Certain situations may indeed call for a utilitarian approach. An appeal to rules in this instance does not, however, negate the improvisation at issue. Following rules is inherently indeterminate and requires improvisation.[34] As Wittgenstein points out,[35] rules themselves fail to eliminate indeterminacy. Moreover, rule-following, in a non-dogmatic sense, relies upon, to use Davidson's terminology, 'passing theories'. One's impetus to consider one rule instead of another as perhaps being appropriate must be in response to the indeterminate situation. Therefore, even rule-following is a situated, improvisational practice – the rules appealed to only make sense guiding one's actions insofar as they are understood from the perspective of *that* situation. Thus, one's appeal to rules, insofar as one is awake to the situation, is indeed improvisatory. The rule that one follows through one's deployment of passing theories strikes one as being appropriate in virtue of one's attending and responding to the situation in which one finds oneself.

What is at issue in the ethical and the improvisational with respect to attending to the *situation* in which one always already is, is captured by Heidegger when he translates Heraclitus's saying, '*ēthos anthrōpōi daimōn*' as: 'The (familiar) abode for man is the open region for the presencing of god (the unfamiliar one).'[36] If the nature of ethics is to maintain this basic affinity with the word *ēthos* in Heraclitus's saying, one cannot think of ethics as separate from the 'abode for man', where 'abode' may be likened to the everyday place or situation of our being-in-the-world. Indeed, in the story Heidegger refers to, Heraclitus is warming himself at his stove; this is the familiar abode for man. The 'presencing of god', we may say, refers to the encounter that initiates one's falling into. When visitors are struck by the banality of Heraclitus's actions (warming himself at his stove, rather than engaging in some curious endeavour of thoughtfulness), Heraclitus says to them, '*Einai gar kai entautha theous*, "here too the gods come to presence".'[37] That is, one encounters the difference or the unfamiliar that initiates one's falling into the improvisational situation in the open region of one's being-in-the-world. It is this 'open region' that Heraclitus connects with *ēthos*. Thus, the ethical, like improvisation, is not to be found in rules, guidelines, or curious acts dislocated from concrete experience but instead emerges from 'the (familiar) abode for man' within which things appear – the improvisational situation. An engagement with the ethical can only be a practical engagement in the form of one's acting in the world. But the action at issue must be a hermeneutical acting – acting and understanding must be reflexive and form the basis of self-understanding and transformation.

One encounters the ethical the same way one encounters the improvisational – by falling into and finding oneself already participating in the situation. Ethical life is lived in the singularity of experience, and one actively attends to the peculiarities and the idiosyncrasies of experience not when the world meets one's prior expectations and is in accord with one's prejudice but when one encounters a certain difference that instigates a falling into the improvisational situation. An original ethics is not determined by right or wrong but rather refers to one's vigilance in one's improvisational traverse; one's commitment to attend and respond to the historical story within which one is enmeshed so that something productive may emerge from one's conversational engagement.

If, as we have seen, one's falling into demarcates a particular region one attends and responds to during one's improvisational traverse, falling into is not merely a 'framing' but equally a 'making space for'. That is, when one encounters difference and falls into the improvisational situation, this falling into makes space for that difference so that one may attend to it. Thus, we notice at the very heart of improvisation what philosopher and political scientist Georgia Warnke refers to as 'an interpretive form of democratic deliberation',[38] for the very basis of improvisation is this making space for, and engagement with, difference. Falling into reflects one of the ways in which Gadamer suggests we ought to attend to the other, which is with a sense of empathy. As we have seen, this improvisational engagement with difference, with that which is beyond oneself, is an attending and responding to such that one allows oneself to receive the language of the thing or other. It begins from the basic premise that the other has something to say, something that perhaps goes against the one who is listening, but the listener strives to understand, nonetheless. What is important, then, is that one listens to the other and engages with the other in an improvisational manner, demonstrating openness to the other. One's falling into an improvisational traverse, then, is essentially ethical, but equally the ethical is bound to the improvisational, for it is improvisation that is indicative of ethical action.

Improvising ethics

Heidegger writes that 'the essential nature of thinking is determined by what there is to be thought about: the presence of what is present'.[39] In a separate passage he says, 'present and presence means: what is with us. And that means: to endure in the encounter.'[40] Pieced together, these excerpts may be presented as follows: 'The essential nature of thinking is determined by what is with us, as it endures in the encounter.' It is this essential nature of thinking that gives rise to the ethical. It is a thinking that is attentive and responsive to that which one encounters, where 'what is with us' endures as we traverse the improvisational situation.

Heidegger writes, 'that thinking which thinks the truth of Being as the primordial element of man, as one who ek-sists, is in itself the original ethics.'[41]

For Heidegger, it is this basic mode of thinking that is tied to one's fundamental mode of understanding and being-in-the-world that is from which an original ethics emerges. Schmidt writes, 'ethics is . . . a matter of an enacting of an understanding that defines the "basis" of our being-in-the-world. It is that for which one bears absolute responsibility since it returns one to that which is most of all one's own'.[42] The ethics at issue here emerges from ontology. The ethical is not a practice or theory applied to human beings. Instead, the ethical, like the hermeneutical and the improvisational, is fundamental to who we are.

This fundamental ethical dimension is present in the thought of both Heidegger and Gadamer, even though neither of them wrote a dedicated treatise on ethics. In Heidegger, it comes forth particularly clearly with respect to his concept of dwelling, where to *be* is to *dwell*. In returning us to that which is most of all one's own, Heidegger directs us back to the place from which both practical and theoretical relations emerge – the world. With respect to dwelling, the 'world' is not something *for* or *produced by* humans. Rather, like the improvisational situation, it is something of which humans are a part. As noted in Part I, Heidegger's fourfold, which is intimately tied to the idea of dwelling, presents the world as the co-responsiveness or happening of earth, sky, divinities and mortals.[43] Earth, sky and the divinities are not for or produced by mortals. Instead, the world only *is* insofar as there is this mutual *belonging* together, or what Heidegger refers to as 'mirror-play',[44] of these four distinct yet related elements. In the idea of dwelling then, one's participation in a particular activity always goes beyond the context of that individual activity. To play music, or participate in any activity, is to participate in the *world*, enacting the oneness of the fourfold, gathering earth, sky, divinities and mortals.

To dwell is to find oneself intimately related to those other elements that belong to the fourfold and attend and respond to that which is given in the enactment of that relationality. Dwelling refers to a topological ordering where one finds oneself already placed as one of four essential elements in the world. To improvise is to encounter the unexpected and the unforeseen in the improvisational situation such that what one encounters and what is produced is not reducible to the subjectivity of the individual but rather comes forth *in* and *from* the improvisational situation. When one improvises one attends and responds to a character of the world that presents itself or is disclosed within the horizon of one's engagement. One receives the world as it is given in the situation and in one's attending and responding to the world makes thematic and celebrates that character of the world. In their openness to receive and engage with the unexpected and unforeseen the improviser does not operate on the basis that their prior understanding of the world is all there is, rather they await the unforeseen (*improviso*), acknowledging an essential richness in that which is concealed. Through improvising one comes to 'be at home' in the indeterminate happening of the world – they come to 'dwell' in the world.

The nature of ethics at issue here is one's living in the light of the co-responsiveness of the fourfold – one's owning up to the topological ordering of existence – and participating in the world in an attentive and responsive – improvisational – manner. Heidegger writes that '*the fundamental character of dwelling is . . .sparing and preserving*'.[45] Rather than objectify the world and attempt to dominate it, control it or use it, a dwelling life calls for one to 'care for' the world, and in the co-responsiveness of being *a part of* the world, allow oneself to be 'cared for by' the world. One awaits and *receives* the world inasmuch as one *gives* to the world, in active participation. This also involves, as Benson acknowledges, 'owning up' to one's responsibility of being with others, where 'any attempt to write oneself out of the picture is *irresponsible*'.[46] To dwell is to own up to the responsibility of being *there* with others in the world.

As noted, an original ethics does not provide rules or guidelines for how to act, rather it simply calls for one to improvise. In improvisation, in attending and responding to the world or situation and uniting the fourfold, there is a certain ethical 'caring for', or, as one reads in Heidegger's essay '. . . Poetically Man Dwells . . .', 'kindness' or 'charity'.[47] Indeed, Malpas takes Heidegger's invocation of 'kindness' to be associated with a form of 'heartfeltness', in the sense of 'attentive responsiveness' to the world that,[48] as Heidegger writes, 'gives heed to the measure'.[49] Dwelling, we may say, is this measured, heartfelt attending and responding to the improvisational situation, which is the happening of the fourfold.

Moreover, thinking dwelling in terms of improvisation, we can make sense of what is sometimes thought to be a tension in Heidegger's thinking. On the one hand, says Heidegger, 'the manner in which we humans *are* on the earth, is *Buan*, dwelling,'[50] and on the other, he insists that 'mortals . . . *must ever learn to dwell*.'[51] The supposed tension at issue here is: Are we always already dwelling, or is it something we must learn? There can be no preconceived method or script for attending and responding to that which is unexpected and unforeseen. To meaningfully engage with those aspects of the world one must be genuinely attentive and responsive. This improvisational engagement is never 'over', as it were – no one ever 'masters' improvisation, just as no one ever masters the world. Equally, no one masters dwelling. Although dwelling is indeed the fundamental way in which mortals *are* in the world, it is a constant task. Like improvisation, it is not something that can simply be set in motion and then forgotten. It is an activity always calling for engagement. We must, as Heidegger says, '*ever learn to dwell*', in much the same way that we must *ever learn to improvise*, since every encounter that calls for improvisational engagement is an encounter in which we learn to improvise anew.

This basic character of being vigilant in one's attentiveness and responsiveness to that which is beyond oneself is equally at issue in the way in which Gadamer appeals to the concept of *Bildung*. An original ethics is particularly evident in Gadamer's model of conversation, which, at its core, asks us to take seriously the idea that the other has something to say to us, and that we do our best to understand what it is they are saying. Gadamer does not prescribe a method for acting ethically during conversation. Rather, he simply calls for one to acknowledge that they may broaden their horizons by being open to and receiving the alterity of the other.

That improvisation cannot be reduced to a set of rules, principles or precepts illuminates how the ethics at issue here is equally irreducible to rules, principles or precepts. Improvisation, like hermeneutics, signals a general comportment towards the world where one is open to receive and engage with that which is beyond oneself. One takes up, or becomes involved in, the ethical encounter with the knowledge available in that situation; one must persevere in one way or another. An original ethics cannot be applied from beyond the situation. Rather, it emerges from the productive engagement of those who participate in the improvisational situation. There can be no overarching rules that do justice to all situations. One can only strive to do one's best in the situation in which one finds oneself by being open to the otherness of the other, allowing oneself to be 'led' by that which one encounters, and being responsive to the indeterminate situation.

Thus, as Warnke writes, 'our understanding of what we ought to do in any particular situation is not the objective knowledge of an observer but the engaged understanding of someone who must act'.[52] An original ethics, then, will always be in tension with rules or guidelines intended to endure, such as the law, for instance. Indeed, Gadamer notes an essential asymmetry between the 'ordered world of law' and the imperfections of human reality.[53] To judge the actions of another, one cannot merely extract the actions of an individual in an objective sense and relate them to what is stipulated by the law. Rather, judging the actions of another relies on a certain hermeneutical comportment. Gadamer notes that such judgement relies upon one's ability to transpose oneself 'fully into the concrete situation of the person who has to act'.[54] The person judging only has a sympathetic understanding of the person acting, asserts Gadamer, if they satisfy 'one requirement, namely that he too is seeking what is right – i.e., that he is united with the other person in this commonality'.[55] Thus, to encounter the ethical in either action or judgement of the actions of another is to take the situation as something that affects oneself. It is to acknowledge the historicality of one's being-in-the-world and acknowledge that one can be transformed through one's actions in that situation. But equally, it is to acknowledge that, as we see so clearly with respect to improvised musical performance, one's engagement with the situation both *influences* and is *influenced by* the happening of that situation.

Consideration of the other should not merely be self-regarding such that one presumes they understand the other better than they understand themselves, for this denies the autonomy and legitimacy of the other's situation and assumes that one can simply substitute their own understanding for the understanding of the other. What is lacking here is an ethical openness where one genuinely strives to transpose oneself into the situation of the other, where one acknowledges that one may be challenged, and one's prejudices questioned. Indeed, this is indicative of the hermeneutic circle where one's acting ethically constitutes a reflexive improvisational traverse where one may undergo a transformative experience.

To argue that an improvisational or hermeneutical ethics is concerned first and foremost with attending to and understanding the other (as best one can) is not to suggest that one must validate or agree with those who hold problematic points of view, those of racists or misogynists, for instance. At issue here, too, is the hermeneutic circle, particularly what we understand as the part-whole relationship, discussed in the preceding chapter. That is, we understand the whole in relation to the part and the part in relation to the whole. While there is, in effect, an infinite number of interpretations, those interpretations must always emerge from out of that basic part-whole relationship. A part not derived from the part-whole structure at issue will not fit, as it were – it will be incoherent within the broader structure. There are, to give an example from music, infinite ways in which a melody can be interpreted, but those interpretations, such that they are indeed interpretations of *that* melody, must bear a certain relationship to the melody being interpreted; one cannot merely play anything. Thus, for those who are sensitive to the teachings of history and open to listening to others, the multiplicity of meanings will, as Warnke points out,[56] include possibilities of neutrality, equality and inclusion, among others, but exclude racial or misogynistic possibilities, for they are incoherent within the broader part-whole structure. The improvisational situation, then, is not void of normative foundations. It is simply that this foundation cannot be prescribed in advance.

A return to factical life

In his call for 'hermeneutic virtue' Gadamer questions philosophy's tendency to move from 'word to concept'. He writes,

> Without bringing concepts to speak and without a common language, I believe we will not be able to find the words that can reach other persons. It is true that we usually move 'from word to concept', but we must also be able to move 'from concept to word' if we wish to reach the other person. Only if we accomplish both will we gain a rational understanding of each other.[57]

Hermeneutics, like improvisation, is not satisfied relegated solely to the realm of the conceptual. Once we have moved from word to concept, it is important to bring the concept back to the word. Therefore, consistent with Aristotle's idea of *phronesis* where practical knowledge is understood as a form of knowledge no less important than *sophia* (theoretical knowledge),[58] Gadamer asserts that hermeneutics is essentially practical philosophy.[59] Schmidt writes, 'philosophical hermeneutics understands that its final gesture must be to enact a *return* to factical life and the realities of ethical life as realities borne and suffered in the singular.'[60]

The basic premise of hermeneutics, that improvisation highlights so well, is that truth and understanding, language and ethics are not applied but encountered. One *participates* in truth and understanding, language and ethics. One encounters truth by receiving the language of a thing, one understands as a result of listening to what the other has to say, and the ethical imperative is encountered in the situation, all of which are consistent with the essential structure of improvisation at issue here. In this sense, insofar as hermeneutics and improvisation describe a fundamental mode of being-in-the-world, truth and understanding, language and the ethical are always already there.

Those seeking a pre-written script for how to live may find this assertion somewhat lacking. But the task of hermeneutics is to return us to our factical existence; to return us to what we each likely already know but rarely acknowledge. Or as Heidegger says in relation to thinking being: 'It is not that this thinking is difficult and would require special arrangements in order to be carried out. If we may speak of a difficulty here, it consists in the fact that to think Being is very simple, but that the simple is for us the most arduous.'[61] The idea of the ethical at issue here, and indeed the idea of the improvisational, is equally simple or basic, but commonly obscured or overlooked. Thus, we require what Heidegger refers to as an 'awakening', where something suddenly 'irrupts into appearance, from non-appearance'.[62] Such an 'awakening' is a falling into and committing to the improvisational traverse where the reflexivity of hermeneutical experience illuminates the essentially ethical nature of our being-in-the-world. The traverse is a genuine caring and being cared for. As such, philosophical hermeneutics does not, and should not, attempt to go beyond itself. Rather it should remind us of the profound limitations of our ability to contribute in advance to the 'riddles' of life,[63] and direct us back to original existence; direct us back to a 'dwelling life' – to an improvisational engagement with the world.

By directing us back to the way in which we *are* in the world hermeneutics reminds us just how high the stakes are. The way in which we understand forges who we are, as Gadamer highlights through the concept of *Bildung*. The reflexivity of hermeneutics illuminates the way in which one's doing reflects back upon and shapes one's understanding of the world. As such we return to the imperative of consistency mentioned earlier. If there was, as it were, a 'teaching' to emerge from the ontology of improvisation presented in this book it might be this: *Improvise in a reflective and informed manner in accord with the structure of improvisation, because how you improvise is what you are becoming.*

Coda
Soon we shall be song

This book began with the idea of improvisation and how it is manifest in improvised musical performance and has ended with an inquiry into the way in which improvisation figures in the very structure of human being-in-the-world. The journey, described earlier as an 'out and back', has been an exploration or an *improvisational traverse* of the improvisational situation. Far from being a linear excursion along a clear and familiar path, by questioning and following the path laid down by improvisation itself, this book has sought to orient our thinking on improvisation within the horizon of its own happening. By orienting oneself within the improvisational situation, that is, by possessing an awareness of the horizon of improvisation, one can guard against any potential misfortunes that may arise from losing sight, or being unaware, of that horizon. American ambient musician Liz Harris (recording under her moniker, Grouper) beautifully illustrates the consequences of losing sight of horizons when she sings of her mother wading into the depths of the ocean, disoriented, having lost sight of the horizon.[1]

To elucidate the topology of improvisation, the main body of this book has been structured in two parts and has progressed over the course of six chapters. In Chapter 1, improvisation was presented as essentially conversational. Drawing on the work of Gadamer and Davidson, it was argued that improvised musical performance relies upon a tripartite structure comprising player, work and other. The conversational character of improvisation provided the first insight into the 'focus' of improvisation; conversation is always in response to a certain *encounter* and therefore occurs on the basis of the topological relationality that emerges from that encounter. One encounters the musical work, text or subject matter that one converses within a particular situation. Thus, conversation is a necessarily situated or topological activity; one encounters some-*thing* some-*where* in order to converse with it.

Given the topological character of both conversation and improvisation, Chapter 2 inquired into the way in which the improvisational situation provides context and content for improvised musical performance. By drawing on a range of examples from the music literature and by appealing to insights from phenomenology, philosophical hermeneutics and philosophy of mind, it was argued that not only is the improvisational situation a distinct place, but also the situation itself structures improvisation. It became apparent that the player is not solely responsible for the coming-into-being of the work. It is better to say that the player *participates* in the happening of the work; they are one element of many that contributes to the coming forth of the work in the improvisational situation. Improvisational engagement, then, is wholly contained in the happening of the situation, and so the 'origin' of improvisation is the *improvisational situation*.

Whereas Chapter 2 focussed on the relationship between improvisation and place in quite broad terms, the final chapter of Part I, Chapter 3, further elucidated the 'where' of improvised musical performance in terms of the way in which improvisation enacts an engagement with the world within a particular 'horizon' or boundary. The relationship between the lifeworld of the player and the poetic world of the musical work was explored, as was the way in which the player listens to the work. Significantly, the topological character of the improvisational situation was worked out by interrogating the nature of timespace with respect to improvised musical performance. It was demonstrated that the event of improvisation must be understood topologically to account for the way in which players participate in improvised musical performance.

The insights uncovered in Part I can be summarized as follows: improvised musical performance is a conversational activity underpinned by the interconnection and interrelation of player, work and other. The 'work', however, cannot be merely understood in terms of a discrete and clearly defined entity but instead should be conceived as a common matter of concern.

That which is of concern to the players comprises myriad things including the contributions of each player, the acoustic properties of the performance venue, one's instrument, the tradition and culture in which one is enmeshed and so forth. Thus, the encounter at issue in the improvisational conversation is an encounter with the improvisational *situation* itself. There is a limit, however, to those common matters of concern. And that limit is the boundary of the improvisational situation; those elements that structure improvisation are all present in a certain place. The relationality at issue in improvisation, where players *participate* in the happening of the work, is topological. The structures that allow the event to happen, such as time and space, do not emerge separately, nor are they reducible to one another, but emerge from place – the improvisational situation. And so, the 'focus', 'origin' and 'horizon' of improvisation turned out to the improvisational situation itself.

Given that the structure of improvisation uncovered in Part I was informed by Gadamer's hermeneutics and turned out to be consistent with the structure of hermeneutics, Part II focussed on reading that account of improvisation back into Gadamer's philosophy. A preliminary overview of Gadamer's hermeneutics was offered in Chapter 4. In Chapter 5, Gadamer's account of truth and understanding was presented as improvisational. The chapter began by inquiring into the relationship between human finitude and improvisation, as well as the improvisational character of ontology where, according to Heidegger, the nature of ontological inquiry is structured by the inquiry itself, which alludes to a distinctly improvisational process. Next, Gadamer's account of hermeneutic engagement was discussed. Drawing upon ideas from Gadamer's work where he claims that one falls into conversation and that truth and understanding emerge from conversational engagement, Chapter 5 elucidated the ways in which the self-presentation of truth and understanding is *participatory*, consistent with the account of improvisation outlined in Part I. Moreover, by considering the way in which Gadamer describes language as conversational, it became apparent that language use is distinctly improvisational.

Chapter 6 focussed on the ethics that emerges from Gadamer's hermeneutics. With respect to key ideas such as awakening to the situation and falling into the ethical, it was argued that a hermeneutical account of ethics relies upon the same, attending and responding to the situation in which one finds oneself that is at issue in improvised musical performance. Thus, ethics, insofar as it emerges from and is an engagement with factical life, turned out to be essentially improvisational; to be genuinely *engaged* with the world is to improvise. What is at the heart of hermeneutical ethics is not the prescription of ethical rules or guidelines but an attentiveness and responsiveness to what the immanent situation calls for.

What was uncovered in Part II is this: improvisation sits at the very heart of philosophical hermeneutics. Therefore, improvisation is at the heart of philosophy more broadly. Given the improvisational character of truth and understanding, language and ethics, improvisation has been presented as universal. Improvisation is central to the way in which we conduct ourselves in factical existence. Thus, it is not so much a matter of asking 'how' one should improvise in the world but whether or not one is improvising in a reflective and informed manner. This book has attempted to offer the appropriate insight so that one can recognize, and live with the understanding of, their improvising in the world.

In light of the discussion presented in the preceding chapters, one may ask what consequences may be derived from this book. Indeed, the breadth of this inquiry, from improvised musical performance to philosophical hermeneutics, situates it within a fairly broad conceptual frame. While the ontology of improvisation was derived from improvised musical performance, the structure of improvisation itself emerged unshackled from any particular form of musical practice. Consequently, the way in which improvisation is at issue in human engagement in the world was uncovered. As a result of this inquiry a renewed understanding of musical practice, improvisation and philosophical hermeneutics has emerged. Rather than offer prescriptions with respect to musical practice or the conduct of life, the significance of this book, to paraphrase Gadamer,[2] lies in its attempt to correct false thinking about music, improvisation and human being-in-the-world.

This book has attempted to provide a foundation for particular ideas concerning music-making, improvisation and philosophical hermeneutics. Given its conceptual nature, it is my hope that this book may provide a framework within which future scholarship concerned with questions pertaining to improvisation may be defined and oriented. For instance, future scholarship may pursue questions such as: What implications does an improvisational understanding of music-making have for authorship and copyright? To what extent is one's improvising inflected by gender, class or culture? How might an improvisational understanding of music reconfigure the way music is taught? What implications does an improvisational account of being-in-the-world have for legal or political matters? What consequences does improvisation have for scientific method or scientific projects such as AI? These are just some of the questions – many of which are already being addressed in varying ways in the literature – that may be seen to stem from, and be informed by, the arguments presented in this book.

In these final pages, I want to explicitly address the relationship between music and philosophy. Given the way in which improvisation is common to both, to follow the path of thinking established throughout this book so far it is necessary to explore this relationship in more detail. It will be argued that there is a certain equivocity at issue with respect to the musical and the hermeneutical. Focussing primarily on the poetic turn in philosophy, where Heidegger and Gadamer turned to aesthetic experience to gain insight into the nature of truth, it will be argued that just as improvised musical performance is essentially hermeneutical, so too is hermeneutics essentially musical. Thus, Heidegger's call to think meditatively and Gadamer's call to hermeneutics, as discussed in Chapter 6, may be understood as a call to think 'musically'. And insofar as we move towards achieving this mode of thinking, as the title of this chapter suggests and as will be discussed further, *soon we shall be song*.

Mousiké

This book has been concerned with noting the ways in which the same improvisational structure is apparent across disparate human activities. Such a concern echoes Gadamer's conviction that 'it is the task of philosophy to discover what is common even in what is different'.[3] The claim that the improvisation manifest in music does not refer to a special mode of being-in-the-world unique to music alone is by no means an attempt to cast aspersions on the practice of music. Rather, the assertion that the improvisation manifest in music is not unique to music calls into question ways in which music might (re-)connect with other fields and disciplines. That is, one might not view the practice of music as being wholly different from the practice of teaching, politics, science, philosophy and so on. One need not think of any of these disciplines as entirely disconnected or isolated. For, to a certain degree, they are each united by an underlying improvisational structure. Improvisation extends not only across the practice of music but also across philosophy and the sciences, across all modes of understanding.

By noting this universal character of improvisation, one may notice ways in which music and other disciplines perhaps have more in common with each other than is typically assumed. Credence might be given to such an idea by considering the ancient Greek term, *mousiké*. While *mousiké* is typically translated as 'music', for Plato the art of music referred to all the arts. Indeed, as the American philosopher Babette Babich writes of Plato's conception of music, 'the "practice of music" . . . included philosophy itself, understood as "a" music'.[4] And as Benson writes, 'in Ancient Greece, to practice *mousiké* was also to be a scholar or a philosopher. Even more broadly, it can simply mean "the cultivation of the soul"'.[5] Thus, the idea that music might be connected to, or provide insight into, a variety of other disciplines is not a new idea, rather it is very old, albeit largely forgotten.

The idea of *mousiké* in the broader context of the discussion here is not of central concern, but it does provide an insightful precedent. It shows how the arts have not always been separate from other forms of knowledge. It gives us reason to pause and consider how art might inform our thinking about the world just as significantly as philosophy or science. As it stands, however, the idea that art has something to teach us is certainly not the dominant view. Indeed, Wittgenstein points out that 'people nowadays think, scientists are there to instruct them, poets, musicians etc. to entertain them. *That the latter have something to teach them*; that never occurs to them.'[6] I do not propose, in these final pages, to address this issue identified by Wittgenstein in any systematic or complete manner. I do, however, want to join the chorus of those who are each contributing to reconstruct an appropriate paradigm for the way in which art can inform our thinking about the world.[7] My (modest) contribution to these discussions – which involves thinking through how we might (re-)connect music with philosophy – emerges from the insight that music and philosophy have more in common with each other than is typically acknowledged – improvisation is essential to both. What follows is an account of how music might help us better understand the task of the philosopher.

The poetic turn in philosophy

To elucidate the structure of improvisation over the course of this book both music and philosophy have been considered. Here, I want to explore what might be referred to as 'musical philosophy', the inverse of the much more common, 'philosophy of music'. It will be demonstrated that the account of music given in the preceding chapters illuminates a certain aspect of what is at issue in the thinking of Heidegger (particularly his later thought) and Gadamer. The thinking at issue here is commonly referred to as 'poetics', where poetry, understood in the broad sense as *poiesis* rather than merely in the literary sense, refers not to traditional metaphysical explanation but to an interpretive Event of being.

An exposé on the musicality of philosophy could focus on an array of different figures – Pythagoras, Plato, Severinus Boethius, G. W. F. Hegel, Arthur Schopenhauer, Nietzsche, Theodor W. Adorno and many others. It may seem odd that an account of the musicality of philosophy should take Heidegger and Gadamer as its focus, given that neither of them had much to say about music. The lack of lengthy and/or explicit engagement with music in their work, however, does not preclude thinking about the relationship between musicality and their respective philosophies. Indeed, while Heidegger has little to say about 'music' per se, one could argue, particularly with respect to his later thought, that he has quite a lot to say about the 'musicality' of thought. For instance, in *On the Way to Language*, he repeatedly speaks of 'listening', 'silence' and 'singing' in a manner that arguably evokes the musicality of poetry, and thus the musicality of thinking more broadly. We will return to this notion of 'musicality' later.

It is the centrality of art and poetics in the thinking of Heidegger and Gadamer that is of interest. Art is not merely another topic to which they have applied themselves. Rather, in Heidegger's later work and more or less the entirety of Gadamer's thinking, their understanding of art is central to their philosophy. Indeed, it is in *poiesis* – the productive activity of making or producing art[8] – that Heidegger seeks the event or experience of understanding or thought, and it is against the backdrop of art, or aesthetic experience, that Gadamer works out his philosophical hermeneutics in *Truth and Method*. Working out the musicality of philosophy with respect to the thought of Heidegger and Gadamer, then, is to highlight not merely the musicality of 'aesthetics' or the 'philosophy of art' but the musicality of philosophy and being-in-the-world more broadly.

Poiesis

It is in the work of Nietzsche that one can derive an appropriate context for why *poiesis* figures so prominently in the work of Heidegger and Gadamer. In book three of *The Gay Science* Nietzsche famously writes, 'God is dead! God remains dead! And we have killed him!'[9] The death of God leaves us in a perilous position, and in our desperate search for knowledge that religion could apparently no longer provide, we turned to science. Heidegger claims it was Nietzsche who first came to recognize the limitations of science's claim to knowledge,[10] citing the following passage by Nietzsche: 'It is not the victory of science that distinguishes our nineteenth century, but the victory of scientific method over science.'[11] With the death of God, religious experience and certain non-scientific knowledge of the world were gradually replaced by the methods of science: methods that exist at 'the mercy of technology',[12] according to Heidegger. What science tends to overlook, Gadamer writes, is our 'ability to become so absorbed in something that we totally forget ourselves in it'.[13] He tells us that this self-forgetfulness, however, 'is one of the great blessings of the experience of art, as well as one of the great promises of religion'.[14] While religion plays a role in both Heidegger's and Gadamer's thinking,[15] it is largely by appealing to art that they seek a certain mode of thinking – an 'entrance' into the world – unaccounted for by science.

Poiesis is important because it refers to the productive activity of bringing something into being. It is the *act* of composing a poem or a song as distinct from the composition being written down as literature or score, which is secondary to *poiesis*. It is this mode of engagement that is essential to and highlighted by the arts that both Heidegger and Gadamer seek in their respective philosophies. From a philosophical perspective, it is a mode of engagement where one does not apprehend things in the world as objects within a framework designed by humans (scientific method), but instead, an engagement where one has, or, better, *undergoes*, a productive and transformative experience with something. Indeed, Heidegger says we must 'undergo' an experience in the sense that 'we endure it, suffer it, receive it as it strikes us and submit to it. It is something itself that comes about, comes to pass, happens'.[16] One might say that the undergoing of an experience is a thoroughly improvisational affair insofar as one falls into a particular set of circumstances that brings about a traverse of the improvisational situation. This undergoing of an experience, this improvisational traverse where one encounters, experiences and is transformed by a thing is what is important for Heidegger and Gadamer with respect to *poiesis*. The encounter is not structured by scientific method, instead it is a genuine encounter with the world.

The *poiesis* at issue in Heidegger's and Gadamer's thinking resonates with the account of improvisation given in the preceding chapters. The language experience that they both strive to account for in their work, Heidegger especially, may indeed be characterized as particularly improvisational, bearing a certain affinity with music. As mentioned, neither Heidegger nor Gadamer explicitly derives this experiential character of philosophy from music, preferring, for the most part, to focus their attention on poetry. This is, however, no different from the discussion of improvisation at issue in this book; while the structure of improvisation is derived from music, this does not preclude its relevance to other disciplines. Thus, in their invocation of *poiesis*, which is not peculiar to poetry alone, there is no reason one may not uncover a certain improvisational musicality in their thinking.

It is precisely 'musicality' that is at issue here. The suggestion is not that philosophy be music or music be philosophy, as if the two might collapse into one. Rather, just as Heidegger employs poetry to highlight the *poiesis* of thinking, one may consider what music might offer or accentuate with respect to that same *poiesis*. Thus, one does not need recourse to any particular philosopher who wrote extensively about music; one can consider how a certain musicality might be at issue in the thinking of Heidegger and Gadamer despite their limited engagement with music as such.[17] The question, then, is: What does the musicality of thinking accentuate with respect to the *poiesis* of thinking that is perhaps backgrounded or passed over by focussing predominately on poetry?

The appeal of poetics, particularly for Heidegger, has to do with the way in which it resists the subjectivity of traditional metaphysics. That is, metaphysics' attempt to understand 'x' via that for which 'x' is an issue, for example, understanding being via an investigation of beings. In contrast to traditional metaphysical thinking, for the later Heidegger being is not determined through the objective or subjective. The turn towards the poetic is a significant departure from the language of metaphysics that seeks to objectify and explain phenomena in terms of absolute truths or enduring essences. While science responds to the wonder of the world by attempting to 'explain' it, which effectively effaces that initial wonderment, poetry (and poetics more broadly) maintains a 'mimetic' character. As such, poetry does not only interpret the world and thus offer insight into the nature of the world but it also, by 're-presenting' the world rather than 'explaining' it, maintains the wonder of the world that it responds to.[18] Thus, our engagement with the work of art, as discussed in Chapter 3 with respect to listening, permits us to experience a certain aspect of the world anew. What is more, by virtue of its non-explanatory character, in aesthetic experience art draws the spectator or audience member in and calls for an *interpretation*. Art calls for us to engage and respond – to participate in its happening; not in the sense that it is an object that is an issue for us, but in the sense of improvisational participation. Gadamer writes,

> When a work of art truly takes hold of us, it is not an object that stands opposite us which we look at in hope of seeing through it to an intended conceptual meaning. Just the reverse. The work is an *Ereignis* – an *event* that 'appropriates us' into itself. It jolts us, it knocks us over, and sets up a world of its own, into which we are drawn, as it were.[19]

The encounter is not relegated to either the objective or the subjective but is instead an active being-present, which is precisely what Heidegger seeks in his abandonment of the language of metaphysics and his turn towards poetics.

What, then, does improvisation and music illuminate of the poetic turn in philosophy? The following discussion takes up four central themes:

1. Performing understanding: Poetry, perhaps even more so than music, is typically associated with a state of fixity, that is, as literature. Music, on the other hand, is more commonly understood as needing to be performed, which draws attention to the playful, dynamic, improvisational character of understanding and being-in-the-world.

2. Music merely is: Music's reputation is that language, analysis and representation fail to account for it. While there is a certain relationship between poetry and exegesis insofar as they are both typically written down, music, especially instrumental music, resists the exegetical. Music, perhaps more so than any other artform, begs us to consider things as they are in active-presence. Music is an exemplar of how one might approach interpreting all things.

3. The singing of language: Heidegger asks us not to 'question' but to 'listen', to listen to the language of things as such.[20] To receive the language of a thing as it merely is, is to receive the song of language, such that when one listens to song, one does not assert oneself onto the song but allows oneself to receive the gift of song.

4. Thinking musically: The mode of thinking worked out here engenders a certain hermeneutical interpretation. Thinking musically, it will be argued, situates us in a certain dissonance at the threshold of the poetic – between the familiar and the strange – a situatedness that allows us to receive the singing of language. Musical thinking highlights the hermeneutics at issue in the musical and the musical at issue in hermeneutics.

Performing understanding

Both poetry and music typically suffer a common ailment – the propensity for people to reduce them to a fixed and enduring artefact; the poem as fixed in literature, music fixed in the recording, for instance. But as already noted, this 'fixing' – the *poesie* (thing made) – is secondary to both poetry and music as such – the *poiesis* (the act of producing). The static and stable representation of both artforms commonly results in the erroneous assumption that the artwork as such should be equally stable or static. But this is to conceal the true nature of art. As Gadamer writes, 'essential to dramatic or musical works is that their performance at different times and on different occasions is, and must be, different.'[21] Gadamer tells us this is true of all artworks – the plastic and literary arts are equally as occasional as music or drama.[22]

The problem with expecting the work to be as stable as its representation is an issue that extends beyond art and into metaphysics. The reduction of phenomena to objective representation conceals the interpretive occasionality of experience. Thus, while Gadamer may be correct when he asserts that 'no one believes that reading music is the same as listening to it',[23] in light of Heidegger's life-long task of overcoming metaphysics, it would seem people typically fail to attend to the performative, the interpretive, the occasional – the improvisational – character of life. That is, if one considers music as a metaphor for life more broadly, it seems there is a long-standing history of people who *do* believe that reading music is the same as listening to it, or at least that reading music provides as much insight as is practical to gain into music as such. Indeed, as the musicologist Lawrence Kramer observes with respect to the dominant analytic approach to theorizing about music (an example that effectively fits with the metaphor at work here), 'reports of formal characteristics are thought to give us the only truth available. . . . [For example,] we cannot deny that [Beethoven's *Coriolan* Overture] is recapitulated at the sub-dominant'.[24] Consequently, understanding is thought to come from reading music (music's non-performative representation) or by studying a particular work's formal characteristics in the context of a certain interpretive framework, rather than from the event of the work's happening. Ending the metaphor, it is simply that music is particularly adept to highlight the error of such thought, that everyone should/would agree that reading music is *not* the same as listening to it.

The significance of poetry for philosophy is its ability to guide the reader into improvisational engagement with a certain subject matter. Poetry does not explain or represent but illuminates a particular character of the world and it does so in a way that draws the reader into an encounter with the subject matter, initiating a falling into. But there is still a certain erroneous residue of literary explanation in poetry for no other reason than poetry is typically written down and read from the literary source, and thus, one may think of poetry in terms of literature, rather than performance.

The performance is integral, not just for works of art but for understanding more generally, as we saw earlier with respect to the improvisational traverse. Poetry situates the reader in a position to have a genuine encounter with a subject matter. It clears the ground for one's falling into. But it is in the performance – the improvisational engagement – where the subject matter truly speaks or, as will be argued later, *sings*. It is through music that we see this particularly clearly. The performance is not incidental but essential. Gadamer writes, 'the performance . . . does not become, as such, thematic, but the work presents itself through it and in it'.[25] The performance is not a thematization of the score or text, for instance, but is the presentation of the work itself. It is only in performance, only in the improvisational situation, as is so well exemplified in music, that one finds oneself in a position to have a genuine transformative experience.

The performance at issue, while highlighted by music, is nonetheless present in poetry. Gadamer writes,

> There is obviously no sharp differentiation between reciting and silent reading. Reading with understanding is always a kind of reproduction, performance, and interpretation. Emphasis, rhythmic ordering, and the like are part of a wholly silent reading too. Meaning and the understanding of it are so closely connected with the corporeality of language that understanding always involves an inner speaking as well.[26]

What the performativity at issue highlights is the occasionality of understanding. All encounters with artworks and phenomena are singular. Again, music illuminates this particularly well. Experiencing music is not necessarily more or less of a temporal experience than experiencing any other form of art because the *work*, as noted above by Gadamer with respect to reading, is always tied to the event of its presentation. The work presents itself in different ways depending on the situation. Music accentuates the performativity at issue in the *working* of art, and experience more generally.

Thus, the understanding at issue in Heidegger's and Gadamer's thinking is highlighted by poetry's ability to facilitate a falling into, and by music's conspicuous relationship with performance, which correlates with the improvisational character of understanding. What music illuminates, perhaps more so than any other artform, is the essentially performative character of experience. Philosophy, insofar as one speaks of a poetic turn, should be understood as a performative thoughtfulness, that is, improvisational engagement. The performance at issue in understanding relates to the idea of the language of the thing itself, discussed in Chapter 5. What one seeks in the poetic turn is to *receive* the language of the thing itself. One encounters and receives such language not by objectifying things but through improvisational participation. The language of the thing always emerges from a certain performance, an improvisational traverse.

Music merely is

There is, undoubtedly, a certain difficulty in speaking and writing about music. Of this difficulty Schmidt writes, 'from the start, a powerful sense of the difference between words and music defines and interrupts every effort to say something about music. This asymmetry between words and music, this untranslatability or impasse . . . impedes every effort to speak words about music'.[27] Nietzsche, too, writes, '*language* . . . can never . . . externalise the innermost depths of music; whenever language attempts to imitate music it only touches the outer surface of music'.[28] Aesthetic experience resists being reduced to the concept and thus exists as a mode of experience that takes us to the limit of language. Schmidt argues that 'aesthetic experience is our way of communicating what cannot be said in the concept'.[29] He notes that aesthetic experience communicates, but the language through which it communicates is 'the language of the secret', that is, 'It *cannot be told*'.[30]

We will return to the tension we experience when we encounter that which goes beyond our standard conceptual language, later. Presently, the central question is: Do we not struggle to talk about other-worldly phenomena in a manner comparable to the way in which we struggle to talk about music? It is not that we have more access to the musical than Nietzsche or Schmidt allow, or that it is easier than we think to talk about music, but that it is perhaps more difficult than we think to talk about other things. The example of music highlights precisely what Gadamer means, in his discussion of Heidegger, when he writes, 'wherever translation, i.e., the illusion of a free and unrestricted transposition of thought, fails, thinking breaks through'.[31] It is precisely this failure of translation that impedes our attempts to talk about music. This untranslatability, as noted, does not point to the end of thinking, however, but to the beginning. The increasingly technical understanding of the world results in objectifying things in order to talk about them. That is, people talk of things as they are an issue for them, not as those things are in their active being-present. Such thinking makes one believe they know where their thinking will lead them. But as Gadamer writes, 'where we believe we know, we only believe that we think'.[32] Music *qua* music resists, perhaps more so than anything else, being reduced to technical or analytic explanation and encourages the mode of thoughtfulness advocated for by Heidegger and Gadamer.

It is precisely because we so easily recognize the rift between analytic explanations of music and the experience of music itself that we readily dismiss analytic explanation as providing any real access to music itself. This discord gives one reason to pause and acknowledge the unsayability of aesthetic experience, and in turn, encourages one to *begin* thinking. What if all reductive and objective analytic explanations of worldly phenomena were treated as suspicious? Would we not similarly encounter issues of thinking with respect to sculpture, fine foods, nature and sport, among other things? This is precisely what the poetic turn in Heidegger's thinking grapples with – how to think things as they are in their active being-present.

Indeed, those elements in Heidegger's later thought sometimes dismissed as a turn towards myth and mysticism demonstrate the profound difficulty of thinking in non-analytic or non-metaphysical terms. Music exemplifies and illuminates a particular character inherent in the poetic turn in philosophy; the difficulty of thinking in such a way that one does not fall back on the language of metaphysics.

What music exemplifies is this: *Music merely is*. Music is without human meaning and feeling, not in the sense of 'absolute' music that is apparently 'for itself' but in the sense that ontologically, music, as a 'thing', is not human; it merely *is*. So too, as English philosopher Simon Critchley writes, 'things merely are . . . . One can say no more.'[33] Nor should we say any more. Indeed, if music asks anything of us, it is not that we say anything but that we listen. Listening is at the heart of Heidegger's poetics. He writes, 'where thinking finds its way to its true destination, it comes to a focus in listening to the promise that tells us what there is for thinking to think upon.'[34] Heidegger counters the dominant view that thinking is 'questioning' and instead presents thinking as 'listening'. Again, music is instructive for this line of philosophy. For how is one to truly encounter and experience music by asking questions of it? To have a musical experience is first and foremost to listen. To question is to question *about* music, to listen is to experience *music* as such.

The listening at issue here is the same listening demonstrated by musicians during improvised musical performance. Players do not ask questions about the work, rather they listen to what it has to say. They are drawn into a conversation with the work. Their responses do not come primarily from questioning but from listening. Such an engagement is not the projection of one's subjectivity onto the music, instead the players attend and respond to the music as it merely is. This is what the poetic turn in philosophy strives to do, attend and respond to things as they merely are, so that something may emerge from the dialecticity of that engagement. The poetic turn asks us to experience things, it calls for a genuine encounter where we do not question but listen – the poetic turn begs for improvisational engagement.

The poetic turn, then, is a call to improvise. The listening at issue here is not passive, it is not a waiting, it is active. Heidegger writes,

> Speaking is at the same time also listening. . . . whenever we are listening to something we are *letting something be said to us* . . . . In our speaking, as a listening to language, we say again the Saying we have heard. We let its soundless voice come to us, and then demand, reach out and call for the sound that is already kept in store for us.[35]

Listening, for Heidegger, is not merely a bringing forth of the presence of the thing, it is equally a being-present. It is an *engagement* where musicians engaged in improvised musical performance are an exemplar. The player's attending and responding to the work brings forth both the player and the work. And so too is the improvisational traverse an active listening – a letting something be said – as one undergoes a transformative experience. It is when one listens to the thing as it merely is, when one attends to the way that it is, as the case of music highlights so well, that one can receive the language of the thing.

The singing of language

'Poetry is song',[36] writes Heidegger. The poetic turn in philosophy might be understood as a turn towards the *singing* of language. As already noted, for Gadamer as for Heidegger, language is not merely syntax and grammar. The *poiesis* at issue in their thinking points towards a primordial understanding of language – the language of experience and transformation. There is something almost primal about music, especially with respect to its affective nature. There is a reason why music is so important for many religious rites; music engenders self-forgetfulness, it is intoxicating, it carries people away. Plato clearly recognized this character of music, for he has Socrates say, 'rhythm and harmony permeate the innermost element of the soul, affect it more powerfully than anything else, and bring it grace'.[37] Music elicits experience and transformation.

British philosopher Andrew Bowie notes the relationship between music and dance. The dancer is not concerned with music in any objective sense, instead the dancer 'behaves in an active-outpouring manner'.[38] A genuine encounter with music is indicative of this relationship between music and dance insofar as one encounters and experiences music as it merely is. The dancer does not objectify the music in their responding to it. In some respects, one may say that for the dancer the music is not central, their real focus consists in their dancing. But the music *is* essential; the dance and music are inseparable. Indeed, the ancient Greeks did not distinguish between music and dance, as noted earlier with respect to the term *mousiké*. Dance is responsive to music – the rhythm of the dance is tied to the rhythm of the music. The dancer does not 'push' the music to be anything other than what it is while being intimately engaged with its happening. Irrespective of how one experiences music, through dancing, seated at an opera house or otherwise, it is this 'letting be' of music – letting the music come to us and affect us such that we undergo an experience – that is key.

It is this character of the encounter offered by art and religious rites where one is drawn into self-forgetfulness, as it were, that philosophers seek in the poetic turn. Indeed, it is this character that Nietzsche claims was lacking in *The Birth of Tragedy* when he laments: 'It ought to have *sung*, this "new soul", and not talked! What a pity it is that I did not dare to say what I had to say at that time as a poet.'[39] The desire for things to sing, to be music, is that music carries us away and illuminates the world to us without explanation. A desire for a text to have sung is a desire for the text not to talk *about* things or explain them but to draw its reader into an encounter with its subject matter so that they encounter it as music, as something that brings forth an experience of self-forgetfulness. As Heidegger writes, 'if our thinking does justice to the matter, then we may never say of the word that it is, but rather that it gives.'[40] The word *gives* when it *sings*. When words sing, they draw the listener into self-forgetfulness and initiate a falling into an improvisational engagement. When words sing rather than talk, they do not explain but direct those who hear their song to wonderment, to think, to ponder, to improvise – to be transformed.

Of the musicality of language, Bowie writes,

> We experience language's essence when it becomes 'music'. The poem's unique combination of elements cannot be reduced to an explanation of the meaning of the elements, and so has to be the '*vollzogen*' [as in, 'carried out'], in Heidegger's sense of 'heard' or 'listened to', rather than actively

constituted by the subject. Otherwise, the subject would just impose its already existing frameworks on those elements.[41]

Receiving the language of a thing – receiving the call from language for a response – is the *singing* of language. It is in the *performance* of a thing – the performance of a jug is its out-pouring, the wine its being savoured, the music its being listened to and so forth – in the sense of singing that one is called to attend and respond to the thing. It is when language sings that one encounters the essence of language. When language sings it gives.

Schmidt notes a relationship between the 'movement of life' and the 'movement of music'.[42] Just as there has been a long-standing argument that language fails to capture the essence of music, so too, Schmidt claims, that same language fails to capture the movement of life. It is the language of metaphysics, as Heidegger describes it, that is indicative of such a shortcoming. The turn towards *poiesis* – the poetic turn – is a turn towards the encounter, the experience, of which music is an exemplary form. The thinking and language that captures things as they merely are is a performative – improvisational – thinking that is best described as listening for the singing of the language of a thing. Thus, the 'poetic turn' might equally be the 'musical turn' in philosophy. In the wake of Heidegger's destruction of metaphysics,[43] we seek a new mode of thought so that we might encounter things as they merely are; a mode of thought that is genuinely *musical*. Perhaps, through such thinking, we can move closer to realizing Hölderlin's insight: having heard the language of one another, 'soon we shall be song'.[44]

Thinking musically

The idea of a certain musicality is explicit in Heidegger's account of the principle of reason. He writes,

> As a recollective anticipatory principle, the principle [*Satz*] is thus a 'vault' [*Satz*] in the sense of a leap [*Sprung*]. If we fully think through the polysemic word *Satz* not only as 'statement,' not only as 'utterance,' not only as 'leap,' but at the same time also in the musical sense of a

'movement,' then we gain for the first time the complete connection to the principle of reason.[45]

To further illuminate the meaning behind his appeal to this 'musical sense of a movement', Heidegger references the writer, musician and visual artist, Bettina von Arnim,[46] who notes the way in which a movement in music is not something merely performed but, consistent with the account of music given in Part I of this book, is something that *leads* the musician. To think musically, then, is not a thinking *about* so much as it is a thinking *with*. In thinking *with* a thing, one is guided or led by the thing itself. Thus, whereas 'a movement' refers to a section or division of music (a sonata typically comprises two, three or four movements, for instance), Heidegger's idea of '*a* movement' may also be thought in the dynamic sense of 'motion'. When one thinks *with* a thing, the thinking one undertakes – the movement of one's thought – is guided by the thing itself, in the sense of improvisational engagement.

This idea of being led, of course, is essential to Gadamer's hermeneutics, as discussed earlier. This movement of thought is also clearly central to the improvisational account of hermeneutics explicated in Part II of this book. The 'movement' at issue here refers to a certain surrendering of oneself to the world – the improvisational situation. That thinking is a being led by that which is beyond oneself, we may think of hermeneutics as a mode of thinking that is an attending to the muses, where the term 'muse' bears an etymological connection to the term *mousiké*, mentioned earlier. We may think of the way in which humans were thought to be delivered messages from the gods by Hermes, whose name, as noted, is commonly invoked as bearing an etymological connection to the term 'hermeneutics'. Musical thinking, we may say, is beholden to the happening of the improvisational situation – beholden to the circumstances that present themselves to us in our engagement with the world that we attend and respond to. It is this participatory engagement with the world that is indicative of being under the sway of, or being led by, the muses. Thus, thinking musically requires us to participate in the happening of the world – the *improvisational situation* – and in so doing, we find ourselves returned to our rightful place – in and of the world as such.

To characterize 'musicality' in this way, as a giving oneself over to the place in which one finds oneself and thinking *with* that which emerges as thought-provoking in the happening of that situation, involves drawing out the equivocity present in the idea of the musical. The 'musical' is that which involves music, that is, the sonorous, but is also that which is involved in the sounding of and listening to music, where the 'musical' goes beyond the merely acoustic. Thus, we can speak of a genuinely, not merely metaphorical, musical thinking. Indeed, one will have likely noticed that key terms employed throughout this book, such as improvisation and hermeneutics, are developed in this equivocal sense, where 'equivocal' does not merely refer to ambiguity, but, following the Latin *aequivocus*, refers to an openness of interpretation, where there may be different interpretations of equal voice or significance. The equivocity at issue here is an attempt to shed light on an essential character of music, hermeneutics and improvisation.

To think musically, to move towards becoming song, is to think *with* a thing or subject matter in a way that allows that which is thought-provoking to take one to the threshold of the poetic. And in one's continual crossing the threshold, insofar as one surrenders oneself to and is led by the situation in which one finds oneself, one is bound to the rhythm of language, such that in receiving the song of the thing – the singing of language – one is 'rhythmed'. Heidegger references Aeschylus's *Prometheus*, where Prometheus says of language, 'in this rhythm I am bound'.[47] Heidegger also notes that the musicologist Thrasybulos Georgiades points out that 'humans do not make rhythm; rather, for the Greeks, the [measure] is the substrate of language, namely the language that approaches us'.[48] As noted, we *receive* the language of the thing by listening to it, by thinking *with* it. To be rhythmed at the threshold of the poetic involves participating in what we might think of as a certain *dissonance*,[49] where we find ourselves on the edge of the unsayable, caught in a certain tension between the ordinary and the poetic, at rest in neither. In this sense, if we are rhythmed by the dissonance of our crossing the threshold, we may think of musical thinking as something we *undergo* by virtue of our thinking *with*. Indeed, while the terminology may be different, this echoes the poetics of Heidegger and Gadamer, although it accents and draws out a certain musical and improvisational character of hermeneutics largely unaccounted for.

Thinking musically, then, turns out to be thinking hermeneutically, and so hermeneutics turns out to be essentially musical. This conclusion reflects the basic path of thinking undertaken throughout this book as a whole. We began by employing hermeneutics to understand music. But this hermeneutical thinking *with* music guided us across a terrain that not only illuminated a certain understanding of music but also led us back through music as a means to understand the hermeneutical. Thus, we uncovered the hermeneutical character of music and the musical character of hermeneutics. Moreover, we uncovered the essentially improvisational character of both music and hermeneutics and thus, the improvisational character of our being-in-the-world.

Notes

Introduction

1 For a broad overview of the disparate fields in which improvisation is finding relevance, see Susanne Ravn, Simon Høffding, and James McGuirk, eds, *Philosophy of Improvisation: Interdisciplinary Perspectives on Theory and Practice* (London: Routledge, 2021); George E. Lewis and Benjamin Piekut, eds, *The Oxford Handbook of Critical Improvisation Studies*, vols. 1 and 2 (New York: Oxford University Press, 2013). DOI: 10.1093/oxfordhb/9780195370935.001.0001; Alessandro Bertinetto and Marcello Ruta, eds, *The Routledge Handbook of Philosophy and Improvisation in the Arts* (New York: Routledge, 2021).

2 In this book 'ontology' is not considered to designate a particular discipline or field of inquiry. Rather, I follow Heidegger who simply writes that '"*Ontology*" means doctrine of being'. The ontological is concerned with the basic structure of existence. See Martin Heidegger, *Ontology: The Hermeneutics of Facticity*, trans. John van Buren (Bloomington: Indiana University Press, 1999), 1.

3 George E. Lewis and Benjamin Piekut, acknowledge the 'pre-eminent position of music in discussions of improvisation'. See George E. Lewis and Benjamin Piekut, 'Introduction: On Critical Improvisation Studies', in *The Oxford Handbook of Critical Improvisation Studies*, vol. 1, ed. George E. Lewis and Benjamin Piekut (New York: Oxford University Press, 2013), 1. DOI: 10.1093/oxfordhb/9780195370935.013.30.

4 The idea of 'jazz' appealed to in this book is understood as a tradition, exemplified by the bebop musicians of the 1940s, where players use pre-composed tunes to structure their improvisations in the sense that, as jazz saxophonist Lee Konitz writes, 'jazz tunes are great vehicles. They are forms that can be used and reused. Their implications are infinite' (Lee Konitz, quoted in Paul F. Berliner, *Thinking in Jazz: The Infinite Art of Improvisation* (Chicago: The University of Chicago Press, 1994), 63). Paul F. Berliner describes this practice as follows: 'It has become the convention for musicians to perform the melody and its accompaniment at the opening and closing of a piece's performance. In between, they take turns improvising solos within the piece's cyclical rhythmic form' (Berliner, *Thinking in Jazz*, 63). It is this broad conception of 'jazz' that is appealed to throughout this book.

5 In line with the central thesis of this book that all musicking is necessarily improvisational, 'free improvisation' should not be thought to invoke a binary between 'improvised' and 'composed' music. Instead, it broadly refers to a practice where the themes and structure of the performance emerge from the happening of the performance itself.

6 Jeff Malpas, *Place and Experience: A Philosophical Topography*, 2nd edn (New York: Routledge, 2018), 15.

7 Malpas, *Place and Experience*.

8 See Donald Davidson, 'Three Varieties of Knowledge', in *A. J. Ayer Memorial Essays: Royal Institute of Philosophy Supplement: 30*, ed. A. Phillips Griffiths (Cambridge: Cambridge University Press, 1991), 153–66.

9 Malpas, *Place and Experience*; Jeff Malpas, ' Placing Understanding/Understanding Place', *Sophia* 56, no. 3 (2017): 379–91.

10 Jeff Malpas, *Heidegger's Topology: Being, Place, World* (Cambridge, MA: The MIT Press, 2006), 6.

11 For an overview of the way in which Heidegger develops the concepts of equipmentality, dwelling and the Event in a musical and improvisational context, see Sam McAuliffe and Jeff Malpas, 'Improvising the Round Dance of Being: Reading Heidegger from a Musical Perspective', in *Heidegger and Music*, ed. Casey Rentmeester and Jeff R. Warren (Lanham: Rowman & Littlefield, 2022), 163–78.

12 Martin Heidegger, *What is Called Thinking?*, trans. J. Glenn Gray (New York: Harper & Row, 2004).

13 My thinking on this issue is strongly influenced by Jeff Malpas – see *Heidegger and the Thinking of Place: Explorations in the Topology of Being* (Cambridge, MA: The MIT Press, 2012), 13.

14 It should be noted that there is a theological background in hermeneutics that might make an immediate connection with music and improvisation, particularly in relation to liturgy, for instance – see Bruce Ellis Benson, *Liturgy as a Way of Life: Embodying the Arts in Christian Worship* (Grand Rapids: Baker, 2013). While philosophical hermeneutics can be said to have developed out of scriptural hermeneutics and textual exegesis, the history of hermeneutics that is of concern in this study begins much later (discussed in Chapters 4 and 5), when hermeneutics begins to diverge from theological hermeneutics and begins its path to 'philosophical' hermeneutics (which is not to suggest that there are no overlaps or that one bears no relevance to the other). While the connection between hermeneutics and theology on the one hand, and music and liturgical worship on the other may well yield interesting ideas with respect to the ways in which improvisation intersects these fields, this is not the path taken in this book.

15 Bruce Ellis Benson and Cynthia R. Nielsen have both explored the relationship between Gadamer's hermeneutics and jazz improvisation in ways that converge with my own work – see for instance 'Indeterminacy, Gadamer, and Jazz', in *The Significance of Indeterminacy: Perspectives from Asian and Continental Philosophy*, ed. Robert H.

Scott and Gregory S. Moss (New York: Routledge, 2019), 215–27; Cynthia R. Nielsen, *Interstitial Soundings: Philosophical Reflections on Improvisation, Practice, and Self-Making* (Eugene: Cascade Books, 2015). If my work represents, in any way, an advance on the work of writers such as these, it is in that I have attempted to set out a definitive case for understanding philosophical hermeneutics as necessarily improvisational.

16 The existence of a relationship between hermeneutics and improvisation (especially improvisation in music) has been noted by both Gary Peters and Benson. Peters is particularly interested in Heidegger's 'playing with words' as an improvisational act – Gary Peters, *The Philosophy of Improvisation* (Chicago: The University of Chicago Press, 2009), 158. Central to his claim that improvisation is essentially a practice of 're-novation', that is, improvisation is more a re-working or 'renovating' the old than the creation of something new, Peters suggests that Heidegger's deployment of obscure words and his interrogation of the meanings of common words is consistent with such an improvisational act of 're-novation'. Benson has highlighted both the hermeneutical character of improvisation in music and the improvisational character of hermeneutic interpretation – Bruce Ellis Benson, *The Improvisation of Musical Dialogue: A Phenomenology of Music* (New York: Cambridge University Press, 2003); Bruce Ellis Benson, 'The Improvisation of Hermeneutics: Jazz Lessons for Interpreters', in *Hermeneutics at the Crossroads*, ed. Keven J. Vanhoozer, James K. A. Smith, and Bruce Ellis Benson (Bloomington: Indiana University Press, 2006), 193–210. With respect to the latter, Benson's concerns are primarily methodological. Comparing the interpretive theories of E. D. Hirsch, Monroe Beardsley, Gadamer, Jacques Derrida and Stanley Fish, Benson argues that jazz improvisation provides a model that comes close to balancing each of these theories and offers something that approximates 'hermeneutical justice' – 'The Improvisation of Hermeneutics', 194.

17 Georgina Born, Eric Lewis and Will Straw argue against universalism, suggesting that an ontological or universal account of improvisation 'is bound to obscure more than it illuminates' – see Georgina Born, Eric Lewis and Will Straw, *Improvisation and Social Aesthetics* (Durham: Duke University Press, 2017), 12. As will become apparent in this book, this is an assertion I contest.

18 Jeff Malpas, 'The Multivocity of Human Rights Discourse', in *The Aporia of Rights: Explorations in Citizenship in the Era of Human Rights*, ed. Anna Yeatman and Peg Birmingham (New York: Bloomsbury, 2014), 38.

19 Dan DiPiero, 'Improvisation as Contingent Encounter, Or: The Song of My Toothbrush', *Critical Studies in Improvisation/Études critiques en improvisation* 12, no. 2 (2018): 7. DOI: https://doi.org/10.21083/csieci.v12i2.4261.

Chapter 1

1 David Borgo has also noted and critiqued the influence that 'methodological individualism has had on the field of improvisation studies' – see 'Openness from Closure: The Puzzle of Interagency in Improvised Music and a Neocybernetic

Solution', in *Negotiated Moments: Improvisation, Sound, and Subjectivity*, ed. Gillian Siddall and Ellen Waterman (Durham: Duke University Press, 2016), 113–30.

2. Eric Lewis, for instance, argues that when musicians improvise on pre-existing melodies (he takes John Coltrane's performance of 'My Favourite Things' as a case study), the performance is best understood as evincing the 'improviser's understanding of the work'. Thus, he attributes the 'outcomes' of improvised musical performance to the 'intent' and 'purposiveness' of the player – see *Intents and Purposes: Philosophy and the Aesthetics of Improvisation* (Ann Arbor: University of Michigan Press, 2019), chapter 5. As will become clear, the emphasis Lewis places on the subject who improvises fails to account for the way in which players are necessarily *responsive* to and *led* by the situation in which they find themselves, such that the player's acting is not solely reducible to their prior understanding and purposiveness.

3. Benson, *Liturgy as a Way of Life*, 154–5.

4. Martin Heidegger, 'The Origin of the Work of Art', in *Poetry, Language, Thought*, trans. Albert Hofstadter (New York: Harper Perennial, 2013), 143.

5. Hans-Georg Gadamer, *Truth and Method*, trans. Joel Weinsheimer and Donald G. Marshal (London: Bloomsbury, 2013), 147.

6. There are, of course, scholars working to temper the hyper-individualist discourse surrounding improvised musical performance. For instance, see Garry Hagberg, 'Ensemble Improvisation, Collective Intention, and Group Attention', in *The Oxford Handbook of Critical Improvisation Studies*, vol. 1, ed. Lewis and Piekut. DOI: 10.1093/oxfordhb/9780195370935.013.011; Cynthia R. Nielsen, 'Hearing the Other's Voice: How Gadamer's Fusion of Horizons and Open-ended Understanding Respects the Other and Puts Oneself in Question', *Otherness: Essays and Studies* 4, no. 1 (2013): 1–25; David Borgo, 'What the Music Wants', in *Soundweaving: Writings on Improvisation*, ed. Franziska Schroder and Micheál Ó hAodha (Newcastle: Cambridge Scholars Publishing, 2014), 33–52. Hagberg, Nielsen and Borgo sketch out anti-subjectivist accounts of improvisation that in some ways converge with my own. In this respect, we each offer different angles or perspectives on the same topic. Thus, despite the different paths taken to arrive at such conclusions, this multiplicity of perspectives ought to be seen positively, as reinforcing the anti-subjectivist view advanced in this book.

7. Davidson, 'Three Varieties of Knowledge', 155.

8. Davidson, 'Three Varieties of Knowledge', 155.

9. Ludwig Wittgenstein, *Philosophical Investigations*, trans. G. E. M. Anscombe, P. M. S. Hacker, and Joachim Schulte, 4th edn (Oxford: Blackwell, 2009).

10. Gadamer, *Truth and Method*, 114.

11. Davidson, 'Three Varieties of Knowledge', 166.

12 Berliner, *Thinking in Jazz*; Ingrid Monson, *Saying Something: Jazz Improvisation and Interaction* (Chicago: The University of Chicago Press, 1997); Keith Sawyer, 'Music and Conversation', in *Musical Communication*, ed. Dorothy Miell, Raymond MacDonald, and David J. Hargreaves (Oxford: Oxford University Press, 2005), 45–60.

13 Graeme B. Wilson and Raymond MacDonald, 'The Sign of Silence: Negotiating Musical Identities in an Improvising Ensemble', *Psychology of Music* 40, no. 5 (2012): 558–73.

14 Wilson and MacDonald, 'The Sign of Silence', 559.

15 It is worth noting that in some quarters jazz and improvisation have been invoked as a model for meaning and linguistic understanding. See Laura Schroeter and François Schroeter, 'A Third Way in Metaethics', *Noûs* 43, no. 1 (2009): 1–30; Kenneth A. Taylor, 'Reference and Jazz Combo Theories of Meaning', in *Reference and Referring*, ed. William P. Kabasenche, Michael O'Rourke, and Matthew H. Slater (Cambridge, MA: MIT Press, 2012), 271–303. While these discussions bear some relevance to this discussion, it is on the work of the aforementioned philosophers that I focus, for their characterization of language and understanding is of particular importance to the specific argument at issue.

16 Benson has made a similar argument, with a particular emphasis on the nature of being 'called' – see *The Improvisation of Musical Dialogue*; 'Taking Responsibility by Letting Go: The Improvisation of Responding to the Call', in *Philosophy of Improvisation: Interdisciplinary Perspectives on Theory and Practice*, ed. Susanne Ravn, Simon Høffding, and James McGuirk (New York: Routledge, 2021), 87–100.

17 Gadamer, *Truth and Method*.

18 Donald Davidson, 'A Nice Derangement of Epitaphs', in *Truth, Language, and History* (Oxford: Clarendon Press, 2005), 93.

19 Davidson, 'A Nice Derangement of Epitaphs', 100.

20 Davidson, 'A Nice Derangement of Epitaphs', 94.

21 Davidson, 'A Nice Derangement of Epitaphs', 95.

22 Davidson, 'A Nice Derangement of Epitaphs', 103–4.

23 Don Ihde, *Listening and Voice: Phenomenologies of Sound*, 2nd edn (Albany: State University of New York Press, 2007), 151.

24 Davidson, 'A Nice Derangement of Epitaphs', 107.

25 Gadamer, *Truth and Method*, 106–34.

26 Cynthia R. Nielsen, 'Gadamer on Play and the Play of Art', in *The Gadamerian Mind*, ed. Theodore George and Gert-Jan van der Heiden (London: Routledge, 2021), 139.

27 Gadamer, *Truth and Method*, 107.

28 Gadamer, *Truth and Method*, 107.

29 Gadamer, *Truth and Method*, 107.

30 Such a view of ensemble interaction is indicative of the musical equivalent of a 'social contract', where individual players selectively interact with certain aspects of the performance and not others, presenting a picture of autonomous self-hood. The ensemble, under such a model, represents a structure where individuals opt for a slight reduction in personal freedom in favour of the benefits that arise from collaborating with others. There is no genuine unity in such a model, only the representation of unity, for each player retains their autonomy. Hagberg convincingly argues against understanding improvised musical performance in terms of a social contract in 'Ensemble Improvisation, Collective Intention, and Group Attention'.

31 Gadamer, *Truth and Method*, 108.

32 The argument here is that improvisation has something of the ontological status characteristic of Gadamer's *Spiel*. While one may be inclined to also make a connection between improvisation and Gadamer's notion of *Sprachlichkeit* – indeed, the relationship between language/conversation and improvisation is explored in Chapter 5 – it is Gadamer's concept of *Spiel* that most clearly and accurately draws out the ontology of improvisation. Nielsen has noted the way in which Gadamer's 'dialogical play structure' is at issue in free jazz – 'Gadamer on the Event of Art, the Other, and a Gesture Toward a Gadamarian Approach to Free Jazz', *Journal of Applied Hermeneutics* (2016): 1–17.

33 Julien Wilson and Stephen Magnusson, 'Stagger', Track 1 on *Kaleidoscopic*, Jazz Head – HEAD113, 2007, CD.

34 *Kaleidoscopic* also features Barney McAll on piano and keyboard, Mark Helias on bass, and Jim Black on drums.

35 Wilson and Magnusson, 'Stagger'.

36 Nielsen has also noted a relationship between Gadamer's account of play and improvisation, writing, 'play involves players, rules, ordered and reciprocal movement, responsiveness, and leeway or creative flexibility; that is, play includes and involves space or room for improvisatory activity' – see 'Gadamer on Play and the Play of Art', 140.

37 'Cartesianism' is often used as placeholder for a larger story in philosophy where one is preoccupied with the 'self', a story that arguably begins with Augustine and continues with Luther, Descartes and Locke.

38 Davidson, 'Three Varieties of Knowledge', 165.

39 I employ the phrase '*belong* together' in a manner consistent with Heidegger's use of the phrase, where things are 'together' *because they belong*; things are *already* placed

in relation to one another. See Martin Heidegger, *Identity and Difference*, trans. Joan Stambaugh (New York: Harper & Row, 1969), 29.

Chapter 2

1 Keith Jarrett, *The Köln Concert*, ECM Records GmbH – ECM 1064/65. 1975, CD.

2 Peter Elsdon, *Keith Jarrett's The Koln Concert* (Oxford: Oxford University Press, 2013), 6.

3 Manfred Eicher, quoted in, Corinna da Fonseca-Wollheim, 'WEEKEND JOURNAL; Leisure & Arts – Masterpiece: A Jazz Night to Remember; The unique magic of Keith Jarrett's "The Köln Concert"', *Wall Street Journal*, Eastern edition, 11 October 2008.

4 Alva Noë, *Out of Our Heads: Why You Are Not Your Brain, and Other Lessons from the Biology of Consciousness* (New York: Hill and Wang, 2009), 101.

5 Edward S. Casey argues that 'culture' is not located in 'mind' or 'history', 'behavioural patterns' or 'symbol systems'. Rather he argues that 'to be cultural, to have a culture, is to inhabit a place sufficiently intensely to cultivate it – to be responsible for it, to respond to it, to attend to it caringly. . . . To be located, culture also has to be *embodied*. Culture is carried into places by bodies.' This is the relationship between culture and place at issue here. See Edward S. Casey, 'How to Get from Space to Place in a Fairly Short Stretch of Time: Phenomenological Prolegomena', in *Senses of Place*, ed. Steven Feld and Keith H. Basso (Santa Fe: School of American Research Press, 1996), 33–4.

6 Timothy Rice, 'Reflections on Music and Identity in *Ethnomusicology*', *Muzikologijas* 7 (2007): 17–38.

7 George E. Lewis, *A Power Stronger Than Itself: The AACM and American Experimental Music* (Chicago: The University of Chicago Press, 2008).

8 Lewis, *A Power Stronger Than Itself*, 1.

9 Lewis, *A Power Stronger Than Itself*, 1.

10 Malpas, *Place and Experience*, 23.

11 Berliner, *Thinking in Jazz*, 22.

12 Berliner, *Thinking in Jazz*, 22.

13 Berliner, *Thinking in Jazz*, 22.

14 Malpas, *Place and Experience*, chap. 1.

15 Doreen Massey, 'Politics and Space/Time', in *Place and the Politics of Identity*, ed. Michael Keith and Steve Pile (London: Routledge, 1993), 139–40.

16 Edward S. Casey, *The Fate of Place: A Philosophical History* (Berkeley: University of California Press, 1998).

17 Derek Bailey, *Improvisation: Its Nature and Practice in Music* (New York: Da Capo Press, 1993), 30.

18 Bailey, *Improvisation*, 30.

19 Jann Pasler, 'Race, Orientalism, and Distinction in the Wake of the "Yellow Peril"' in *Western Music and Its Others: Difference, Representation, and Appropriation in Music*, ed. Georgina Born and David Hesmondhalgh (Berkeley: University of California Press, 2000), 87.

20 Jeff R. Warren, *Music and Ethical Responsibility* (New York: Cambridge University Press, 2014), 118.

21 Edward W. Said, *Musical Elaborations* (New York: Columbia University Press, 1991), 70.

22 Carol S. Gould and Kenneth Keaton, 'The Essential Role of Improvisation in Musical Performance', *The Journal of Aesthetics and Art Criticism* 58, no. 2 (2000): 146.

23 Monson, *Saying Something*, 5.

24 Lydia Goehr, *The Imaginary Museum of Musical Works: An Essay in the Philosophy of Music* (New York: Oxford University Press, 2007), 145.

25 Monson, *Saying Something*, 176.

26 Said, *Musical Elaborations*, 29.

27 Warren, *Music and Ethical Responsibility*, 118.

28 Monson, *Saying Something*, 18.

29 Peters, *The Philosophy of Improvisation*, 91.

30 David Toop, *Into the Maelstrom: Music, Improvisation and the Dream of Freedom Before 1970* (New York: Bloomsbury, 2016), 77.

31 Andy Hamilton, 'The Art of Improvisation and the Aesthetics of Imperfection', *British Journal of Aesthetics* 40, no. 1 (2000): 171.

32 Jean-François Augoyard, and Henry Torgue, eds, *Sonic Experience: A Guide to Everyday Sounds*, trans. Andra McCartney and David Paquette (London: McGill-Queen's University Press, 2005), 12.

33 Augoyard and Torgue, *Sonic Experience*, 17.

34 Georgina Born, Introduction to *Music, Sound and Space: Transformations of Public and Private Experience*, ed. Georgina Born (Cambridge: Cambridge University Press, 2013), 57.

35 Lee B. Brown, David Goldblatt, and Theodore Gracyk, *Jazz and the Philosophy of Art* (New York: Routledge, 2018), 227.

36 Malpas, *Heidegger's Topology*, 40.

37 Gadamer, *Truth and Method*, 315.

38 *Oxford English Dictionary*, 3rd edn, s.v. 'situation', https://www-oed-com.ezproxy.lib.monash.edu.au/view/Entry/180520?redirectedFrom=situation& (accessed 24 July 2020).

39 Malpas, *Place and Experience*, 112.

40 Juhani Pallasmaa, 'Place and Atmosphere', in *The Intelligence of Place: Topographies and Poetics*, ed. Jeff Malpas (London: Bloomsbury, 2017), 133.

41 Malpas, *Place and Experience*, 31.

42 Pallasmaa, 'Place and Atmosphere', 135.

43 Malpas, *Heidegger's Topology*, 176–7.

44 Hans-Georg Gadamer, 'The Universality of the Hermeneutical Problem', in *Philosophical Hermeneutics*, trans. and ed. David E. Linge (Berkeley: University of California Press, 2008), 3–17. The idea of 'prejudice' (German *Vorurteil*) at issue here, and, indeed, at issue throughout this book, refers to the idea of 'pre-judgement', where all judgements are, as Chris Lawn and Niall Keane say, 'conditioned' by prejudgements. All judgement, all understanding, is made possible by prejudice or pre-judgement. See Chris Lawn and Niall Keane, *The Gadamer Dictionary* (London: Continuum, 2011), 115.

45 Gadamer, 'The Universality of the Hermeneutical Problem', 9.

46 Gadamer acknowledges that prejudices can be unjustified and erroneous – 'The Universality of the Hermeneutical Problem', 9. The point that Gadamer is making by employing the term 'prejudice' is that they are 'simply condition[s] whereby we experience something'. Thus, the idea that one can have a completely unbiased and prejudiceless understanding (the goal of science, for instance) is, according to Gadamer, misguided. See 'The Universality of the Hermeneutical Problem', 9–10.

47 Malpas, *Heidegger's Topology*, 177–8.

48 Malpas, *Heidegger's Topology*, 178.

49 Malpas, *Heidegger's Topology*, 58–9, 214–18.

50 Although there is a commonplace tendency to think of the Event as temporal, the Event ought properly to be understood as encompassing both the temporal *and* the spatial – as, in fact, topological (place being both temporal and spatial). In the *Contributions*, for instance (in which the Event emerges as a central idea), time and space are dealt with as 'time-space' (*Zeit-raum*) – see Martin Heidegger, *Contributions to Philosophy (Of the Event)*, trans. Richard Rojcewicz and Daniela Vallega-Neu (Bloomington: Indiana University Press, 2012), 293–306.

51 Gadamer, *Truth and Method*, 111.

52 Martin Heidegger, 'Building Dwelling Thinking', in *Poetry, Language, Thought*.

53 Martin Heidegger, 'The Thing', in *Poetry, Language, Thought*, 177–9.

54 Heidegger, *Identity and Difference*, 36–40.

55 Heidegger, 'The Thing', 178.

56 Heidegger, 'The Origin of the Work of Art'.

57 In his writing Heidegger writes of both 'the gods' (*die Götter*) and 'the divinities' (*die Göttlichen*). I have employed 'the divinities' throughout for the sake of consistency. As Julian Young points out, the distinction between 'the gods' and 'the divinities' need not be overly stressed – see *Heidegger's Later Philosophy* (Cambridge: Cambridge University Press, 2002), 94n3.

58 See Malpas, *Heidegger's Topology*, 274–6; Young, *Heidegger's Later Philosophy*, 94–102.

59 Heidegger, *Contributions to Philosophy*, 246.

60 Gadamer, *Truth and Method*, 364.

61 Miles Davis, 'So What', track 1 on *Kind of Blue*, Columbia, CK 64935, 1997, compact disc.

62 Peters, for instance, speaks of the 'certainty' of improvisation. Adopting a Kantian perspective, Peters argues it is the cultivation of 'taste' that occurs across the '*life of the artist*' that structures the actions of the player in the event, suggesting that the possible outcomes of improvised performances are significantly narrower than performers often care to admit. The result of cultivating one's aesthetic taste between performances, Peters argues, assures a degree of certainty in the performance itself. See Gary Peters, 'Certainty, Contingency, and Improvisation', *Critical Studies in Improvisation / Études critiques en improvisation* 8, no. 2 (2012), DOI: https://doi.org/10.21083/csieci.v8i2.2141.

63 Mandy-Suzanne Wong and Nina Sun Eidsheim, '*Corregidora*: Corporeal Archaeology, Embodied Memory, Improvisation', in Siddall and Waterman, *Negotiated Moments*, 217.

64 Wong and Eidsheim, '*Corregidora*', 218.

65 Gayl Jones, *Corregidora* (Boston: Beacon Press, 1975).

66 Wong and Eidsheim, '*Corregidora*', 219.

67 Wong and Eidsheim, '*Corregidora*', 220.

68 Wong and Eidsheim, '*Corregidora*', 220.

69 Edward S. Casey, 'Between Geography and Philosophy: What Does It Mean to Be in the Place-World?' *Annals of the Association of American Geographers* 91, no. 4 (2001): 688.

70 Edward S. Casey, *Remembering: A Phenomenological Study*, 2nd edn (Bloomington: Indiana University Press, 2000), 182.

71 Casey, *Remembering*, 182.

72 Malpas, *Place and Experience*, 102.

73 Malpas, *Place and Experience*, 102–15.

74 Malpas also notes a topographical structure in Ulric Neisser's account of memories, where just as places are nested within larger places, certain memories of things or events are topologically nested within a memory of a larger event or process. See Malpas, *Place and Experience*, 109–12; Ulric Neisser, 'Nested Structure in Autobiographical Memory', in *Autobiographical Memory*, ed. David C. Rubin (Cambridge: Cambridge University Press, 1989), 71–81.

75 Malpas, *Place and Experience*, 106.

76 Bailey, *Improvisation*, 107.

77 Bailey, *Improvisation*, 107.

78 Bailey, *Improvisation*, 108.

79 See, for instance, Andy Clark and David J. Chalmers, 'The Extended Mind', *Analysis* 58, no. 1 (1998): 7–19; Mark Johnson, *Embodied Mind, Meaning, and Reason: How Our Bodies Give Rise to Understanding* (Chicago: The University of Chicago Press, 2017); Shaun Gallagher, *Enactivist Interventions: Rethinking the Mind* (Oxford: Oxford University Press, 2017); Noë, *Out of Our Heads*. For discussion on the distinction between 'extended mind' and 'enactive cognition', see Daniel D. Hutto and Erik Myin, *Radicalizing Enactivism: Basic Minds without Content* (Cambridge, MA: The MIT Press, 2013), chap. 7.

80 Noë, *Out of Our Heads*, 186.

81 Noë, *Out of Our Heads*, 79.

82 Noë, *Out of Our Heads*, 78–9.

83 Noë, *Out of Our Heads*, 79.

84 Alva Noë, *Varieties of Presence* (Cambridge, MA: Harvard University Press, 2012), 7–9. Noë criticizes Heidegger's differentiation between 'absence' and 'presence', arguing that what Heidegger refers to as a form of 'absence' is in fact 'presence'. Interestingly, the conclusion Noë reaches on page 9, where he writes, supposedly contra Heidegger, 'the baseball player's glove, or the carpenter's hammer, although withdrawn, and in that sense absent, are not absent *tout court*. Theirs is a lively absence, not a dead one', is largely consistent with Heidegger's argument. When Heidegger argues that things are not apprehended thematically and are therefore unthought or absent, he is not suggesting those things are altogether not present, that is, non-existent, but rather, despite them *being there with us*, requiring us to 'find our bearings in regard to them' (Martin Heidegger, *Basic Problems of Phenomenology*,

trans. Albert Hofstadter (Bloomington: Indiana University Press, 1982), 163), there is a difference between those things that are 'thematically apprehended for deliberate thinking' (Heidegger, *Basic Problems of Phenomenology*, 163), and those things that are there, yet absent in the sense that one does not consider them thematically or directly. Thus, while Noë and Heidegger understand the terms 'presence' and 'absence' differently, their broader arguments are perhaps not in as stark an opposition as Noë suggests.

85 Martin Heidegger, *Being and Time*, trans. John Macquarrie and Edward Robinson (New York: Harper & Row, 2008), 97.

86 Heidegger, *Being and Time*, 116.

87 See Clark and Chalmers, 'The Extended Mind;' Shaun Gallagher, 'Body Schema and Intentionality', in *The Body and the Self*, ed. José Luis Bermúdez, Anthony Marcel, and Naomi Eilan (Cambridge, MA: The MIT Press, 2001), 225–44; Noë, *Out of Our Heads*.

88 Noë, *Out of Our Heads*, 100.

89 I employ the term *topos* here in a manner consistent with Malpas's account, where *topos* refers to a certain bounded region that allows for an openness or extendedness within. It is a domain of interrelatedness and irreducible interconnection between elements *there* in that open, bounded region. To know the *topos* of an instrument is to possess an understanding of the relationality at issue when one plays the instrument in the place in which one *is*. See Malpas, *Place and Experience*, 26–8. Paloma Puente-Lozano gives an overview of Malpas's account of *topos* in 'Jeff Malpas: From Hermeneutics to Topology', in *Place, Space and Hermeneutics*, ed. Bruce B. Janz (Cham: Springer, 2018), 303.

90 Mark Johnson, *The Aesthetics of Meaning and Thought: The Bodily Roots of Philosophy, Science, Morality, and Art* (Chicago: The University of Chicago Press, 2018), 15.

91 Johnson, *The Aesthetics of Meaning and Thought*, 15.

92 Johnson, *The Aesthetics of Meaning and Thought*, 26.

93 Gallagher, 'Body Schema and Intentionality', 226.

94 Gallagher, 'Body Schema and Intentionality', 226.

95 Noë, *Out of Our Heads*, 100.

96 Gallagher, 'Body Schema and Intentionality', 237.

97 Gallagher, 'Body Schema and Intentionality', 237.

98 Gallagher, 'Body Schema and Intentionality', 236.

99 Noë, *Out of Our Heads*, 98.

100 Noë, *Out of Our Heads*, 97–128.

101 Noë, *Out of Our Heads*, 111.

102 Félix Ravaisson, *Of Habit*, trans. Clare Carlisle and Mark Sinclair (London: Continuum, 2008), 55.

103 Ravaisson, *Of Habit*, 55.

104 Noë, *Out of Our Heads*, 127.

105 Pallasmaa, 'Place and Atmosphere', 133.

106 Pallasmaa, 'Place and Atmosphere', 135.

107 Johnson, *The Aesthetics of Meaning and Thought*, 15.

108 Benson has also acknowledged the relevance of Gadamer's account of tact for improvisation in music – see Bruce Ellis Benson, 'Improvisation', in *The Oxford Handbook of Western Music and Philosophy*, ed. Tomás McAuley, Nanette Nielsen, and Jerrold Levinson, with Ariana Phillips-Hutton, assoc. ed. (New York: Oxford University Press, 2021), 446.

109 Gadamer, *Truth and Method*, 15.

110 Gadamer, *Truth and Method*, 15.

111 Gadamer, *Truth and Method*, 15.

112 Gadamer, *Truth and Method*, 16.

113 Nicholas Davey, *Unquiet Understanding: Gadamer's Philosophical Hermeneutics* (Albany: State University of New York Press, 2006), 89.

114 Hilmar Jensson, 'Larf', track 2 on *Ditty Blei*, Songlines Recordings SGL SA1547-2, 2004, CD.

115 Davey, *Unquiet Understanding*, 89.

116 Gadamer, *Truth and Method*, 405.

Chapter 3

1 The question of 'listening', of course, extends beyond the player to the audience; players and audience members listen to the same work. While much aesthetic theory tends to focus on the audience who listens at the expense of the player, this chapter takes as its focus the player who listens to the music that they are playing, and leaves questions related to the audience to one side.

2 Hannah Arendt famously asked, 'where are we when we think?' in *The Life of the Mind*, vol. 1 (San Diego: Harcourt, 1978). Günther Anders, too, asked, sometime

between 1929 and 1930 in an unpublished manuscript, 'where are we when listening to music?' – see Veit Erlmann, *Reason and Resonance: A History of Modern Aurality* (New York: Zone Books, 2010), chap. 8.

3   Peter Sloterdijk, 'Where Are We When We Hear Music?' in *The Aesthetic Imperative: Writings on Art*, ed. Peter Weibel, trans. Karen Margolis (Cambridge: Polity, 2017), 77–127.

4   Sloterdijk, 'Where Are We When We Hear Music?' 95.

5   Sloterdijk, 'Where Are We When We Hear Music?' 84.

6   While Sloterdijk employs terminology related to spatiality and topology, he offers little to no interrogation or questioning of these concepts either on their own terms or with respect to music and hearing.

7   Archytas of Tarentum, quoted in Casey, *The Fate of Place*, 4.

8   Harri Mäcklin, 'Going Elsewhere: A Phenomenology of Aesthetic Immersion', (PhD diss., University of Helsinki, 2018), 146, https://helda.helsinki.fi/handle/10138/271647 (accessed 26 November 2020).

9   Mäcklin, 'Going Elsewhere', 148.

10 Mäcklin, 'Going Elsewhere', 159.

11 Mäcklin, 'Going Elsewhere', 160.

12 Mikel Dufrenne, *The Phenomenology of Aesthetic Experience*, trans. Edward S. Casey et al. (Evanston: Northwestern University Press, 1973), 149.

13 Heidegger, *Basic Problems of Phenomenology*, 163.

14 See 'Max Neuhaus: Times Square, 1977', Dia (website), https://www.diaart.org/media/_file/webpdfs/neuhaus-brochure-3-to-printer.pdf (accessed 11 August 2021).

15 Jeff Malpas, 'The Threshold of the World', in *Funktionen des Lebendigen*, ed. Thiemo Breyer and Oliver Müller (Berlin: De Gruyter, 2016), 161–8.

16 Malpas, 'The Threshold of the World'.

17 Mäcklin, 'Going Elsewhere'.

18 Ren Walters, 'What is Improvisation?', *Sam McAuliffe* (blog), 11 August 2017, https://sjmcauliffe.files.wordpress.com/2017/08/ren-walters.pdf (accessed 26 November 2020).

19 Ren Walters and Stephen Magnusson, 'Raphsody', Track 4 on *de flection*, 2004, online recording, https://renwaltersandstephenmagnusson.bandcamp.com/album/de-flection (accessed 11 June 2021).

20 Jean-Luc Nancy, *Listening*, trans. Charlotte Mandell (New York: Fordham University Press, 2007), 13.

21 Nancy, *Listening*, 14.

22 Heidegger, *Contributions to Philosophy*.

23 Casey defines 'temporocentrism' as 'a belief in the hegemony of time'. See Casey, *The Fate of Place*, x.

24 Edward Campbell, *Music after Deleuze* (London: Bloomsbury, 2013), 99.

25 Edward Sarath, *Music Theory through Improvisation: A New Approach to Musicianship Training* (New York: Routledge, 2010), 7.

26 Gary Peters, 'It Gives: The There and the Given in Improvisation Space', *Land2*, http://land2.leeds.ac.uk/symposia/spectral-traces/it-gives/ (accessed 7 February 2018).

27 Max Neuhaus, 'Program Notes', in *Sound Works, Volume I: Inscription*, ed. Markus Hartman (Ostfildern: Cantz, 1994), 34.

28 Christoph Cox, 'From Music to Sound: Being as Time in the Sonic Arts', in *Sound: Documents of Contemporary Art*, ed. Caleb Kelly (London: Whitechapel Gallery and The MIT Press, 2011), 84.

29 Henri Bergson, *Time and Free Will: An Essay on the Immediate Data of Consciousness*, trans. F. L. Pogson (Mineola: Dover, 2001), 91.

30 Bergson, *Time and Free Will*, 91.

31 Bergson, *Time and Free Will*, 100.

32 Martin Heidegger, *Logic: The Question of Truth*, trans. Thomas Sheehan (Bloomington: Indiana University Press, 2010), 207.

33 Jeff Malpas, 'Timing Space – Spacing Time', in *Performance and Temporalisation: Time Happens*, ed. Stuart Grant, Jodie McNeilly, and Maeva Veerapen (Hampshire: Palgrave Macmillan, 2015), 34.

34 Malpas, 'Timing Space – Spacing Time', 33.

35 Heidegger, *Contributions to Philosophy*, 303.

36 George Lewis, quoted in, Andrys Onsman and Robert Burke, *Experimentation in Improvised Jazz: Chasing Ideas* (New York: Routledge, 2019), 106.

37 Ellen Waterman, 'Improvised Trust: Opening Statements', in *The Improvisation Studies Reader: Spontaneous Acts*, ed. Rebecca Caines and Ajay Heble (London: Routledge, 2015), 59.

38 Onsman and Burke, *Experimentation in Improvised Jazz*, 129.

39 Hagberg provides an excellent examination of why subjectivity or intention alone is not adequate to understand the unity at issue in improvised musical performance – see Hagberg, 'Ensemble Improvisation, Collective Intention, and Group Attention'.

40 Daniel Fischlin, '(Call and) Responsibility: Improvisation, Ethics, Co-creation', in *The Improvisation Studies Reader*, ed. Caines and Heble, 290.

41 Edmund Husserl, *The Phenomenology of Internal Time-Consciousness*, ed. Martin Heidegger, trans. James S. Churchill (Bloomington: Indiana University Press, 1964), 43–111.

42 Barry Dainton, 'Temporal Consciousness', in *Stanford Encyclopedia of Philosophy*, article published 6 August 2010; last modified 28 June 2017, https://plato.stanford.edu/entries/consciousness-temporal/ (accessed 27 June 2019).

43 Gary Peters, 'Improvisation and Time-Consciousness', in *The Oxford Handbook of Critical Improvisation Studies*, vol. 1, ed. Lewis and Piekut, 443, DOI: 10.1093/oxfordhb/9780195370935.013.002.

44 Onsman and Burke, *Experimentation in Improvised Jazz*.

45 Peters, 'Improvisation and Time-Consciousness', 445.

46 Malpas, 'Timing Space – Spacing Time', 35.

47 Bruce Ellis Benson, '*Creatio ex improvisatione*: Chrétien on the Call', in *Music and Transcendence*, ed. Férdia J. Stone-Davis (London: Routledge, 2016), 54. In contradistinction to the way in which creativity is commonly described, following Kant, in terms of the 'solitary genius', where the genius is typically presented as a 'lone' creator who somehow gets ideas independently of others, which alludes to a conception of creativity as *creatio ex nihilo*, Benson asserts that creativity is a necessarily situated activity. That is, one arrives at creative ideas by virtue of being situated in a particular culture and tradition. According to Benson, the act of creation is *not* producing something where nothing was before but fabricating something from what is conveniently 'on hand'.

48 Benson, '*Creatio ex improvisatione*', 55.

49 See Edmund Husserl, *The Crisis of European Sciences and Transcendental Phenomenology*, trans. David Carr (Evanston: Northwestern University Press, 1978), 161–4.

50 See Nancy, *Listening*, 21.

51 See Ihde, *Listening and Voice*, 103–14.

52 Heidegger, 'Building Dwelling Thinking', 152.

53 Ihde, *Listening and Voice*, 109.

54 Ihde, *Listening and Voice*, 110.

55 Ihde, *Listening and Voice*, 106.

56 Casey O'Callaghan, *Sounds: A Philosophical Theory* (Oxford: Oxford University Press, 2007), 9–10.

57 Pierre Schaeffer, *Treatise on Musical Objects: An Essay across Disciplines*, trans. Christine North and John Dack, Oakland: University of California Press, 2017.

58 O'Callaghan, *Sounds*, 28.

59 O'Callaghan, *Sounds*, 46.

60 O'Callaghan, *Sounds*, 47–56.

61 Jim Denley, *Through Fire, Crevice + the Hidden Valley*, Splitrec – CD16. 2006, CD.

62 'Through Fire, Crevice + the Hidden Valley', splitrec.com, https://splitrec.com/through-fire-crevice-the-hidden-valley-jim-denley/ (accessed 25 June 2019).

63 Scott Tinkler, *Simon Barker/Scott Tinkler May 7 2016* (online video, 24 June 2019), https://www.youtube.com/watch?v=goE_u91EAOU (accessed 27 July 2019).

64 Rob Wallace, 'Kick Out the Jazz!', in *People Get Ready: The Future of Jazz is Now!*, ed. Ajay Hebel and Rob Wallace (Durham: Duke University Press, 2013), 131.

65 Malpas, *Place and Experience*, 39.

Chapter 4

1 Francisco Gonzalez, 'Hermeneutics in Greek Philosophy', in *The Routledge Companion to Hermeneutics*, ed. Jeff Malpas and Hans-Helmuth Gander (London: Routledge, 2015), 13.

2 Jeff Malpas, 'Place and Situation', in *The Routledge Companion to Hermeneutics*, ed. Malpas and Gander, 354.

3 Gonzalez, 'Hermeneutics in Greek Philosophy'.

4 Jean Grondin, *Introduction to Philosophical Hermeneutics*, trans. Joel Weinsheimer (New Haven: Yale University Press, 1994), 1.

5 For a comprehensive overview of the history of hermeneutics, see Grondin, *Introduction to Philosophical Hermeneutics*.

6 Grondin, *Introduction to Philosophical Hermeneutics*, 2.

7 Grondin, *Introduction to Philosophical Hermeneutics*, 98.

8 Heidegger, *Being and Time*, 62.

9 Heidegger, *Ontology*. For insight into the influence of these lectures on Gadamer's thinking, see Grondin, *Introduction to Philosophical Hermeneutics*, 2 and 98–100.

10 Heidegger, quoted in, Grondin, *Introduction to Philosophical Hermeneutics*, 2.

11 For an overview of twentieth-century hermeneutics, see Nicholas Davey, 'Twentieth-Century Hermeneutics', in *The Routledge Companion to Twentieth-Century Philosophy*, ed. Dermot Moran (Abingdon: Routledge, 2008), 693–735. There are numerous edited collections and monographs dedicated to Gadamer's work, for example, Jeff Malpas and Santiago Zabala, eds, *Consequences of Hermeneutics: Fifty Years After Gadamer's Truth and Method* (Evanston: Northwestern University Press, 2010); Davey, *Unquiet Understanding*; Günter Figal, *Objectivity: The Hermeneutical and Philosophy*, trans. Theodore D. George (New York: State University of New York Press, 2010); Rudolf A. Makkreel, *Orientation and Judgment in Hermeneutics* (Chicago: The University of Chicago Press, 2015); Robert J. Dostal, ed., *The Cambridge Companion to Gadamer* (Cambridge: Cambridge University Press, 2002); Bruce Krajewski, ed., *Gadamer's Repercussions: Reconsidering Philosophical Hermeneutics* (Berkeley: University of California Press, 2004).

12 Hans-Georg Gadamer, *Plato's Dialectical Ethics: Phenomenological Interpretations Relating to the Philebus*, trans. Robert M. Wallace (New Haven: Yale University Press, 1991).

13 Jean Grondin, *The Philosophy of Gadamer*, trans. Kathryn Plant (Chesham: Acumen, 2003), 4.

14 Hans-Helmuth Gander, 'Gadamer: The Universality of Hermeneutics', in *The Routledge Companion to Hermeneutics*, ed. Malpas and Gander, 137.

15 Gadamer, *Truth and Method*, 5.

16 Grondin, *The Philosophy of Gadamer*, 19.

17 Gadamer, *Truth and Method*, xxvi.

18 Gadamer, *Truth and Method*, 10.

19 Grondin, *The Philosophy of Gadamer*, 25.

20 Paul Fairfield, 'Hermeneutics and Education', in *The Routledge Companion to Hermeneutics*, ed. Malpas and Gander, 544.

21 The broad appeal of hermeneutics is reflected in Malpas and Gander, eds, *The Routledge Companion to Hermeneutics*; Niall Keane and Chris Lawn, eds, *The Blackwell Companion to Hermeneutics* (Chichester: Wiley Blackwell, 2016). Richard E. Palmer provides a comprehensive list of books in English by and about Gadamer published prior to 2001 in Hans-Georg Gadamer, *Gadamer in Conversation: Reflections and Commentary*, ed. and trans. Richard E. Palmer (New Haven: Yale University Press, 2001), 134–9.

22 Benson, *Liturgy as a Way of Life*, 17.

23 Benson, *Liturgy as a Way of Life*, 17.

24 Benson, *Liturgy as a Way of Life*, 17.

Chapter 5

1 The idea of 'truth' at issue here, as will be discussed later in this chapter, should not be understood as being in opposition to the more common idea of truth as 'correctness'. Indeed, while Ernst Tugendhat famously critiqued Heidegger's account of truth as unconcealment (*aletheia*), arguing that unconcealment lacks a normative dimension that would allow truth to be contrasted with falsity, Tugendhat seems not to acknowledge that unconcealment does not *replace* correctness but is rather the *ground* for correctness. Heidegger does not deny truth as correctness in his characterization of truth as unconcealment, rather he seeks the ontological ground of truth itself. For a discussion on the twofold nature of truth in Heidegger's thinking, see Jeff Malpas, 'The Twofold Character of Truth: Heidegger, Davidson, Tugendhat', in *The Multidimensionality of Hermeneutic Phenomenology*, ed. Babette Babich and Dimitri Ginev (Cham: Springer, 2014), 243–66. For Tugendhat's critique of Heidegger, see Ernst Tugendhat, 'Heidegger's Idea of Truth', in *Hermeneutics and Truth*, ed. Brice R. Wachterhauser (Evanston: Northwestern University Press, 1994), 83–97.

2 Gadamer, 'Heidegger's Later Philosophy', in *Philosophical Hermeneutics*, 222.

3 Gadamer, 'Heidegger's Later Philosophy', 223.

4 Gadamer, *Truth and Method*, 120.

5 Gadamer, 'Heidegger's Later Philosophy', 224.

6 Grondin, *The Philosophy of Gadamer*, 149.

7 Gadamer, *Truth and Method*, chap. 3.

8 Grondin, *Introduction to Philosophical Hermeneutics*, 123.

9 Plato, quoted in Gadamer, *Truth and Method*, 502.

10 Gadamer, *Truth and Method*, 502.

11 Gadamer, 'The Universality of the Hermeneutical Problem', 16.

12 Gadamer, *Truth and Method*, 181.

13 Heidegger, *Being and Time*, 195.

14 See Gunter Scholtz, 'Ast and Schleiermacher: Hermeneutics and Critical Philosophy', in *The Routledge Companion to Hermeneutics*, ed. Malpas and Gander, 65.

15 Jean Grondin, 'The Hermeneutic Circle', in *The Blackwell Companion to Hermeneutics*, ed. Keane and Lawn, 300–1.

16 Richard E. Palmer, *Hermeneutics: Interpretation Theory in Schleiermacher, Dilthey, Heidegger, and Gadamer* (Evanston: Northwestern University Press, 1988), 86.

17 Palmer, *Hermeneutics*, 88–90.

18 Makkreel, *Orientation and Judgment in Hermeneutics*, 25.

19 Heidegger, *Ontology*, 1.

20 Heidegger, *Ontology*, 1.

21 Jeff Malpas, 'The Beckoning of Language: Heidegger's Hermeneutic Transformation of Thinking', in *Hermeneutical Heidegger*, ed. Michael Bowler and Ingo Farin (Evanston: Northwestern University Press, 2016), 203–21.

22 Heidegger, *Being and Time*, 26.

23 Heidegger, *Being and Time*, 32.

24 Jeff Malpas, 'The Transcendental Circle', *Australasian Journal of Philosophy* 75, no. 1 (1997): 11.

25 Heidegger, *Being and Time*, 249.

26 Malpas, 'The Transcendental Circle', 12.

27 Heidegger, *Being and Time*, 257.

28 Heidegger, *Being and Time*, 195.

29 Wilhelm Dilthey, quoted in, Palmer, *Hermeneutics*, 101.

30 Palmer, *Hermeneutics*, 111.

31 Heidegger, *Being and Time*, 62.

32 Dermot Moran, Introduction to *The Shorter Logical Investigations*, by Edmund Husserl, trans. J. N. Findlay (London: Routledge, 2001), xxxii.

33 Daniel Dahlstrom, 'Martin Heidegger', in *The Routledge Companion to Phenomenology*, ed. Sebastian Luft and Søren Overgaard (London: Routledge, 2012), 54.

34 Palmer, *Hermeneutics*, 144.

35 Thomas S. Kuhn, *The Structure of Scientific Revolutions*, 3rd edn (Chicago: The University of Chicago Press, 1996).

36 Grondin, *Introduction to Philosophical Hermeneutics*, 98.

37 Grondin, *Introduction to Philosophical Hermeneutics*, 99.

38 Grondin, *Introduction to Philosophical Hermeneutics*, 99.

39 Gadamer, 'The Universality of the Hermeneutical Problem', 9.

40 Grondin, *Introduction to Philosophical Hermeneutics*, 115.

41 Gadamer, *Truth and Method*, 307.

42 Gadamer, *Truth and Method*, 307.

43 Gadamer, *Truth and Method*, 307.

44 Gadamer, *Truth and Method*, 310.

45 Gadamer, *Truth and Method*, 127.

46 Gadamer, *Truth and Method*, 187.

47 Gadamer, *Truth and Method*, 186.

48 Gadamer, *Truth and Method*, 187.

49 Gadamer, *Truth and Method*, 500.

50 Hans-Georg Gadamer, 'Reflections on My Philosophical Journey', in *The Philosophy of Hans-Georg Gadamer*, ed. Lewis Edwin Hahn (Chicago: Open Court, 1997), 47.

51 Heidegger, 'The Origin of the Work of Art', 68.

52 Heidegger, 'The Origin of the Work of Art', 35.

53 Heidegger, 'The Origin of the Work of Art', 50.

54 Heidegger, 'The Origin of the Work of Art', 51.

55 Martin Heidegger, 'The Question Concerning Technology', in *The Question Concerning Technology and Other Essays*, trans. William Lovitt (New York: Garland, 1977), 45.

56 Heidegger, *Being and Time*, 376.

57 Hans-Georg Gadamer, 'Hermeneutics on the Trail', in *Hermeneutics between History and Philosophy*, ed. and trans. Pol Vandevelde and Arun Iyer (London: Bloomsbury Academic, 2019), 188.

58 Hans-Georg Gadamer, 'Praise of Theory', in *Praise of Theory: Speeches and Essays*, trans. Chris Dawson (New Haven: Yale University Press, 1998), 31. The German language and translation included in this quote are taken from Robert J. Dostal, 'The Experience of Truth for Gadamer and Heidegger: Taking Time and Sudden Lightning', in *Hermeneutics and Truth*, ed. Brice R. Wachterhauser (Evanston: Northwestern University Press, 1994), 62.

59 See Figal, *Objectivity*, 3–4.

60 Gadamer, *Truth and Method*, 148.

61 Malpas, 'The Beckoning of Language'.

62 Gadamer, *Truth and Method*, 91.

63 Malpas, 'Placing Understanding/Understanding Place', 381.

64 Gadamer, *Truth and Method*, 401. The original German translated here as 'we fall into a conversation', reads 'wir in ein Gespräch geraten' – Hans-Georg Gadamer, *Gesammelte Werke 1: Hermeneutik I: Wahrheit und Methode: Grundzüge einer philosophischen Hermeneutik* (Tübingen: Mohr Siebeck, 1990), 387. *Geraten* can carry

a range of senses including, 'stumbling into', 'getting into', 'coming upon', captured here as 'falling into'. Gadamer does not himself put any special emphasis on *geraten* as such, his point being simply that conversation is indeed something that happens spontaneously. But the idea of 'falling into' also captures something important about the way this spontaneity is experienced, and for that reason it provides a useful way of elaborating spontaneity as it occurs in the conversational and improvisational context of understanding. It should be clear, of course, that the sense of 'falling' at issue in 'falling into' is quite distinct from the sense of 'falling' that Heidegger identifies, in *Being and Time*, as a basic structure of *Dasein*, and for which he uses the term *Verfallen*.

65 Gadamer, 'On the Problem of Self Understanding', in *Philosophical Hermeneutics*, 51.

66 Gadamer, *Truth and Method*, 116.

67 Gadamer, 'Hermeneutics on the Trail', 192.

68 Gadamer, 'Hermeneutics on the Trail', 192.

69 Gadamer, 'Hermeneutics on the Trail', 192.

70 Gadamer, 'Hermeneutics on the Trail', 193.

71 Gadamer, *Truth and Method*, 349.

72 Gadamer, *Truth and Method*, 401.

73 Gadamer, *Truth and Method*, 107.

74 Gadamer, *Truth and Method*, 406, 600–1.

75 James Risser, 'Gadamer's Hidden Doctrine: The Simplicity and Humility of Philosophy', in *Consequences of Hermeneutics*, ed. Malpas and Zabala, 9.

76 Risser, 'Gadamer's Hidden Doctrine', 11.

77 Gadamer, *Truth and Method*, 407.

78 Gadamer, 'Hermeneutics on the Trail', 187.

79 Gadamer, 'Man and Language', in *Philosophical Hermeneutics*, 65.

80 Gadamer, *Truth and Method*, 462.

81 Grondin, *The Philosophy of Gadamer*, 144.

82 Heidegger, 'Language', in *Poetry, Language, Thought*, 189.

83 Martin Heidegger, 'The Nature of Language', in *On the Way to Language*, trans. Peter D. Hertz (New York: Harper & Row, 1982), 63.

84 James Risser, 'Language and Alterity', in *The Blackwell Companion to Hermeneutics*, ed. Keane and Lawn, 124.

85 Gadamer, *Truth and Method*, 386.

86 Gadamer, *Truth and Method*, 47, 310, 415. Davey has discussed this topic in detail, highlighting the difference between 'disclosive' (*aletheic*) and 'propositional' (*apophantic*) language, where the former is ontologically prior to the latter (see Heidegger, *Being and Time*, 199). It is the 'disclosive' character of language that is Gadamer's primary concern. Aesthetic experience is the experience of something being 'disclosed' through art – *Unfinished Worlds: Hermeneutics, Aesthetics and Gadamer* (Edinburgh: Edinburgh University Press, 2013), chap. 6. Nielsen, too, has discussed the way in which artworks speak. She writes, 'art speaks to us not through words or by being translated in words or reduced to propositions; rather, art's material content, given its art-ful arrangement of symbols, figures, colours, and sounds, all of which arise from and are shaped by broader historical and cultural horizons, communicates something meaningful' – 'Harsh Poetry and Art's Address: Romare Bearden and Hans-Georg Gadamer', *Estetyka i Krytyka: The Polish Journal of Aesthetics* 4 (2016): 113.

87 Hans-Georg Gadamer, 'Hermeneutics as Practical Philosophy', in *The Gadamer Reader: A Bouquet of the Later Writings*, ed. and trans. Richard E. Palmer (Evanston: Northwestern University Press, 2007), 243.

88 Gadamer, 'Man and Language', 60.

89 Nicholas Davey, 'Dialogue, Dialectic and Conversation', in *The Gadamerian Mind*, ed. Theodore George and Gert-Jan van der Heiden (London: Routledge, 2021), 65.

90 Gadamer, *Truth and Method*, 474.

91 Gadamer, *Truth and Method*, 474.

92 Gadamer, 'Language and Understanding', in *The Gadamer Reader*, 92.

93 Grondin, *The Philosophy of Gadamer*, 133.

94 Augustine, *On the Trinity: Books 8–15*, ed. Gareth B. Matthews, trans. Stephen McKenna (Cambridge: Cambridge University Press, 2002), 187.

95 Gadamer, 'Language and Understanding', 93.

96 Gadamer, 'Language and Understanding', 93.

97 Daniel Dahlstrom, 'Language and Meaning', in *The Routledge Companion to Hermeneutics*, ed. Malpas and Gander, 278.

98 Gadamer, 'Man and Language', 65.

99 Gadamer, *Truth and Method*, 386.

100 Gadamer, *Truth and Method*, 387.

101 Davey describes Gadamer's 'subject matter' in a way largely consistent with how I have characterized 'a common matter of concern' when he writes, 'a subject-matter in Gadamer's sense of the term is not to be understood as an entity with a determinate

meaning but as a constellation of meanings which cross relate, interpenetrate and, sometimes, disrupt one another'. See Nicholas Davey, 'In Between Word and Image: Philosophical Hermeneutics, Aesthetics and the Inescapable Heritage of Kant', in *Critical Communities and Aesthetic Practices: Dialogues with Tony O'Connor on Society, Art, and Friendship*, ed. Francis Halsall, Julia Jansen, and Sinéad Murphy (Dordrecht: Springer, 2012), 29.

102 Gadamer, 'The Nature of Things and the Language of Things', in *Philosophical Hermeneutics*, 71–2.

103 David Tolley, 'Improvisation and our Great Western Music Tradition', *David Tolley ~ artist-musician-composer-teacher-improviser* (blog), 23 August 2012, https://davidtolley.wordpress.com/category/texts/ (accessed 16 April 2018).

104 Gadamer, *Truth and Method*, 503.

105 Gadamer, *Truth and Method*, 504.

106 Gadamer, *Truth and Method*, 476.

107 Günter Figal, 'The Doing of the Thing Itself: Gadamer's Hermeneutic Ontology of Language', trans. Robert J. Dostal, in Dostal, *The Cambridge Companion to Gadamer*, 110–11.

108 Gadamer, 'Hermeneutics on the Trail', 194.

109 Grondin, *The Philosophy of Gadamer*, 148.

110 Grondin, *The Philosophy of Gadamer*, 148.

111 I would like to acknowledge Nicholas Davey for drawing my attention to this relationship between circularity and repetition.

112 Gadamer, *Truth and Method*, 407.

113 Heidegger, *Ontology*.

114 Gadamer, 'On the Problem of Self Understanding', 49.

115 Gadamer, 'On the Problem of Self Understanding', 49.

116 Gadamer, 'On the Problem of Self Understanding', 50.

117 Gadamer, 'On the Problem of Self Understanding', 50.

118 It should be noted that the *Augenblick* does not originate with Heidegger, it is an idea that he adopts primarily from Nietzsche.

119 Dostal argues, in 'The Experience of Truth for Gadamer and Heidegger', that there is a tension between Heidegger's account of truth and Gadamer's: one is immediate and the other is mediated, one occurs in a momentary flash of revelation and the other is worked out conversationally (see Dostal, 'The Experience of Truth for Gadamer and Heidegger', 48–9). But although there are differences in the way each develops

their account of truth, Dostal's identification of a significant tension between the two is overstated, even Dostal significantly moderates and qualifies his own claim in the course of his discussion. Dostal devotes significant attention to the contrast between the staying with things that occur in conversation ('lingering' or 'tarrying') – in German *Verweilen* – as characteristic of Gadamer's account and contrasts this with Heidegger's emphasis on the 'authentic moment' (the *Augenblick*). Dostal acknowledges that *Verweilen* also appears in *Being and Time*, but claims that it 'drops out almost entirely from Heidegger's writing' (see Dostal, 'The Experience of Truth for Gadamer and Heidegger', 63). Arguably, however, what is at issue in *Verweilen* does not disappear from Heidegger's work at all, being instead taken up in the later discussions of 'dwelling' (*Wohnen*), and also in the idea of 'abode' or 'dwelling-place' (*Aufenthalt*). Significantly, Heidegger's discussion of *Verweilen* in *Being and Time* does not reduce 'the moment' (*Augenblick*) to merely a temporal 'flash', but connects it to *Verweilen* and to *Aufenthalt*. In a key passage that Dostal appears to ignore, Heidegger writes that 'through the awaiting which leaps after . . . the making-present is abandoned more and more to itself. It makes present for the sake of the Present. It thus entangles itself in itself, so that the distracted not-tarrying [*Unverweilen*] becomes *never-dwelling-anywhere* [*Aufenthaltlosigkeit*]. This latter mode of the Present is the counter-phenomenon at the opposite extreme from the *moment of vision*. In never dwelling anywhere, Being-there is everywhere and nowhere. The moment *of vision* [*Augenblick*], however, brings existence into the Situation and discloses the authentic "there"' – see *Being and Time*, 398. The 'being there' in the situation that is central here is something revealed in a 'moment', but what is revealed is not restricted merely to a moment.

Chapter 6

1 Martin Heidegger, *Discourse on Thinking*, trans. John M. Anderson and E. Hans Freund (New York: Harper & Row, 1966).

2 Gadamer, 'From Word to Concept: The Task of Hermeneutics as Philosophy', in *The Gadamer Reader*, 108–22.

3 See Husserl, *The Crisis of European Sciences and Transcendental Phenomenology*.

4 Gadamer, 'From Word to Concept', 119.

5 Heidegger, *Discourse on Thinking*, 56.

6 Gadamer, 'From Word to Concept', 119.

7 Ingo Farin, 'Heidegger: Transformation of Hermeneutics', in *The Routledge Companion to Hermeneutics*, ed. Malpas and Gander, 120.

8 Gadamer, 'Reflections on my Philosophical Journey'.

9   Plato, *Statesman*, ed. and trans. C. J. Rowe (Warminster: Aris and Phillips LTD, 1995).

10 Plato, *Statesman*, 103.

11 Plato, *Statesman*, 103.

12 Miguel de Beistegui, *The New Heidegger* (London: Continuum, 2005), 125.

13 Luigi Pareyson, 'The Necessity of Philosophy', in *Truth and Interpretation*, trans. Robert T. Valgenti, rev. and ed. Silvia Benso (Albany: State University of New York Press, 2013), 168–9.

14 Pareyson, 'The Necessity of Philosophy', 169.

15 Gadamer, 'The Universality of the Hermeneutical Problem', 11.

16 Heidegger, 'The Origin of the Work of Art'.

17 Pareyson, 'The Necessity of Philosophy', 174.

18 Julian Young, *Heidegger's Philosophy of Art* (Cambridge: Cambridge University Press, 2004), 11.

19 Young, *Heidegger's Philosophy of Art*, 11.

20 Bruce Pascoe, *The Little Red Yellow Black Book: An Introduction to Indigenous Australia* (Canberra: Aboriginal Studies Press, 2008), 10.

21 Pascoe, *The Little Red Yellow Black Book*, 10.

22 Fiona Magowan, *Melodies of Mourning: Music and Emotion in Northern Australia* (Crawley: University of Western Australia Press, 2007), 15.

23 Pareyson, 'The Necessity of Philosophy', 171.

24 Gadamer, *Truth and Method*, 322.

25 Davey, *Unquiet Understanding*, 12.

26 Martin Heidegger, 'Letter on Humanism', in *Basic Writings*, ed. David Farrell Krell (New York: HarperCollins, 1993), 258.

27 Dennis J. Schmidt, 'Hermeneutics as Original Ethics', in *Difficulties of Ethical Life*, ed. Shannon Sullivan and Dennis J. Schmidt (New York: Fordham University Press, 2008), 36.

28 Schmidt, 'Hermeneutics as Original Ethics', 36.

29 Schmidt, 'Hermeneutics as Original Ethics', 42.

30 Gadamer, *Truth and Method*, 332.

31 The idea of 'seeing' here is not meant to refer explicitly to visual perception but is rather, in response to Gadamer's idea of 'blindness', a placeholder for the *awareness* that guides one's attending and responding to the situation.

32 Gadamer, *Truth and Method*, 324.

33 Grondin, *The Philosophy of Gadamer*, 106.

34 Andrew Bowie discusses improvisation and rule-following in *Philosophical Variations: Music as 'Philosophical Language'* (Malmö: NSU Press, 2010), 59–69.

35 Wittgenstein, *Philosophical Investigations*, 39–40.

36 Heidegger, 'Letter on Humanism', 258.

37 Heraclitus, quoted in Heidegger, 'Letter on Humanism', 257.

38 Georgia Warnke, 'Hermeneutics, Ethics, and Politics', in *The Cambridge Companion to Gadamer*, ed. Dostal, 79.

39 Heidegger, *What is Called Thinking?*, 244.

40 Heidegger, *What is Called Thinking?*, 234.

41 Heidegger, 'Letter on Humanism', 258.

42 Dennis J. Schmidt, 'Hermeneutics and Ethical Life: On the Return to Factical Life', in *The Blackwell Companion to Hermeneutics*, ed. Keane and Lawn, 66.

43 Heidegger, 'The Thing', 177.

44 Heidegger, 'The Thing', 177.

45 Heidegger, 'Building Dwelling Thinking', 147.

46 Benson, 'Taking Responsibility by Letting Go', 94.

47 Heidegger, '…Poetically Man Dwells…', in *Poetry, Language, Thought*, 226; Jeff Malpas, *Rethinking Dwelling: Heidegger, Place, Architecture* (London: Bloomsbury, 2021), chap. 2.

48 Malpas, *Rethinking Dwelling*, chap. 2.

49 Heidegger, '…Poetically Man Dwells…', 227.

50 Heidegger, 'Building Dwelling Thinking', 145.

51 Heidegger, 'Building Dwelling Thinking', 159.

52 Warnke, 'Hermeneutics, Ethics, and Politics', 86.

53 Gadamer, *Truth and Method*, 328.

54 Gadamer, *Truth and Method*, 332.

55 Gadamer, *Truth and Method*, 332.

56 Warnke, 'Hermeneutics, Ethics, and Politics', 100.

57 Gadamer, 'From Word to Concept', 120.

58 Gadamer, *Truth and Method*, 19–21,

59 Gadamer, 'Hermeneutics as Practical Philosophy', 227–45.

60 Schmidt, 'Hermeneutics and Ethical Life', 68.

61 Martin Heidegger, *Parmenides*, trans. André Schuwer and Richard Rojcewicz (Bloomington: Indiana University Press, 1992), 149.

62 Heidegger, *Parmenides*, 149.

63 Schmidt, 'Hermeneutics and Ethical Life', 71.

Coda

1 Grouper, 'Headache', track 1 on *Paradise Valley*, Yellow Electric – GR-015, 2016, LP.

2 In the introduction to *Truth and Method* Gadamer writes, 'it is not my intention to make prescriptions for the sciences or the conduct of life, but to try to correct false thinking about what they are' – *Truth and Method*, xxii.

3 Hans-Georg Gadamer, 'The Relevance of the Beautiful', in *The Relevance of the Beautiful and Other Essays*, trans. Nicholas Walker, ed. Robert Bernasconi (Cambridge: Cambridge University Press, 1998), 12.

4 Babette Babich, *The Hallelujah Effect: Philosophical Reflections on Music, Performance Practice, and Technology* (Surrey: Ashgate, 2013), 170.

5 Benson, *Liturgy as a Way of Life*, 34.

6 Ludwig Wittgenstein, *Culture and Value*, ed. Georg Henrik von Wright in collaboration with Heikki Nyman, trans. Peter Winch (Oxford: Blackwell, 1998), 42.

7 That art might offer ways of responding to philosophical questions, or that it is paradigmatic of human experience and therefore of central concern to those seeking to understand human nature, is increasingly being taken up by philosophers. For example, see Benson, *Liturgy as a Way of Life*; Andrew Bowie, *Music, Philosophy, and Modernity* (Cambridge: Cambridge University Press, 2007); Johnson, *The Aesthetics of Meaning and Thought*; Alva Noë, *Strange Tools: Art and Human Nature* (New York: Hill and Wang, 2015); Santiago Zabala, *Why Only Art Can Save Us: Aesthetics and the Absence of Emergency* (New York: Columbia University Press, 2017).

8 Gadamer, 'The Artwork in Word and Image: "So True, So Full of Being!"', in *The Gadamer Reader*, 201.

9 Friedrich Nietzsche, *The Gay Science: With a Prelude in German Rhymes and an Appendix of Songs*, ed. Bernard Williams, trans. Josefine Nauckhoff (Cambridge: Cambridge University Press, 2007), 120.

10 Heidegger, 'The Nature of Language', 74.

11 Nietzsche, quoted in Heidegger, 'The Nature of Language', 74. The quote from Nietzsche is from *The Will to Power*, ed. Walter Kaufmann, trans. Walter Kaufmann and R. J. Hollingdale (New York: Vintage Books, 1968), 261.

12 Heidegger, 'The Nature of Language', 74.

13 Gadamer, 'From Word to Concept', 120.

14 Gadamer, 'From Word to Concept', 120.

15 On the relationship between religion and aesthetics in Heidegger's and Gadamer's thinking, see Davey, 'Art, Religion, and the Hermeneutics of Authenticity', in *Performance and Authenticity in the Arts*, ed. Salim Kemal and Ivan Gaskell (Cambridge: Cambridge University Press, 1999), 66–94.

16 Heidegger, 'The Nature of Language', 57.

17 This is not the place to hypothesize as to why Heidegger in particular wrote so little about music. However, both Young and Bowie have offered thoughts on the matter. See Young, *Heidegger's Philosophy of Art*, 168–70; Bowie, *Music, Philosophy, and Modernity*, 302–3.

18 See Malpas, *Heidegger and the Thinking of Place*, 255–6.

19 Gadamer, *Gadamer in Conversation*, 71.

20 Heidegger, 'The Nature of Language', 75.

21 Gadamer, *Truth and Method*, 147.

22 Gadamer, *Truth and Method*, 147–8.

23 Gadamer, *Truth and Method*, 147.

24 Lawrence Kramer, *Expression and Truth: On the Music of Knowledge* (Berkeley: University of California Press, 2012), 21.

25 Gadamer, *Truth and Method*, 123–4.

26 Gadamer, *Truth and Method*, 160.

27 Dennis J. Schmidt, 'Keeping Pace with the Movement of Life: On Words and Music', *Research in Phenomenology* 43, no. 2 (2013): 194.

28 Friedrich Nietzsche, *The Birth of Tragedy and Other Writings*, ed. Raymond Geuss and Ronald Speirs, trans. Ronald Speirs (Cambridge: Cambridge University Press, 2007), 36.

29 Dennis J. Schmidt, *Lyrical and Ethical Subjects: Essays on the Periphery of the Word, Freedom, and History* (Albany: State University of New York Press, 2005), 13.

30 Schmidt, *Lyrical and Ethical Subjects*, 13–14.

31 Hans-Georg Gadamer, 'The Way in the Turn', in *Heidegger's Ways*, trans. John W. Stanley (Albany: State University of New York Press, 1994), 137.

32 Gadamer, 'The Way in the Turn', 137.
33 Simon Critchley, *Things Merely Are: Philosophy in the Poetry of Wallace Stevens* (London: Routledge, 2005), 74.
34 Heidegger, 'The Nature of Language', 75.
35 Heidegger, 'The Way to Language', in *On the Way to Language*, 123–4.
36 Heidegger, 'The Nature of Language', 77.
37 Plato, *The Republic*, trans. C. D. C. Reeve (Indianapolis: Hackett, 2004), 401d.
38 Bowie, *Music, Philosophy, and Modernity*, 294.
39 Nietzsche, *The Birth of Tragedy and Other Writings*, 6.
40 Heidegger, 'The Nature of Language', 88.
41 Bowie, *Music, Philosophy, and Modernity*, 304.
42 Schmidt, 'Keeping Pace with the Movement of Life'.
43 For a discussion of Heidegger's destruction of metaphysics, see Santiago Zabala, *The Remains of Being: Hermeneutic Ontology after Metaphysics* (New York: Columbia University Press, 2009), chap. 1.
44 Friedrich Hölderlin, 'Celebration of Peace', in *Selected Poems and Fragments*, trans. Michael Hamburger, ed. Jeremy Adler (London: Penguin Books, 1998), 215.
45 Martin Heidegger, *The Principle of Reason*, trans. Reginald Lilly (Bloomington: Indiana University Press, 1991), 89.
46 Heidegger, *The Principle of Reason*, 89.
47 Martin Heidegger and Eugen Fink, *Heraclitus Seminar*, trans. Charles H. Seibert (Alabama: The University of Alabama Press, 1979), 55.
48 Heidegger and Fink, *Heraclitus Seminar*, 55.
49 Schmidt notes a certain 'musical dissonance' in Heidegger's thought. While the way in which I am employing the term 'dissonance' here is not identical to the way in which Schmidt employs it, my deployment of this terminology was inspired by Schmidt's account. See Schmidt, *Lyrical and Ethical Subjects*, 73–5.

Bibliography

Arendt, Hannah. *The Life of the Mind*. Vol. 1. San Diego: Harcourt, 1978.
Augoyard, Jean-François, and Henry Torgue, eds. *Sonic Experience: A Guide to Everyday Sounds*. Translated by Andra McCartney and David Paquette. London: McGill-Queen's University Press, 2005.
Augustine. *On the Trinity: Books 8–15*. Edited by Gareth B. Matthews. Translated by Stephen McKenna. Cambridge: Cambridge University Press, 2002.
Babich, Babette. *The Hallelujah Effect: Philosophical Reflections on Music, Performance Practice, and Technology*. Surrey: Ashgate, 2013.
Bailey, Derek. *Improvisation: Its Nature and Practice in Music*. New York: Da Capo Press, 1993.
Benson, Bruce Ellis. 'Creatio ex improvisatione: Chrétien on the Call'. In *Music and Transcendence*, edited by Férdia J. Stone-Davis, 49–64. London: Routledge, 2016.
Benson, Bruce Ellis. 'Improvisation'. In *The Oxford Handbook of Western Music and Philosophy*, edited by Tomás McAuley, Nanette Nielsen, and Jerrold Levinson, with Ariana Phillips-Hutton, associate editor, 437–50. New York: Oxford University Press, 2021.
Benson, Bruce Ellis. 'The Improvisation of Hermeneutics: Jazz Lessons for Interpreters'. In *Hermeneutics at the Crossroads*, edited by Keven J. Vanhoozer, James K. A. Smith, and Bruce Ellis Benson, 193–210. Bloomington: Indiana University Press, 2006.
Benson, Bruce Ellis. *The Improvisation of Musical Dialogue: A Phenomenology of Music*. New York: Cambridge University Press, 2003.
Benson, Bruce Ellis. 'Indeterminacy, Gadamer, and Jazz'. In *The Significance of Indeterminacy: Perspectives from Asian and Continental Philosophy*, edited by Robert H. Scott and Gregory S. Moss, 215–27. New York: Routledge, 2019.
Benson, Bruce Ellis. *Liturgy as a Way of Life: Embodying the Arts in Christian Worship*. Grand Rapids: Baker, 2013.
Benson, Bruce Ellis. 'Taking Responsibility by Letting Go: The Improvisation of Responding to the Call'. In *Philosophy of Improvisation: Interdisciplinary Perspectives on Theory and Practice*, edited by Susanne Ravn, Simon Høffding, and James McGuirk, 87–100. New York: Routledge, 2021.
Bergson, Henri. *Time and Free Will: An Essay on the Immediate Data of Consciousness*. Translated by F. L. Pogson. Mineola: Dover, 2001.
Berliner, Paul F. *Thinking in Jazz: The Infinite Art of Improvisation*. Chicago: The University of Chicago Press, 1994.

Bertinetto, Alessandro, and Marcello Ruta, eds. *The Routledge Handbook of Philosophy and Improvisation in the Arts*. New York: Routledge, 2021.

Borgo, David. 'Openness from Closure: The Puzzle of Interagency in Improvised Music and a Neocybernetic Solution'. In *Negotiated Moments: Improvisation, Sound, and Subjectivity*, edited by Gillian Siddall and Ellen Waterman, 113–30. Durham: Duke University Press, 2016.

Borgo, David. 'What the Music Wants'. In *Soundweaving: Writings on Improvisation*, edited by Franziska Schroder and Micheál Ó hAodha, 33–52. Newcastle: Cambridge Scholars, 2014.

Born, Georgina. 'Introduction'. In *Music, Sound and Space: Transformations of Public and Private Experience*, edited by Georgina Born, 1–70. Cambridge: Cambridge University Press, 2013.

Born, Georgina, Eric Lewis, and Will Straw. *Improvisation and Social Aesthetics*. Durham: Duke University Press, 2017.

Bowie, Andrew. *Music, Philosophy, and Modernity*. Cambridge: Cambridge University Press, 2007.

Bowie, Andrew. *Philosophical Variations: Music as 'Philosophical Language'*. Malmö: NSU Press, 2010.

Brown, Lee B., David Goldblatt, and Theodore Gracyk. *Jazz and the Philosophy of Art*. New York: Routledge, 2018.

Campbell, Edward. *Music after Deleuze*. London: Bloomsbury, 2013.

Casey, Edward S. 'Between Geography and Philosophy: What Does It Mean to Be in the Place-World?' *Annals of the Association of American Geographers* 91, no. 4 (2001): 683–93.

Casey, Edward S. *The Fate of Place: A Philosophical History*. Berkeley: University of California Press, 1998.

Casey, Edward S. 'How to Get from Space to Place in a Fairly Short Stretch of Time: Phenomenological Prolegomena'. In *Senses of Place*, edited by Steven Feld and Keith H. Basso, 13–52. Santa Fe, NM: School of American Research Press, 1996.

Casey, Edward S. *Remembering: A Phenomenological Study*. 2nd edn. Bloomington: Indiana University Press, 2000.

Clark, Andy, and David J. Chalmers. 'The Extended Mind'. *Analysis* 58, no. 1 (1998): 7–19.

Cox, Christoph. 'From Music to Sound: Being as Time in the Sonic Arts'. In *Sound: Documents of Contemporary Art*, edited by Caleb Kelly, 80–7. London: Whitechapel Gallery and the MIT Press, 2011.

Critchley, Simon. *Things Merely Are: Philosophy in the Poetry of Wallace Stevens*. London: Routledge, 2005.

da Fonseca-Wollheim, Corinna. 'WEEKEND JOURNAL; Leisure & Arts – Masterpiece: A Jazz Night to Remember; The Unique Magic of Keith Jarrett's "The Koeln Concert"'. *Wall Street Journal*, Eastern ed. October 11, 2008.

Dahlstrom, Daniel. 'Language and Meaning'. In *The Routledge Companion to Hermeneutics*, edited by Jeff Malpas and Hans-Helmuth Gander, 277–86. London: Routledge, 2015.

Dahlstrom, Daniel. 'Martin Heidegger'. In *The Routledge Companion to Phenomenology*, edited by Sebastian Luft and Søren Overgaard, 50–61. London: Routledge, 2012.

Dainton, Barry. 'Temporal Consciousness'. In *Stanford Encyclopedia of Philosophy*. Article published August 6, 2010; last modified June 28, 2017. https://plato.stanford.edu/entries/consciousness-temporal/ (Accessed 27 June 2019).

Davey, Nicholas. 'Art, Religion, and the Hermeneutics of Authenticity'. In *Performance and Authenticity in the Arts*, edited by Salim Kemal and Ivan Gaskell, 66–94. Cambridge: Cambridge University Press, 1999.

Davey, Nicholas. 'Dialogue, Dialectic and Conversation'. In *The Gadamerian Mind*, edited by Theodore George and Gert-Jan van der Heiden, 61–77. London: Routledge, 2021.

Davey, Nicholas. 'In Between Word and Image: Philosophical Hermeneutics, Aesthetics and the Inescapable Heritage of Kant'. In *Critical Communities and Aesthetic Practices: Dialogues with Tony O'Connor on Society, Art, and Friendship*, edited by Francis Halsall, Julia Jansen, and Sinéad Murphy, 23–36. Dordrecht: Springer, 2012.

Davey, Nicholas. 'Twentieth-Century Hermeneutics'. In *The Routledge Companion to Twentieth-Century Philosophy*, edited by Dermot Moran, 693–735. Abingdon: Routledge, 2008.

Davey, Nicholas. *Unfinished Worlds: Hermeneutics, Aesthetics and Gadamer*. Edinburgh: Edinburgh University Press, 2013.

Davey, Nicholas. *Unquiet Understanding: Gadamer's Philosophical Hermeneutics*. Albany: State University of New York Press, 2006.

Davidson, Donald. 'Three Varieties of Knowledge'. In *A. J. Ayer Memorial Essays: Royal Institute of Philosophy Supplement: 30*, edited by A. Phillips Griffiths, 153–66. Cambridge: Cambridge University Press, 1991.

Davidson, Donald. *Truth, Language, and History*. Oxford: Clarendon Press, 2005.

de Beistegui, Miguel. *The New Heidegger*. London: Continuum, 2005.

Dia. 'Max Neuhaus: Times Square, 1977'. https://www.diaart.org/media/_file/webpdfs/neuhaus-brochure-3-to-printer.pdf (Accessed 11 August 2021).

DiPiero, Dan. 'Improvisation as Contingent Encounter, Or: The Song of My Toothbrush'. *Critical Studies in Improvisation/Études critiques en improvisation* 12, no. 2 (2018). DOI: https://doi.org/10.21083/csieci.v12i2.4261.

Dostal, Robert J., ed. *The Cambridge Companion to Gadamer*. Cambridge: Cambridge University Press, 2002.

Dostal, Robert J. 'The Experience of Truth for Gadamer and Heidegger: Taking Time and Sudden Lightning'. In *Hermeneutics and Truth*, edited by Brice R. Wachterhauser, 47–67. Evanston: Northwestern University Press, 1994.

Dufrenne, Mikel. *The Phenomenology of Aesthetic Experience*. Translated by Edward S. Casey, Albert A. Anderson, Willis Domingo, and Leon Jacobson. Evanston: Northwestern University Press, 1973.

Elsdon, Peter. *Keith Jarrett's The Koln Concert*. Oxford: Oxford University Press, 2013.

Erlmann, Veit. *Reason and Resonance: A History of Modern Aurality*. New York: Zone Books, 2010.

Fairfield, Paul. 'Hermeneutics and Education'. In *The Routledge Companion to Hermeneutics*, edited by Jeff Malpas and Hans-Helmuth Gander, 541–9. London: Routledge, 2015.

Farin, Ingo. 'Heidegger: Transformation of Hermeneutics'. In *The Routledge Companion to Hermeneutics*, edited by Jeff Malpas and Hans-Helmuth Gander, 107–26. London: Routledge, 2015.

Figal, Günter. 'The Doing of the Thing Itself: Gadamer's Hermeneutic Ontology of Language'. Translated by Robert J. Dostal. In *The Cambridge Companion to Gadamer*, edited by Robert J. Dostal, 102–25. Cambridge: Cambridge University Press, 2002.

Figal, Günter. *Objectivity: The Hermeneutical and Philosophy*. Translated by Theodore D. George. New York: State University of New York Press, 2010.

Fischlin, Daniel. '(Call and) Responsibility: Improvisation, Ethics, Co-creation'. In *The Improvisation Studies Reader: Spontaneous Acts*, edited by Rebecca Caines and Ajay Heble, 289–95. London: Routledge, 2015.

Gadamer, Hans-Georg. *Gadamer in Conversation: Reflections and Commentary*. Edited and translated by Richard E. Palmer. New Haven: Yale University Press, 2001.

Gadamer, Hans-Georg. *The Gadamer Reader: A Bouquet of the Later Writings*. Edited and translated by Richard E. Palmer. Evanston: Northwestern University Press, 2007.

Gadamer, Hans-Georg. *Gesammelte Werke 1: Hermeneutik I: Wahrheit und Methode: Grundzüge einer philosophischen Hermeneutik*. Tübingen: Mohr Siebeck, 1990.

Gadamer, Hans-Georg. *Heidegger's Ways*. Translated by John W. Stanley. Albany: State University of New York Press, 1994.

Gadamer, Hans-Georg. *Hermeneutics between History and Philosophy*. Edited and translated by Pol Vandevelde and Arun Iyer. London: Bloomsbury, 2019.

Gadamer, Hans-Georg. *Philosophical Hermeneutics*. Translated and edited by David E. Linge. Berkeley: University of California Press, 2008.

Gadamer, Hans-Georg. *Plato's Dialectical Ethics: Phenomenological Interpretations Relating to the Philebus*. Translated by Robert M. Wallace. New Haven: Yale University Press, 1991.

Gadamer, Hans-Georg. 'Praise of Theory'. In *Praise of Theory: Speeches and Essays*. Translated by Chris Dawson, 16–36. New Haven: Yale University Press, 1998.

Gadamer, Hans-Georg. 'Reflections on My Philosophical Journey'. In *The Philosophy of Hans-Georg Gadamer*, edited by Lewis Edwin Hahn, 3–63. Chicago: Open Court, 1997.

Gadamer, Hans-Georg. *The Relevance of the Beautiful and Other Essays*. Translated by Nicholas Walker. Edited by Robert Bernasconi. Cambridge: Cambridge University Press, 1998.

Gadamer, Hans-Georg. *Truth and Method*. Translated by Joel Weinsheimer and Donald G. Marshall. London: Bloomsbury, 2013.

Gallagher, Shaun. 'Body Schema and Intentionality'. In *The Body and the Self*, edited by José Luis Bermúdez, Anthony Marcel, and Naomi Eilan, 225–44. Cambridge: The MIT Press, 2001.

Gallagher, Shaun. *Enactivist Interventions: Rethinking the Mind*. Oxford: Oxford University Press, 2017.

Gander, Hans-Helmuth. 'Gadamer: The Universality of Hermeneutics'. In *The Routledge Companion to Hermeneutics*, edited by Jeff Malpas and Hans-Helmuth Gander, 137–48. London: Routledge, 2015.

Goehr, Lydia. *The Imaginary Museum of Musical Works: An Essay in the Philosophy of Music*. New York: Oxford University Press, 2007.

Gonzalez, Francisco. 'Hermeneutics in Greek Philosophy'. In *The Routledge Companion to Hermeneutics*, edited by Jeff Malpas and Hans-Helmuth Gander, 13–22. London: Routledge, 2015.

Gould, Carol S., and Kenneth Keaton. 'The Essential Role of Improvisation in Musical Performance'. *The Journal of Aesthetics and Art Criticism* 58, no. 2 (2000): 143–8.

Grondin, Jean. 'The Hermeneutic Circle'. In *The Blackwell Companion to Hermeneutics*, edited by Niall Keane and Chris Lawn, 299–305. Chichester: Wiley Blackwell, 2016.

Grondin, Jean. *Introduction to Philosophical Hermeneutics*. Translated by Joel Weinsheimer. New Haven: Yale University Press, 1994.

Grondin, Jean. *The Philosophy of Gadamer*. Translated by Kathryn Plant. Chesham: Acumen, 2003.

Hagberg, Garry. 'Ensemble Improvisation, Collective Intention, and Group Attention'. In *The Oxford Handbook of Critical Improvisation Studies*. Vol. 1, edited by George E. Lewis and Benjamin Piekut. New York: Oxford University Press, 2013. DOI: 10.1093/oxfordhb/9780195370935.013.011.

Hamilton, Andy. 'The Art of Improvisation and the Aesthetics of Imperfection'. *British Journal of Aesthetics* 40, no. 1 (2000): 168–85.

Heidegger, Martin. *Basic Problems of Phenomenology*. Translated by Albert Hofstadter. Bloomington: Indiana University Press, 1982.

Heidegger, Martin. *Basic Writings*. Edited by David Farrell Krell. New York: HarperCollins, 1993.

Heidegger, Martin. *Being and Time*. Translated by John Macquarrie and Edward Robinson. New York: Harper & Row, 2008.

Heidegger, Martin. *Contributions to Philosophy (Of the Event)*. Translated by Richard Rojcewicz and Daniela Vallega-Neu. Bloomington: Indiana University Press, 2012.

Heidegger, Martin. *Discourse on Thinking*. Translated by John M. Anderson and E. Hans Freund. New York: Harper & Row, 1966.

Heidegger, Martin. *Identity and Difference*. Translated by Joan Stambaugh. New York: Harper & Row, 1969.

Heidegger, Martin. *Logic: The Question of Truth*. Translated by Thomas Sheehan. Bloomington: Indiana University Press, 2010.

Heidegger, Martin. *On the Way to Language*. Translated by Peter D. Hertz. New York: Harper & Row, 1982.

Heidegger, Martin. *Ontology: The Hermeneutics of Facticity*. Translated by John van Buren. Bloomington: Indiana University Press, 1999.

Heidegger, Martin. *Parmenides*. Translated by André Schuwer and Richard Rojcewicz. Bloomington: Indiana University Press, 1992.

Heidegger, Martin. *Poetry, Language, Thought*. Translated by Albert Hofstadter. New York: Harper Perennial, 2013.

Heidegger, Martin. *The Principle of Reason*. Translated by Reginald Lilly. Bloomington: Indiana University Press, 1991.

Heidegger, Martin. *The Question Concerning Technology and Other Essays*. Translated by William Lovitt. New York: Garland, 1977.

Heidegger, Martin. *What is Called Thinking?* Translated by J. Glenn Gray. New York: Harper & Row, 2004.

Heidegger, Martin, and Eugen Fink. Heraclitus Seminar. Translated by Charles H. Seibert. Alabama: The University of Alabama Press, 1979.

Hölderlin, Friedrich. *Selected Poems and Fragments*. Translated by Michael Hamburger. Edited by Jeremy Adler. London: Penguin Books, 1998.

Husserl, Edmund. *The Crisis of European Sciences and Transcendental Phenomenology*. Translated by David Carr. Evanston: Northwestern University Press, 1978.

Husserl, Edmund. *The Phenomenology of Internal Time-Consciousness*. Edited by Martin Heidegger. Translated by James S. Churchill. Bloomington: Indiana University Press, 2019.

Hutto, Daniel D., and Erik Myin. *Radicalizing Enactivism: Basic Minds without Content*. Cambridge: The MIT Press, 2013.

Ihde, Don. *Listening and Voice: Phenomenologies of Sound*. 2nd edn. Albany: State University of New York Press, 2007.

Johnson, Mark. *The Aesthetics of Meaning and Thought: The Bodily Roots of Philosophy, Science, Morality, and Art*. Chicago: The University of Chicago Press, 2018.

Johnson, Mark. *Embodied Mind, Meaning, and Reason: How Our Bodies Give Rise to Understanding*. Chicago: The University of Chicago Press, 2017.

Jones, Gayl. *Corregidora*. Boston: Beacon Press, 1975.

Keane, Niall, and Chris Lawn, eds. *The Blackwell Companion to Hermeneutics*. Chichester: Wiley Blackwell, 2016.

Krajewski, Bruce, ed. *Gadamer's Repercussions: Reconsidering Philosophical Hermeneutics*. Berkeley: University of California Press, 2004.

Kramer, Lawrence. *Expression and Truth: On the Music of Knowledge*. Berkeley: University of California Press, 2012.

Kuhn, Thomas S. *The Structure of Scientific Revolutions*. 3rd edn. Chicago: The University of Chicago Press, 1996.

Lawn, Chris, and Niall Keane. *The Gadamer Dictionary*. London: Continuum, 2011.

Lewis, Eric. *Intents and Purposes: Philosophy and the Aesthetics of Improvisation*. Ann Arbor: University of Michigan Press, 2019.

Lewis, George E. *A Power Stronger Than Itself: The AACM and American Experimental Music*. Chicago: The University of Chicago Press, 2008.

Lewis, George E., and Benjamin Piekut, eds. *The Oxford Handbook of Critical Improvisation Studies*. Vols. 1 and 2. New York: Oxford University Press, 2013. DOI: 10.1093/oxfordhb/9780195370935.001.0001.

Lewis, George E., and Benjamin Piekut. 'Introduction: On Critical Improvisation Studies'. In *The Oxford Handbook of Critical Improvisation Studies*. Vol. 1, edited by George E. Lewis and Benjamin Piekut. New York: Oxford University Press, 2013. DOI: 10.1093/oxfordhb/9780195370935.013.30.

Mäcklin, Harri. 'Going Elsewhere: A Phenomenology of Aesthetic Immersion'. PhD diss., University of Helsinki, 2018. https://helda.helsinki.fi/handle/10138/271647 (Accessed 26 November 2020).

Magowan, Fiona. *Melodies of Mourning: Music and Emotion in Northern Australia*. Crawley: University of Western Australia Press, 2007.

Makkreel, Rudolf A. *Orientation and Judgment in Hermeneutics*. Chicago: The University of Chicago Press, 2015.

Malpas, Jeff. 'The Beckoning of Language: Heidegger's Hermeneutic Transformation of Thinking'. In *Hermeneutical Heidegger*, edited by Michael Bowler and Ingo Farin, 203–21. Evanston: Northwestern University Press, 2016.

Malpas, Jeff. *Heidegger and the Thinking of Place: Explorations in the Topology of Being.* Cambridge: The MIT Press, 2012.

Malpas, Jeff. *Heidegger's Topology: Being, Place, World.* Cambridge: The MIT Press, 2006.

Malpas, Jeff. 'The Multivocity of Human Rights Discourse'. In *The Aporia of Rights: Explorations in Citizenship in the era of Human Rights*, edited by Anna Yeatman and Peg Birmingham, 37–52. New York: Bloomsbury, 2014.

Malpas, Jeff. *Place and Experience: A Philosophical Topography.* 2nd ed. New York: Routledge, 2018.

Malpas, Jeff. 'Place and Situation'. In *The Routledge Companion to Hermeneutics*, edited by Jeff Malpas and Hans-Helmuth Gander, 354–66. London: Routledge, 2015.

Malpas, Jeff. 'Placing Understanding/Understanding Place'. *Sophia* 56, no. 3 (2017): 379–91.

Malpas, Jeff. *Rethinking Dwelling: Heidegger, Place, Architecture.* London: Bloomsbury, 2021.

Malpas, Jeff. 'The Threshold of the World'. In *Funktionen des Lebendigen*, edited by Thiemo Breyer and Oliver Müller, 161–8. Berlin: De Gruyter, 2016.

Malpas, Jeff. 'Timing Space – Spacing Time'. In *Performance and Temporalisation: Time Happens*, edited by Stuart Grant, Jodie McNeilly, and Maeva Veerapen, 25–36. Hampshire: Palgrave Macmillan, 2015.

Malpas, Jeff. 'The Transcendental Circle'. *Australasian Journal of Philosophy* 75, no. 1 (1997): 1–20.

Malpas, Jeff. 'The Twofold Character of Truth: Heidegger, Davidson, Tugendhat'. In *The Multidimensionality of Hermeneutic Phenomenology*, edited by Babette Babich and Dimitri Ginev, 243–66. Cham: Springer, 2014.

Malpas, Jeff, and Hans-Helmuth Gander, eds. *The Routledge Companion to Hermeneutics.* London: Routledge, 2015.

Malpas, Jeff, and Santiago Zabala, eds. *Consequences of Hermeneutics: Fifty Years After Gadamer's Truth and Method.* Evanston: Northwestern University Press, 2010.

Massey, Doreen. 'Politics and Space/Time'. In *Place and the Politics of Identity*, edited by Michael Keith and Steve Pile, 139–59. London: Routledge, 1993.

McAuliffe, Sam, and Jeff Malpas. 'Improvising the Round Dance of Being: Reading Heidegger from a Musical Perspective'. In *Heidegger and Music*, edited by Casey Rentmeester and Jeff R. Warren, 163–78. Lanham: Rowman and Littlefield, 2022.

Monson, Ingrid. *Saying Something: Jazz Improvisation and Interaction.* Chicago: The University of Chicago Press, 1997.

Moran, Dermot. *Introduction to The Shorter Logical Investigations*, by Edmund Husserl. Translated by J. N. Findlay, xxv–lxxviii. London: Routledge, 2001.

Nancy, Jean-Luc. *Listening.* Translated by Charlotte Mandell. New York: Fordham University Press, 2007.

Neisser, Ulric. 'Nested Structure in Autobiographical Memory'. In *Autobiographical Memory*, edited by David C. Rubin, 71–81. Cambridge: Cambridge University Press, 1989.

Neuhaus, Max. 'Program Notes'. In *Sound Works, Volume I: Inscription.* Edited by Markus Hartman, 34. Ostfildern: Cantz, 1994.

Nielsen, Cynthia R. 'Gadamer on Play and the Play of Art'. In *The Gadamerian Mind*, edited by Theodore George and Gert-Jan van der Heiden, 139–54. London: Routledge, 2021.

Nielsen, Cynthia R. 'Gadamer on the Event of Art, the Other, and a Gesture Toward a Gadamarian Approach to Free Jazz'. *Journal of Applied Hermeneutics* (2016): 1–17.

Nielsen, Cynthia R. 'Harsh Poetry and Art's Address: Romare Bearden and Hans-Georg Gadamer'. *Estetyka i Krytyka: The Polish Journal of Aesthetics* 4 (2016): 101–22.

Nielsen, Cynthia R. 'Hearing the Other's Voice: How Gadamer's Fusion of Horizons and Open-ended Understanding Respects the Other and Puts Oneself in Question'. *Otherness: Essays and Studies* 4, no. 1 (2013): 1–25.

Nielsen, Cynthia R. *Interstitial Soundings: Philosophical Reflections on Improvisation, Practice, and Self-Making*. Eugene: Cascade Books, 2015.

Nietzsche, Friedrich. *The Birth of Tragedy and Other Writings*. Edited by Raymond Geuss and Ronald Speirs. Translated by Ronald Speirs. Cambridge: Cambridge University Press, 2007.

Nietzsche, Friedrich. *The Gay Science: With a Prelude in German Rhymes and an Appendix of Songs*. Edited by Bernard Williams. Translated by Josefine Nauckhoff. Cambridge: Cambridge University Press, 2007.

Nietzsche, Friedrich. *The Will to Power*. Edited by Walter Kaufmann. Translated by Walter Kaufmann and R. J. Hollingdale. New York: Vintage Books, 1968.

Noë, Alva. *Out of Our Heads: Why You Are Not Your Brain, and Other Lessons from the Biology of Consciousness*. New York: Hill and Wang, 2009.

Noë, Alva. *Strange Tools: Art and Human Nature*. New York: Hill and Wang, 2015.

Noë, Alva. *Varieties of Presence*. Cambridge: Harvard University Press, 2012.

O'Callaghan, Casey. *Sounds: A Philosophical Theory*. Oxford: Oxford University Press, 2007.

Onsman, Andrys, and Robert Burke. *Experimentation in Improvised Jazz: Chasing Ideas*. New York: Routledge, 2019.

Oxford English Dictionary. 3rd ed. s.v. 'situation'. https://www.oed.com/view/Entry/180520?redirectedFrom=situation& (Accessed 24 July 2020).

Pallasmaa, Juhani. 'Place and Atmosphere'. In *The Intelligence of Place: Topographies and Poetics*, edited by Jeff Malpas, 129–56. London: Bloomsbury, 2017.

Palmer, Richard E. *Hermeneutics: Interpretation Theory in Schleiermacher, Dilthey, Heidegger, and Gadamer*. Evanston: Northwestern University Press, 1988.

Pareyson, Luigi. *Truth and Interpretation*. Translated by Robert T. Valgenti. Revised and edited by Silvia Benso. Albany: State University of New York Press, 2013.

Pascoe, Bruce. *The Little Red Yellow Black Book: An Introduction to Indigenous Australia*. Canberra: Aboriginal Studies Press, 2008.

Pasler, Jann. 'Race, Orientalism, and Distinction in the Wake of the "Yellow Peril"'. In *Western Music and Its Others: Difference, Representation, and Appropriation in Music*, edited by Georgina Born and David Hesmondhalgh, 86–118. Berkeley: University of California Press, 2000.

Peters, Gary. 'Certainty, Contingency, and Improvisation'. *Critical Studies in Improvisation / Études critiques en improvisation* 8, no. 2 (2012). DOI: https://doi.org/10.21083/csieci.v8i2.2141.

Peters, Gary. 'Improvisation and Time-Consciousness'. In *The Oxford Handbook of Critical Improvisation Studies*. Vol. 1, edited by George E. Lewis and Benjamin Piekut. New York: Oxford University Press, 2013. DOI: 10.1093/oxfordhb/9780195370935.013.002.

Peters, Gary. 'It Gives: The There and the Given in Improvisation Space'. *Land2*. http://land2.leeds.ac.uk/symposia/spectral-traces/it-gives/ (Accessed 7 February 2018).
Peters, Gary. *The Philosophy of Improvisation*. Chicago: The University of Chicago Press, 2009.
Plato. *The Republic*. Translated by C. D. C. Reeve. Indianapolis: Hackett, 2004.
Plato. *Statesman*. Edited and translated by C. J. Rowe. Warminster: Aris and Phillips, 1995.
Puente-Lozano, Paloma. 'Jeff Malpas: From Hermeneutics to Topology'. In *Place, Space and Hermeneutics*, edited by Bruce B. Janz, 301–16. Cham: Springer, 2018.
Ravaisson, Félix. *Of Habit*. Translated by Clare Carlisle and Mark Sinclair. London: Continuum, 2008.
Ravn, Susanne, Simon Høffding, and James McGuirk, eds. *Philosophy of Improvisation: Interdisciplinary Perspectives on Theory and Practice*. London: Routledge, 2021.
Rice, Timothy. 'Reflections on Music and Identity in *Ethnomusicology*'. *Muzikologijas* 7 (2007): 17–38.
Risser, James. 'Gadamer's Hidden Doctrine: The Simplicity and Humility of Philosophy'. In *Consequences of Hermeneutics: Fifty Years After Gadamer's Truth and Method*, edited by Jeff Malpas and Santiago Zabala, 5–24. Chicago: Northwestern University Press, 2010.
Risser, James. 'Language and Alterity'. In *The Blackwell Companion to Hermeneutics*, edited by Niall Keane and Chris Lawn, 122–9. Chichester: Wiley Blackwell, 2016.
Said, Edward W. *Musical Elaborations*. New York: Columbia University Press, 1991.
Sarath, Edward. *Music Theory through Improvisation: A New Approach to Musicianship Training*. New York: Routledge, 2010.
Sawyer, Keith. 'Music and Conversation'. In *Musical Communication*, edited by Dorothy Miell, Raymond MacDonald, and David J. Hargreaves, 45–60. Oxford: Oxford University Press, 2005.
Schaeffer, Pierre. *Treatise on Musical Objects: An Essay across Disciplines*. Translated by Christine North and John Dack. Oakland: University of California Press, 2017.
Schmidt, Dennis J. 'Hermeneutics and Ethical Life: On the Return to Factical Life'. In *The Blackwell Companion to Hermeneutics*, edited by Niall Keane and Chris Lawn, 65–71. Chichester: Wiley Blackwell, 2016.
Schmidt, Dennis J. 'Hermeneutics as Original Ethics'. In *Difficulties of Ethical Life*, edited by Shannon Sullivan and Dennis J. Schmidt, 35–47. New York: Fordham University Press, 2008.
Schmidt, Dennis J. 'Keeping Pace with the Movement of Life: On Words and Music'. *Research in Phenomenology* 43, no. 2 (2013): 193–203.
Schmidt, Dennis J. *Lyrical and Ethical Subjects: Essays on the Periphery of the Word, Freedom, and History*. Albany: State University of New York Press, 2005.
Scholtz, Gunter. 'Ast and Schleiermacher: Hermeneutics and Critical Philosophy'. In *The Routledge Companion to Hermeneutics*, edited by Jeff Malpas and Hans-Helmuth Gander, 62–73. London: Routledge, 2015.
Schroeter, Laura, and François Schroeter. 'A Third Way in Metaethics'. *Noûs* 43, no. 1 (2009): 1–30.
Sloterdijk, Peter. 'Where Are We When We Hear Music?' In *The Aesthetic Imperative: Writings on Art*. Edited by Peter Weibel. Translated by Karen Margolis, 77–127. Cambridge: Polity, 2017.

Splitrec. 'Through Fire, Crevice + the Hidden Valley'. https://splitrec.com/through-fire-crevice-the-hidden-valley-jim-denley/ (Accessed 25 June 2019).

Taylor, Kenneth A. 'Reference and Jazz Combo Theories of Meaning'. In *Reference and Referring*, edited by William P. Kabasenche, Michael O'Rourke, and Matthew H. Slater, 271–303. Cambridge: MIT Press, 2012.

Tolley, David. 'Improvisation and our Great Western Music Tradition'. *David Tolley ~ artist-musician-composer-teacher-improviser* (blog). August 23, 2012. https://davidtolley.wordpress.com/category/texts/ (Accessed 6 April 2018).

Toop, David. *Into the Maelstrom: Music, Improvisation and the Dream of Freedom Before 1970*. New York: Bloomsbury, 2016.

Tugendhat, Ernst. 'Heidegger's Idea of Truth'. In *Hermeneutics and Truth*, edited by Brice R. Wachterhauser, 83–97. Evanston: Northwestern University Press, 1994.

Wallace, Rob. 'Kick Out the Jazz!' In *People Get Ready: The Future of Jazz Is Now!*, edited by Ajay Hebel and Rob Wallace, 111–37. Durham: Duke University Press, 2013.

Walters, Ren. 'What is Improvisation?' *Sam McAuliffe* (blog). August 11, 2017. https://sjmcauliffe.files.wordpress.com/2017/08/ren-walters.pdf (Accessed 26 November 2020).

Warnke, Georgia. 'Hermeneutics, Ethics, and Politics'. In *The Cambridge Companion to Gadamer*, edited by Robert J. Dostal, 79–101. Cambridge: Cambridge University Press, 2002.

Warren, Jeff R. *Music and Ethical Responsibility*. New York: Cambridge University Press, 2014.

Waterman, Ellen. 'Improvised Trust: Opening Statements'. In *The Improvisation Studies Reader: Spontaneous Acts*, edited by Rebecca Caines and Ajay Heble, 59–62. London: Routledge, 2015.

Wilson, Graeme B., and Raymond MacDonald. 'The Sign of Silence: Negotiating Musical Identities in an Improvising Ensemble'. *Psychology of Music* 40, no. 5 (2012): 558–73.

Wittgenstein, Ludwig. *Culture and Value*. Edited by Georg Henrik von Wright in collaboration with Heikki Nyman. Translated by Peter Winch. Oxford: Blackwell, 1998.

Wittgenstein, Ludwig. *Philosophical Investigations*. Translated by G. E. M. Anscombe, P. M. S. Hacker, and Joachim Schulte. 4th ed. Oxford: Blackwell, 2009.

Wong, Mandy-Suzanne, and Nina Sun Eidsheim. '*Corregidora*: Corporeal Archaeology, Embodied Memory, Improvisation'. In *Negotiated Moments: Improvisation, Sound, and Subjectivity*, edited by Gillian Siddall and Ellen Waterman, 217–32. Durham: Duke University Press, 2016.

Young, Julian. *Heidegger's Later Philosophy*. Cambridge: Cambridge University Press, 2002.

Young, Julian. *Heidegger's Philosophy of Art*. Cambridge: Cambridge University Press, 2004.

Zabala, Santiago. *The Remains of Being: Hermeneutic Ontology After Metaphysics*. New York: Columbia University Press, 2009.

Zabala, Santiago. *Why Only Art Can Save Us: Aesthetics and the Absence of Emergency*. New York: Columbia University Press, 2017.

Discography and multimedia

Grouper. 'Headache'. Track 1 on *Paradise Valley*. Yellow Electric – GR-015. 2016, LP.
Hilmar Jensson. 'Larf'. Track 2 on *Ditty Blei*. Songlines Recordings – SGL SA1547-2. 2004, CD.
Jim Denley. *Through Fire, Crevice + the Hidden Valley*. Splitrec – CD16. 2006, CD.
Julien Wilson and Stephen Magnusson. 'Stagger'. Track 1 on *Kaleidoscopic*. Jazz Head – HEAD113. 2007, CD.
Keith Jarrett. *The Köln Concert*. ECM Records GmbH – ECM 1064/65. 1975, CD.
Miles Davis. 'So What'. Track 1 on *Kind of Blue*. Columbia – CK 64935. 1997, CD.
Ren Walters and Stephen Magnusson. 'Raphsody'. Track 4 on *de flection*. 2004, online recording. https://renwaltersandstephenmagnusson.bandcamp.com/album/de-flection (Accessed 11 June 2021).
Scott Tinkler. *Simon Barker/Scott Tinkler*, 7 May 2016 (online video, 24 June 2019). https://www.youtube.com/watch?v=goE_u91EAOU (Accessed 27 July 2019).

Index

aesthetic experience   24, 26-7, 66-7, 102, 113, 118, 133, 163, 166, 168, 172-3, 203 n.86
aesthetics/philosophy of art   143, 166
aletheia/unconcealedness/unconcealment   43, 69, 79, 113, 115, 199 n.1
appropriate(d)   42-4, 48-50, 60, 68, 132, 168
art   9, 13, 24, 30, 62, 66, 68, 72, 95-6, 102-3, 105, 107, 114-15, 117, 120, 122, 142-4, 164, 166, 168, 170-2, 176, 203 n.86, 208 n.7
artform   169-70, 172
artwork   14, 16, 26-8, 113, 127-9, 131, 133, 135, 172
atmosphere(s)/atmospheric   38-9, 52, 59-61, 67
attend and respond/attending and responding/attentiveness and responsiveness   1, 3-4, 6-7, 17-18, 20, 23-4, 26, 29, 31-2, 45, 62-4, 80, 83, 86, 88-91, 108, 113, 118, 121-2, 125, 130-1, 134, 145-54, 162, 174-5, 177-8, 206 n.31
awaken/awaken to the situation   148, 161

Bailey, Derek   49, 50
being   3, 26, 60, 89, 98, 102, 105, 107-11, 114-15, 117, 126, 130, 132, 134-7, 151, 157, 165, 167-8, 181 n.2
being in the moment/caught up in/in the moment/moment/taken up by   42, 65, 74-8, 80, 90, 111, 114, 116, 127

being-in-the-world   3, 10, 32, 37, 53-7, 108-9, 131-2, 134-5, 145, 150, 152, 155, 157, 159, 162-3, 166, 169, 180
Benson, Bruce Ellis   13, 79-80, 100, 153, 164, 182 n.15, 183 n.16, 185 n.16, 193 n.108, 196 n.47
Bergson, Henri   72-3, 76-7
Berliner, Paul F.   18, 34
Bildung/becoming cultured   98-9, 112, 125, 147, 154, 158
body schema   50, 54-7, 60, 62
boundary   7, 9, 31, 39-41, 64, 66, 71, 78, 80-1, 84, 87, 120, 122-3, 160-1

Casey, Edward S.   35, 47-9, 187 n.5
circumstance(s)   3, 7, 14-15, 17, 29, 31, 35-7, 40-2, 44, 50, 58, 62-3, 121, 129, 146, 167, 178
common matter of concern/of concern   16-17, 23, 25, 31, 39, 45, 52, 63, 66, 80-1, 83-4, 90, 120, 126, 131, 160-1, 203 n.101
conversation/conversational/conversationally   1, 5-8, 14-16, 18-20, 22-5, 28-9, 31-2, 35, 39-42, 44, 60, 62-4, 67, 69-71, 78, 89-90, 99, 101, 103-4, 112, 114, 116, 118-21, 124, 126-7, 129-31, 133-7, 154, 159-61, 174, 202 n.64, 204-5 n.119
Cox, Christoph   72
creative/create/creativity   1, 4, 13, 18, 24-5, 28, 73, 79-80, 82-3, 85, 90, 127, 133, 142-4, 183 n.16, 196 n.47

Davey, Nicholas 60–2, 127, 203 n.86, 203 n.101
Davidson, Donald 3, 7, 14–17, 19–23, 27–8, 149, 159
Davis, Miles 45, 87
Denley, Jim 83–4, 120, 122, 147
dialogue 15, 61–2, 104–5, 114, 123, 128, 131
dissonance 169, 179, 210 n.49
duration/durational 30, 59, 71–4, 76–7, 85, 87
dwell/dwelling 3, 152–4, 157, 182 n.11, 205 n.119

epistemology/epistemological/epistemologically 27–8, 97, 99, 103, 106, 111, 140
equipment/equipmentality 3, 38, 51, 56
equivocity/equivocal 10, 163, 179
ethics/ethical/ethically 2, 6, 8, 100, 139, 142–55, 157, 161–2
event 3, 14–15, 18, 20, 22, 24, 27, 42–5, 63, 69, 71–4, 76–8, 97, 102–3, 113–16, 118, 123, 127–9, 134, 136–8, 147, 160–1, 165–6, 168, 170, 172, 189 n.50, 190 n.62, 191 n.74
extempore/of the moment 74, 77, 89, 114, 118

facticity/factical existence/factical experience/factical life 8, 96, 111, 113, 117–18, 136, 145–7, 157, 162
falling into/fallen/fallen into/falls/falls into 120–4, 126, 134, 137, 146, 151, 161, 167
finitude 98, 104–5, 117–18, 135, 161
Fischlin, Daniel 75–6
'focus' 4, 6, 14, 16, 28–9, 52, 63–5, 80, 90, 120, 159, 161
fourfold 3, 42–4, 69, 152–3
fusion of horizons 125–6, 130, 132, 134

Gadamer, Hans-Georg 2–3, 5–8, 10, 14–17, 19–20, 22–8, 37, 40, 42–4, 59–60, 63, 90, 96–107, 111–14, 116–20, 122–42, 145–8, 151–2, 154–9, 161–3, 165–8, 170–3, 175, 178–9, 182 n.15, 183 n.16, 186 n.32, 186 n.36, 189 n.46, 193 n.108, 203 n.86, 203 n.101, 204–5 n.119, 206 n.31
Gallagher, Shaun 55–6
Grondin, Jean 96–8, 104, 110–11, 126, 135, 148

habit(s)/habitually/habituate(d) 33, 44, 54–5, 57–63, 121
Harris, Liz 159
Heidegger, Martin 3–4, 10, 13–14, 28, 42–4, 51, 67, 69, 71, 73–4, 79, 81, 96–8, 100, 102, 104–11, 113–17, 124, 126, 132, 136–7, 139–41, 143, 145–6, 150–4, 157, 161, 163, 165–70, 172–9, 181 n.2, 183 n.16, 186 n.39, 191–2 n.84, 199 n.1, 202 n.64, 204–5 n.119, 210 n.49
hermeneutical ethics 155, 162
hermeneutic circle/circularity/circular/circularity of understanding/part-whole 5, 8, 105–9, 111, 119, 124, 129, 155–6
hermeneutics/hermeneutical/hermeneutically/philosophical hermeneutics 2, 3, 5–6, 8, 10, 14–16, 19, 61, 90–1, 95–101, 103–14, 116–21, 123–4, 126, 136–40, 142, 145–6, 150, 152, 154–8, 160–3, 166, 169, 178–80, 182 n.14, 182–3 n.15, 183 n.16
hermeneutic thinking 141
hermeneutic understanding 119, 148
hermeneutic virtue 140–1, 156
historical situatedness/historical situation 16, 37, 104, 110
historicity 8, 98, 105, 109–10, 117–18, 124, 136
horizon 4, 7, 39–40, 45, 64, 69, 71, 75, 81, 85, 87, 90, 109, 120, 125, 129, 135, 153–4, 159–61
horizonal field 7, 84, 87–90, 120, 122–3, 125

Index

horizontal limit 85
Husserl, Edmond 76, 81, 109–10

Ihde, Don 23, 81
imperative of consistency 148, 158
improvisation/improvisational/
  improvisatory 1–10, 13–4, 17–21,
  24–8, 32, 34, 38–42, 44, 46, 48,
  50, 52–4, 56–8, 60, 63–6, 68, 70,
  74–81, 83–7, 89–91, 99–106, 108, 114,
  116–20, 122–5, 127–8, 130–2, 134–9,
  145–65, 167–72, 174, 177–80, 181 n.4,
  182 n.5, 182 n.14, 183 n.15, 183 n.16,
  183 n.17, 183 n.1, 185 n.15, 186 n.32,
  190 n.62, 202 n.64
improvisational musicality 167
improvisational situation 4, 6–7, 14, 16,
  20, 22, 26–30, 33, 37–45, 49–50, 52–3,
  56–60, 63–6, 69, 71–2, 74, 77–8, 80–1,
  83–5, 88–90, 113, 119–20, 122–4, 126,
  129–31, 133–8, 146–8, 150–4, 156,
  159–61, 167, 171, 178
improvisational traverse/traverse/
  traversing 63, 88–9, 122–6, 130, 133,
  136–8, 146–7, 150–1, 155, 157, 159,
  167, 171–2, 175
improvisation as conversation 18–19
Improvised musical performance 2, 4,
  6–7, 13–17, 19–20, 22–5, 27–33, 41, 43,
  46, 48–9, 53–4, 56, 59, 61–7, 71–4, 78–
  81, 84–5, 87–90, 102, 118–19, 121–2,
  130, 137, 155, 159–60, 162–3, 174–5,
  184 n.2, 184 n.6, 186 n.30, 195 n.39
improviso/unforeseen 44–5, 63, 70–1,
  74, 79, 117–21, 123, 130, 137, 152–4
indeterminate/indeterminacy 1, 17, 21,
  23, 29, 44, 46, 54, 56–7, 63, 79, 86–7,
  99, 108, 117, 119, 123–4, 127, 130, 135,
  146–9, 153, 155
intend/intending 47, 55–7, 119–20
intentional/intentionality/
  intentionally 18, 28, 50, 55–8, 76, 77,
  98, 113, 119, 121, 133, 145
intersubjective/intersubjectivity 7,
  15–18, 26–7, 109

Jarrett, Keith 31–2, 49
Jazz 1–2, 14, 18, 21, 23, 25, 30–1, 33–4,
  45, 54, 58, 61, 84, 86, 99, 135, 181 n.4,
  182 n.15, 183 n.16, 185 n.15
Jensson, Hilmar 61–2
Johnson, Mark 54, 59, 61

Kramer, Lawrence 170

language of the thing 131, 133–4, 151,
  172, 175, 179
Lewis, George E. 33–4, 74
Lichtung/clearing/lighting 115–16,
  118, 136–7
limit(s)/limited 7, 9, 28, 39–40, 64, 80–1,
  84, 88, 90, 120, 122, 142, 144, 161, 173
linguistics/linguisticality 125–8, 131,
  133, 185 n.15
listen/listened/listening 7, 17, 23, 45,
  61, 64–6, 69–71, 74, 77–81, 83–6,
  90, 132–3, 141, 151, 156–7, 160, 165,
  168–71, 174–7, 179, 193 n.1

Mäcklin, Harri 66–9
Magnusson, Stephen 25–6, 70
Malpas, Jeff 2, 9, 36–8, 41, 48–9, 73, 78,
  88, 108, 119, 153, 191 n.74, 192 n.89
meditative thinking/think
  meditatively 139, 141, 163
metaphysics 103–4, 111, 145, 168–70,
  174, 177
mousiké 164, 176, 178
musicality 10, 34, 87, 165–8, 176–7, 179
musical thinking 169, 178–9

Nancy, Jean-Luc 71, 74
Neuhaus, Max 68, 72
Nietzsche, Friedrich 96, 165–6, 172–3,
  176, 204 n.118
Noë, Alva 32, 50–2, 55, 57, 191–2 n.84

objective/objectify/objectifies/objectification/
  objectively/objectivity 15–16, 27, 36,
  63, 106, 110, 124, 131, 135, 141, 145,
  148, 153, 168–70, 172–3, 175–6

O'Callaghan, Casey 82
ontology/ontological/ontologically 2, 8, 10, 13, 28, 42, 62, 82, 96, 105–11, 113–15, 117–18, 124, 136, 139–40, 145, 148, 152, 158, 161–2, 174, 181 n.2, 183 n.17, 186 n.32, 199 n.1, 203 n.86
orient/orientation/oriented/orienting 7, 15–16, 21, 25–6, 28–30, 36, 42–6, 48, 55, 58–64, 67–8, 70–1, 81–3, 88, 110, 115, 117, 122–4, 126, 134, 136, 145, 159, 163
origin 4, 7, 13, 28–9, 32–3, 52, 63–5, 80, 90, 114–15, 120, 160–1
original ethics 146–8, 150–5

Pareyson, Luigi 141–4
participating/participate/participation/participatory 28, 44–5, 48, 74, 78–80, 83, 85, 87–8, 103, 108, 113–14, 116, 118–21, 123, 126–7, 131, 145, 150, 152–4, 157, 160–1, 168, 172, 178, 179
passing theories/passing theory 20–2, 40, 121, 149
perception 31, 54, 59, 81–3, 206 n.31
phenomenology/phenomenological/phenomenologically 39, 66, 76, 81, 105, 109–10, 118, 139, 160
philosophical topography 2, 3, 88
place 2–4, 7, 29–31, 33–42, 46–50, 52–3, 56, 58–9, 62–3, 65–6, 71–4, 77–8, 81, 83–4, 88–90, 115, 119–22, 131, 133, 144, 146, 150, 152, 160–1, 178–9, 187 n.5, 189 n.50, 192 n.89
Plato 95, 104, 141, 164–5, 175
played 26–7, 32, 42–3, 53
poeticization 69
poetics 165–6, 168, 169, 174, 179
poetic turn 10, 163, 169, 172–7
poetic world 66–70, 74, 77–9, 89–90, 160
poiesis 10, 165–8, 170, 175, 177
possibilities 24–6, 31, 39–45, 49, 61, 63, 67–8, 70–1, 79–80, 84–8, 90, 122, 131–2, 134, 146, 156

prejudice(s) 39–40, 43, 46, 48–9, 52, 87, 104, 106, 108, 111–12, 121, 124, 136, 142, 150, 155, 189 n.44, 189 n.46
prior theories/prior theory 20, 22–3
purposiveness 14, 18, 24–5, 130, 184 n.2

Ravaisson, Félix 58
region 3–4, 7, 31, 39–40, 66, 81, 84–5, 87–9, 120, 122, 150–1, 192 n.89
Risser, James 125–6
rules 19–20, 22–3, 57, 67, 121, 128, 134, 143, 145–50, 153–5, 162

Schmidt, Dennis J. 146–7, 152, 157, 172–3, 177, 210 n.49
scientific thinking 140–5
self-understanding 5, 33, 110, 112, 117, 150
set in place 38–41, 62
silence 7, 54, 69, 79, 81, 85–7, 165
singularity 9, 74, 110, 150
situation/situated 1, 3–4, 6–7, 14–15, 17–18, 20–1, 23, 27–9, 31–2, 34–46, 48–50, 52–65, 70–1, 73–4, 77–80, 83–90, 102, 108, 110, 113–26, 130–3, 135–8, 145–50, 153–5, 157, 160, 162, 172, 179, 184 n.2, 205 n.119, 206 n.31
Sloterdijk, Peter 65, 194 n.6
space 4, 35, 38–9, 48, 70–4, 78, 82, 89, 102, 133, 151, 161, 189 n.50
spatiality/spatial/spatialized 35, 38, 55, 72–3, 82, 89, 189 n.50, 194 n.6
Spiel/play 3, 24–6, 28, 32, 41–2, 44–5, 53, 58, 99, 102, 114, 118, 124, 137, 186 n.32, 186 n.36
spontaneous/spontaneity/spontaneously 1, 21, 29, 44, 46, 53–4, 56, 59–60, 62–3, 76, 117, 119, 121–2, 130–1, 146, 148, 202 n.64
subjective/subjectism/subjectively/subjectivist/subjectivities/subjectivity 3, 6–7, 14–16, 18, 24–8, 36, 48, 53, 62, 75, 77, 79, 107, 109–10, 113–14, 119–21, 131, 133, 141, 146, 152, 168–9, 174, 184 n.6, 195 n.39

subject-object   17, 132, 136
succession   71–4, 77, 89, 138

tacit knowledge   44, 52, 54, 60
tact/tactful/tactfully/tactfulness   44, 54, 59–63, 125, 148
technology/technological   139–41, 145, 166
temporal/temporality/temporalization   48, 71–7, 89, 109, 137, 172, 189 n.50, 205 n.119
thinking musically   169, 178, 180
thinking *with*   178–80
threshold   66–9, 71, 74, 77–9, 89–90, 169, 179
time   71–7, 82, 89, 137, 161, 189 n.50
timespace   72–4, 78, 89, 160
Tinkler, Scott and Simon Barker   86–7
Tolley, David   132–3
topology/topography/topological/topologically/*topos*   2–3, 6, 33, 36–7, 42, 49, 53, 55–6, 65, 72, 77, 83–4, 88, 103, 123–5, 137, 145, 152–3, 159–61, 189 n.50, 191 n.74, 192 n.89, 194 n.6
transforms/transformation/transformative/transformed   6, 27, 78, 125, 150, 155, 167, 171, 175–6
triangulation   3, 14, 16, 21, 23
truth(s)   2, 6, 8, 10, 18, 27, 40, 98, 100, 102–7, 110–11, 113–18, 122–3, 126, 129, 131, 133–4, 136–40, 143, 151, 157, 161–3, 168, 170, 199 n.1, 204–5 n.119

unifying concept/unifying structure   4, 9, 10
universal/universalism/universality   1, 9, 23, 99–100, 103–5, 111, 113, 129, 145, 162, 164, 183 n.17

Walters, Ren   70–1
Warnke, Georgia   151, 155–6
Wilson, Graeme B. and Raymond MacDonald   18–19
Wilson, Julien   25
Wittgenstein, Ludwig   17, 149, 164
Wong, Mandy-Suzanne and Nina Sun Eidsheim   46–7
work (of art)   3–4, 6–7, 13–26, 28, 31, 37, 40–5, 50, 52, 54, 58–9, 61–70, 77–90, 102–3, 115, 117, 119–20, 122, 130, 132–3, 137–8, 147, 159–61, 168, 170–2, 174–5, 184 n.2, 193 n.1
world   1, 3–4, 7, 15–16, 27–9, 32–3, 37, 40, 42–3, 46, 49–51, 53–6, 58–9, 65–72, 74, 77–80, 82–3, 89–90, 98, 102, 104–6, 108, 110, 116–17, 119–20, 123–4, 126–7, 129–34, 136, 140–3, 145, 150, 152–4, 157–8, 160, 162, 164, 166–8, 171, 173, 176, 178

www.ingramcontent.com/pod-product-compliance
Lightning Source LLC
Chambersburg PA
CBHW062218300426
44115CB00012BA/2114